GATEWAYS TO
HEALTH & HARMONY
WITH
REFLEXOLOGY
Ann Gillanders

GATEWAYS TO HEALTH AND HARMONY WITH REFLEXOLOGY
ISBN 0-9511868-4-1
British Library Cataloguing in Publication Data.
A catalogue record for this book is available from the British Library.

Illustrations by Eleanor Tanner.
Cover design, book design and typesetting by Eleanor Tanner.
Prepared for publication by
Eleanor Tanner Design, 25 Godfrey Way, Great Dunmow, Essex CM6 2AY.

Printed and bound in Great Britain by The Alden Press, Oxford.
Published by Ann Gillanders.

Ann Gillanders
The British School of Reflexology
92 Sheering Road
Old Harlow
Essex CM17 0JW Telephone 01279 429060 Fax 01279 445234

Contents

About the author

ANN GILLANDERS is the Principal of **The British School of Reflexology**. She and her brother **Tony Porter** were the true pioneers of Reflexology some 25 years ago and were responsible for the development of Reflexology throughout the United Kingdom. Ann's career has been both extensive and varied, mainly directed to the fields of medicine and writing.

In 1973 she was introduced to Reflexology. At that time it was little known as a science but was often ridiculed. Ann trained with Dwight Byers, Director of The International Institute of Reflexology, where she and her brother promoted Reflexology and set up the United Kingdom side of that Institute, establishing training schools in London, Manchester, Switzerland, Paris and Israel. In 1986 Ann founded **The British School of Reflexology** and now has her own training centre in Harlow, Essex, where students attend for training from all over the world.

In 1989 she studied Acupressure and Remedial Massage with Dr Louis Chung, Director of the Oriental School of Medicine in Peking, and obtained a qualification.

Ann is author of the following books:
Reflexology, the Ancient Answer to Modern Ailment,
No Mean Feet (Autobiography, Ann Gillanders),
Reflexology – The Theory and Practice,
Reflexology – Step by Step (published by Gaia Books, London),
The Joy of Reflexology (Littlebrown & Co., USA),
Gateways to Health and Harmony with Reflexology.

Ann has increased her knowledge of healing over the years and has become involved with nutrition, vitamins and particularly herbalism, so has included more information on complementary medicine to enhance the skills of the practitioner and to promote wider knowledge in this book, **Gateways to Health and Harmony with Reflexology**.

Dedications

To Eleanor, a great artist and treasured friend:

Thank you for all your help and support in the design and artwork of **Gateways to Health and Harmony with Reflexology**.

To Tony, my brother:

With gratitude for your inspiration and guidance through the early years of Reflexology.

Introduction

Introduction

The purpose of this book is to introduce you to a pathway to better health, harmony and to the ability to enjoy life to the full, appreciating that life on this planet is not a dress rehearsal. We cannot come back on this level, and 'do it all again'.

In order to get the best out of life we need 'to be the best we can be' – to *feel good, look good,* and experience as much pleasure and joy that is possible.

The whole process of health and healing is under review at this time with the increased concern about the side effects from many orthodox medical treatments and the damaging effects of the ever growing, extensive range of synthetic drugs.

Healing was meant to be gentle and simple. It is man who has complicated the issue in the so-called 'progress' that we have made in this twentieth century.

With a greater understanding of the link between the mind, body and spirit, a truly holistic approach to health and healing can be achieved. No man is an island. He is surrounded by influences of life, externally with the universe and internally through emotions and feelings of his own mind and life experiences.

New drugs which were discovered in the 1940s and 1950s appeared to produce such miraculous results that the public at large became conditioned to their common use without questioning such things as side effects. A few doctors stood out against the use of these synthetic chemicals and were scorned – that was until the thalidomide tragedy shocked the world. Hundreds of babies were born deformed, the main deformity being the absence of arms and legs.

As the drug had not been officially licensed by the Federal Food and Drug Administration in the United States, the Americans were spared its tragic results. The drug was used for the control of sickness in early pregnancy!

Never before have we had so much terminal disease, and never before have we had such a selection of drugs. Healing means getting to the root causes of the illness, treating the person not the disease.

'There is no such thing as an incurable disease, only an incurable person!'

Sometimes illness or debilitation may be the only way an individual can be forced to take stock of his spiritual life or his need for additional psychological or inner growth and often quite disastrous situations are required to force a person to look at his life from a new perspective. Hours spent lying on your back looking up to the ceiling may force you to take a look at the speed you had been living at; maybe that speed was the reason why you had the road accident – an enforcement to stop, look and listen to your inner self.

Every deed and every thought of an individual is imprinted onto a magnetic field of energy, much like words being typed onto a computer. Those messages, internal arguments as well as positive messages translate into concrete daily happenings that can sometimes bring positive conditions and opportunities, or can act like a boomerang, returning to shock the person to the core of his being.

No research has revealed a cure for nerve paralysis, muscular dystrophy, epilepsy or retardation. Millions of people suffer pain or have physical impairment. Heart attacks, cancer, diabetes, rheumatoid arthritis, osteoporosis, kidney failure, brain tumours and accidents hit rich and poor alike, noble and vindictive, saints and sinners without any discrimination.

Why do people get sick? There is no simple answer to that vast question. Illness is always a surface manifestation of some problem that exists somewhere in the overall system. In reality, illness may play a far more important role in life than is readily apparent.

While it is all too easy to decry the shortcomings of the medical profession, in spite of their drugs, where technology is concerned many miracles have been created. The use of lasers has restored the sight of many, ear operations have enabled the deaf to hear again, and the strides achieved in transplant operations have enabled many to enjoy a long, active life. Remember, a lot of our problems today are due to our living much longer than was ever expected a century ago, and consequently our skeletal system in particular is exposed to many more years of wear and tear.

It is very hard to grasp the fact that complementary medicines are so simple, non-invasive and comforting. Frequently practitioners of the various sciences use their hands and nothing else to effect a good result, and we hear it said so frequently: 'Why don't doctors use these treatments more readily if they are so successful?' The answer is simply that doctors are trained to treat the body as a mechanical machine that has broken down and have little recognition of the fact that the illness of the patient has been brought about by many different aspects – emotional, spiritual, the stress levels of the individual, his diet, his smoking, drinking, lack of exercise and the side effects of all the drugs that he has been taking for too long to try and bring about some relief for his suffering.

Luckily things are changing. Many doctors are listening and are using these therapies, because their patients are asking for them.

Patients often get well by just being handled by a pleasant doctor with a pleasing manner who seems to have a way of treating the person as an individual, not a body in a bed.

This is exactly what happened in the healing temples of one of the earliest civilizations, when the healer priests would don the mask of Anubis (Egyptian god of anaesthetics) before putting a patient 'under' for surgery so that the sufferer sincerely believed that the god himself was with him and would see him through the operation.

The same thing also took place in Greece and Rome, where those suffering from nervous breakdowns would be treated by incubation therapy or narcosis, the last thing that they were shown as they drifted off to sleep being a priestess garbed to represent the goddess Isis.

A considerable amount of research is being undertaken at present to discover the origin of pain, especially of the sort for which there is no obvious physical reason. New methods of treatment are achieving excellent results in this area and doctors concerned are taking into account the psychological factors – the mind punishing its body as a protest against its inner frustrations.

It is refreshing to see physicians and psychologists working side by side, which is as it should be.

Surely, the most important factor in all forms of healing is the ultimate health of the patient, not the pet theories of doctors, nor the fear of the medical profession losing its power. So whether it be the acupuncturist, the praying priest, the manipulator or the psychotherapist, perhaps the time is right for the ultimate good result to be *the* most important factor in the field of healing.

'The only medicine
for suffering crime
and all other
woes of mankind
is wisdom.'
Thomas Henry Hassle

CHAPTER 1

Herbs and healing

1 Herbs and healing

Herbal medicine or herbalism, as it is more popularly called, goes back a very long way. In days past most villages in Britain and Europe had a wise woman whose knowledge of the healing properties of herbs had been passed down to her from earlier times. Such people were often members of what is now known as 'the old religion'.

The therapeutic use of herbs being so ancient, we may assume it to be part of that instinctive knowledge that is most common among animals and primitive man. You will all have seen an animal tear and eat some long grasses, or graze on a particular shrub or bush, or break off and grind down the wood from the bark of a tree. They obviously still have an inbuilt knowledge of what they need to stay healthy and to heal themselves when sickness occurs.

Although herbs are in everyday culinary use and therefore readily available to everyone, to the trained herbalist they possess other properties which place them firmly in the therapeutic bracket.

Herbal medicine has even been tied in with magic and astrology, each plant resonating to a given planet or astrological sign and constituting part of an arcane knowledge, the basis of which has been long forgotten. Gifted clairvoyants, members of the 'old religion' and pursuants of Druidic lore are believed to have an inner understanding of the healing quality of plants.

In the west of Ireland the belief still lingers that the right herb to treat an illness can only be found if one allows the fairies to guide one to it. Since that particular coastline can count among its legends the arrival of the Fairy People, this is little wonder.

It also tends to confirm my own belief that all legends which allude to the arrival of highly knowledgeable and advanced people from 'across the seas', be it in South America, the British Isles, China or Egypt, came from a common source.

The practice of clinical herbalism continued throughout the Middle Ages, becoming more and more sophisticated as time went on. Instead of single herbs, physicians would make mixtures which they felt were appropriate to the disease, and animal substances were frequently added for the supposed effect.

In the seventeenth century Nicholas Culpeper compiled his famous *Herbal*. Culpeper trained as an apothecary, which was the equivalent in those times to our modern GP. He believed in astrology and its importance in the lives of both plants and animals. In those days such beliefs were not as contrary to science as they are today.

Sir Isaac Newton himself was a firm believer in astrology. As medicine became a more exact science, however, the astrological aspect was cautiously dropped.

Simple herbal remedies slowly gave way to synthetic drugs, which were believed to be as effective as their herbal originals and more reliable. The advent of the twentieth century saw medicine and commerce marching hand in hand, with patent medicines slowly taking over from the old herbal remedies. Names like Thomas Beecham and Jesse Boot still adorn our bottles and shop fronts to this day. Although the herbalists were replaced by the chemists, the practice of herbalism continued and the Society of Medical Herbalists is still in existence.

Following the exposure of the damaging side effects of many drugs, herbalism is now enjoying a revival.

The Times Educational Supplement, December 1981, states, 'Free courses in phytotherapy (healing through plants) are being offered to members of the French medical profession by the privately financed Institut d'Enseignement de Phytothérapie (IEP).'

In the last three years the demand in France for herbal cures has increased enormously. The Institute was only started comparatively recently and its courses have attracted more than 300 hundred people at a time including dentists, pharmacists, biologists, veterinary surgeons and medical students. Dr Moatti, IEP President, hopes the Institute will soon be recognized officially.

The true benefit of herbalism depends upon the knowledge of the practitioner in advising on the right concoction of herbs to treat the sick person effectively. The administering of herbs by an unskilled person can lead to most unpleasant side effects and prove totally useless. Be sure therefore to seek out a well-qualified medical herbalist before you undertake herbal treatment.

Echinacea

Echinacea is an excellent herbal remedy for improving general healing in the body. Its benefits are antiseptic, anti-inflammatory and detoxicant. It is therefore a natural antibiotic and can be used safely when the body is in an infectious state.

It does not work directly on the virus but gets to the root cause of the problem and stimulates the immune response.

Royal jelly

Queen bee jelly. This is a secretion from the salivary glands of the worker bee. It is rich in amino acids, vitamins and metabolites. It is a concentrated food which gives extraordinary powers to the queen bee, enabling her to live 30 times longer than the other bees. It is royal jelly that enables the queen to grow larger than the others, and it also increases her fertility.

Its action is as a stimulant to the endocrine gland (hence its fertility link) and it is therefore beneficial in cases of distressing symptoms associated with the menopause, and also to those having difficulty in conceiving. It also has antibiotic properties and is a digestive stimulant, so is a valuable source as an energy stimulant in the aged. Royal jelly contains vitamins B1, B2, B3, B5, B6, biotin, inositol, folic acid and vitamin C.

Spirulina

Past civilizations harvested algae for food bulk. Algae have blood purifying properties which is made possible by their high chlorophyll content.

The product comes from Japan where the algae are cultivated in large water reservoirs. The product does, however, grow naturally on alpine lakes and is valuable for its high protein, vitamins and minerals.

Its exceptional level of vitamin B12 is of special interest to vegetarians, vegans and non-meat eaters who, unless they study their diet carefully, may be deficient in this important vitamin. It has therefore been used effectively in the treatment of AIDS.

It is also rich in iodine necessary for the efficient function of the thyroid gland, so is highly recommended for those suffering from hypothyroidism or hyperthyroidism.

Cinchona bark

Cinchona bark, or Peruvian bark, was originally used in the treatment of malaria. Its main effectiveness is in controlling fever.

The Countess of Cinchona, wife of the Viceroy of Peru, was cured of malarial fever with the powdered bark in 1638. News of her recovery spread like wildfire throughout the high society circles of Europe and this started a world demand for the bark. Its temperature-reducing effect is really powerful.

Ginseng

Ginseng is said to be more suitable for men than for women. It is a revitalizer in old age and was used by the People's Republic of China for a wide range of disorders, often inducing a feeling of well-being.

It has been used in the Far East for over 4,000 years. All ginsengs enhance the recuperative power of healing in the body. It is a natural anti-inflammatory.

The Chinese have great faith in using ginseng to increase fertility and it is still promoted widely today for fertility problems.

Gotu kola

Gotu kola is mentioned in most Eastern religions and medical systems. It has a reputation for longevity.

Under the name of Po-ti-tieng it was prescribed and taken by Professor Li Ching-Yu, a Chinese herbalist, who died in 1930 at the reputed age of 256.

The herb has a long history in treating leprosy and tumours, and some success has been reported in using it for the treatment of cancer of the cervix and other painful and distressing conditions of the female reproductive system.

Research reports that such success has been achieved in improving memory and overcoming stress and fatigue. It would therefore be recommended in assisting in the treatment of Alzheimer's disease.

Mistletoe

The juice of the mistletoe berry has been applied to external cancers since the time of the Druids, and Hippocrates records its use in epilepsy and tumours.

It acts as a tranquillizer and vasodilator. It will reduce blood pressure in those with hypertension and is sometimes used as a beta blocker when conventional drugs cause skin rashes and the like.

Again, another immune enhancer, it has been used as an adjunct to surgery and radiotherapy for patients for whom cytotoxic drugs are inappropriate because of adverse side effects.

Onions

It has been said that 'an onion a day keeps arteriosclerosis at bay.' Onions clear the arteries of fat.

They are a great expectorant and are therefore recommended in the treatment of bronchitis and asthma. Boiled onions strained and mixed with honey are a very good remedy for coughs and colds.

Onions promote bile flow and share some of the properties of garlic.

Olive oil

Olive oil is beneficial in increasing high density lipoprotein (HDL) and in decreasing low density lipoprotein (LDL) which can have a detrimental effect upon the blood when in excess.

Taken orally, the oil forms a barrier on the surface of the stomach thus arresting the secretion of gastric juice. It has therefore been used with success for gastric and duodenal ulcers.

Olive oil is said to prevent heart disease, and a dessertspoonful a day is the recommended amount.

Opium poppy

In an age before modern drugs and anaesthetics this was one of the few solaces available. Even today there are a few situations for which this deep acting pain killer is indicated as, for instance, in wounds healed but not without pain.

Prescription is by a medical practitioner only as it contains morphine alkaloids and codeine, analgesic and a narcotic.

Disease begins with a very small imbalance in the body which ultimately becomes a very large problem. If symptoms were regarded as good warning signs from the body instead of being disregarded and immediately tackled with synthetic drugs which bang the symptoms on the head but never get to the root cause of the problem, serious diseases would rarely occur and we would all eventually die from a worn-out body and fade away in our sleep – not suffer from agonizing pain and disability and end our days in anguish both mentally and physically.

Poor elimination causes a build-up of toxic waste in all the organs of elimination – the bowel, the lungs, the kidneys, the skin and the lymphatic system.

Nature tackles an excess of toxicity by creating a fever, a furnace to burn the waste, a healing crisis. We regard fever as a worrying condition and immediately seek medication to relieve us of our symptoms. Drugs are toxins, so we replace exactly what the body is trying to eliminate.

To be out of the running because of a physical breakdown when one is at or nearing the peak of social, business and professional life is disastrously disappointing. Rightly, life should not be marked with unfulfilled beginnings or with brilliant promise never brought to fruition because time must be spent in regaining health.

As a rule, your body has a warning period which you should heed, before succumbing to the ravages of illness. As an alarm clock wakes you from sound sleep, these warnings are a bodily alarm reaction which should be sufficient to awaken you to the need for checking your daily routine, to learn whether and where you are out of step with those laws of nature which were devised for the human machine.

Chronic fatigue is one such warning. Suddenly, you may find that you are easily fatigued. A night's rest does not remove this sense of fatigue and you are exhausted when you rise in the morning. The day's work ceases to give you any pleasure. You give up one outside activity after the other. You may have real mental ability and know you have it in you to do very much better than you are doing – if only you could get rid of this ever-present tired feeling.

Occasionally you do have a good day, when you feel equal to

anything and everything the day demands. You accomplish much and wonder why you can't feel like this all the time.

If you have chronic fatigue, let us first check up on the amount of time you sleep at night. When do you go to bed? When do you get up in the morning?

Remember that artificial lighting after sundown was invented by man. The present time-table of daily activities aided by artificial lighting is not the time-table set by nature. Nature's time-table of lighting begins at sunrise and ends with sunset. Though it is impractical for most of us who need to live in relation to the modern tempo set around us to begin our work at sunrise and end it at sunset, we must nevertheless balance work and rest as nearly as possible in keeping with nature's wise plan. One essential is to get as many hours in bed before midnight as you can.

We know of individuals, of course, who require only a few hours of sleep to bring them fresh to the beginning of the new day. But we are not among them if we have developed chronic fatigue with loss of the will to win.

CHAPTER 2

The medicines of the soil

2 The medicines of the soil

Vitality is the energy of life, call it your life force, 'chi', 'god' or whatever is comfortable for you to interpret.

Vitality makes the heart beat, the brain function, the endocrine glands pump hormones into our bloodstream as chemical messengers.

Energy abounds in every aspect of our life. We live on a planet that rotates on an energy force field, moving at such a speed that if it reduced its speed the result would be complete turmoil.

Living beings have an energy: that is how the body is enabled to repair itself, even after the most serious accident. Good health is not just the absence of disease.

Energy is a snowdrop forcing itself through the ground on a cold winter's day. The flight of a bird on the wind. A good scattering of manure will produce more prolific vegetables and flowers than if we had not bothered, so like flowers and trees, when our living conditions are good, our vitality is high.

The best way to restore vitality and health is to pay attention to the very basics of life – water, sunlight, fresh air, correct diet and comfort. The object of good nutrition is to promote and restore health by encouraging self-healing within and, whether you like to accept it or not, you really are 'what you eat'.

Sugar is not a food, it has no food value at all and today it is in so many foods that have a high fat content and this combination of fat and sugar is responsible for a whole range of diseases from breast cancer to Crohn's disease and candida.

Our consumption of coffee is increasing by the year, one or two cups daily will increase our alertness, any more than this and we are putting our systems on 'red alert', increasing our heart beat, bowel function and hormonal output of adrenalin.

Could this be the reason for our increase in anxiety-based illness?

In high doses coffee can produce a variety of negative symptoms, nervousness and insomnia to name but two.

Tea has the same basic effect but if it is taken in a very diluted form, there is no definite evidence that tea drinking is responsible for any specific disease. Large amounts of very, very strong tea have been linked to bladder cancer.

We all eat too much salt. In fact we take 20 times the amount that we need. Excesses of salt are in most of the tinned, packaged and frozen dishes that we buy, and only a small amount actually comes from what we add as an extra to our food.

The wide variety of additives have certain reactions on certain people, which just goes to prove that we are all individual in our reaction to the ingestion of additives.

Artificial sweeteners often cause a reaction in the respiratory system in some sensitive individuals, such as wheezing or skin irritation. Many colourings in food are responsible for attacks of migraine and eczema.

Most of what we need to live a healthy and productive life was provided for us, so when deciding what foods we should, or should not, eat, just cast your mind back to the fruits, roots, shrubs, vegetables, fish and meats that were available on this planet in its profusion before man came along and changed it all.

Yes, I do believe we were meant to eat meat, otherwise we would not have 'tearing' teeth.

However, because of the adulteration of our meat and fish with chemicals and steroids to boost the body weight of cattle and the dreadful way our animals are slaughtered, it may not be the most appetizing food after all, but that is a matter for each individual.

A good vegetarian diet, if balanced in the correct amount of vitamins and minerals, is to be recommended. True vegetarians seldom get cancer.

Honey

Honey is a predigested sugar, digested in the stomach of the honey bee. Honey is a food which needs no digestion by the human body so it is ready to be used by the body immediately. It is therefore excellent as a pick-me-up and often soothes a fractious baby as it has a sedative property, therefore inducing sound sleep.

The pollen of many flowers has a higher vitamin C content than almost any fruit or vegetable. Honey contains pollen, so the higher the amount of pollen, the more concentrated the vitamin C content will be.

Honey is a builder food packed with things the body needs for the release of energy, which makes it appealing as a breakfast food, mixed with a cereal, to start the day right.

As one of the medicines of the soil it has so many advantages. Firstly, it is very easy to obtain. Try to get a pure blend at your local health food shop or, if you have a source, from a local beekeeper.

Try a dessertspoon three times a day for that over-active, highly strung child or individual and I am sure you will notice a change in behaviour within a month.

Honey for burns

In folk medicine honey has been long used as a very successful treatment for burns.

When applied directly to the afflicted area it relieves the pain and prevents the formation of blisters. Healing of the burned area is very rapid.

The honeycomb treatment

Honeycomb has, for many years, been used for the relief of respiratory tract infections and allergic reactive illnesses such as hay fever, asthma and bronchitis.

Chewing the comb daily during the hay fever season gives instant relief.

Colour and food

It should be very easy to learn how certain colours in natural foods give identity to certain parts of the body, and should be eaten when diseases prevail and affect specific functions.

Black and dark brown foods

These purify the kidneys; therefore be encouraged to eat blackberries, aubergines, mushrooms, olives, nuts, black grapes and kidney beans. Kidney beans are even kidney shaped and so should provide a good cleansing to the urinary system.

White foods

These help the lungs: among them are onions, shallots, potatoes, white fish, garlic, pears and celery.

Most of us older readers will have been brought up with boiled onion juice and garlic to treat bronchitis. My grandmother was a sufferer from bronchitis, never went near a doctor and treated her attacks in this way. She lived until the great age of 93 and never resorted to antibiotics for anything in her life.

Yellow, orange and tan foods

These control the spleen. Among them are carrots, oranges, lemons, limes and pineapple, all full of vitamin C. Were we not encouraged to drink hot lemon and honey when we suffered a heavy cold?

Green foods

These govern the liver. They include kiwi fruits, peas, lettuce, watercress, courgettes and green beans. All help cleanse the liver. Eat plenty of these if you have indulged in too much rich food and drink and are suffering a hangover.

Red foods

These boost the heart. Strawberries, raspberries, cherries, beetroot and blackcurrants all help the health of the arteries and heart muscle itself. Strawberries and raspberries are even heart-shaped themselves.

Colour and healing

Colour is a powerful aid to healing and is very necessary for our mental health and happiness.

Hospitals have now accepted that patients recover faster when nursed in a pleasant, colourful room with attractive curtains and drapes, than in the wards of long ago when patients often only looked out onto drab, grey buildings and on equally unattractive surroundings within.

If you are lucky enough to be hospitalized where there are gardens and can actually look out onto a view, that is a great bonus to your recovery.

Colours have meaning and we are dominated through our life with all the colours of the rainbow.

Red

We say that we saw red when expressing our feelings over a volatile situation. Red is a strong colour, it represents leadership, makes you stand out in a crowd. The red traffic light brings you quickly to a halt. Red describes power and is an energy colour.

Orange

Orange is an emotional colour. Many personalities who are the risk takers of this life, such as the racing car driver, often choose orange for their car or choose a protective suit in that hue.

Yellow

Yellow is representative of the coward, but also represents the thinkers of this world, and many inventors are very attracted to the colour yellow.

Green

Green is a very balanced colour, the true colour of nature with all its wide variety of shades, particularly in the spring. Many business people, accountants and the like choose the colour green for their offices. We also say that we were green with envy.

Blue

Blue is the colour of love. We say we feel blue when we are

suffering from a break-up of an emotional relationship.

Baby boys were always dressed in very pale blue, so it also represents, infancy, dependency.

Lavender

The attractive lavender shades are the artistic, healing colours. If you look at any stained glass window in a church you will see a dominance of lavender shades in which the saints and disciples of Christ were dressed. They represent the very centre of our being.

Colour and advertising

Advertising today is yet another powerful way of using colour to attract. Cola is sold in bright red cans for a reason: to make them stand out, to represent power. That is why so many are sold.

If the products advertised on our television screens were in black and white, very few people would bother to buy them.

We are what we eat

We are dying today from diseases of affluence, not poverty. Arteriosclerosis, cancer, the demylinating diseases of the nervous system, arthritis and the like are very common in our Western lifestyle.

We are killing ourselves with what we are putting into our mouths and what we are doing to our planet.

It always amazes me how much money parents spend on equipping their babies with all their practical needs, expensive prams and all the other aids and the right equipment, and, we must all admit, there is so much choice. Then as they grow older, with all the expensive, latest-style clothes, so little trouble is taken on what goes down their throats.

There is only one way children can become addicted to sweets, chocolates, crisps, cola drinks, ice cream and chips, and that is because they were introduced to them by their mothers at a very young age.

The reason they won't eat vegetables and fruit is because they were not encouraged to do so as toddlers. Every child should be encouraged to eat a small portion of a variety of vegetables, try a different one every day, just a teaspoonful to start. They will soon become a basic part of their diet, instead of something that must be avoided at all costs.

I see toddlers in fast-food outlets with their mothers, eating beefburgers and chips with tomato sauce at 11 in the morning. How they expect to build a good immune system with poor quality food I will never know. You can't put rubbish in and expect to get good health out.

How many of us put the best petrol, oil and chemical additives into our cars and then put any old rubbish down our throats? The human body has to last far longer than the average car, which probably will be in the nearest rubbish dump within 10 years. *Nothing is more important than good health.* If you lose it, everything else you possess will be unimportant.

Money does not give good health; common sense, education and good personal effort do.

Coronary artery disease causes 990,000 people to drop dead every year – heart attacks: we hear about these fatalities occurring every day.

A man in his prime dropped dead with a massive heart attack. He seemed so well, say his friends and family. That would have been an impossibility: nobody was fit on Friday and had a heart attack on the following Monday.

The gradual furring up of our arteries takes years and years. In fact some investigations into the health of teenagers conducted at a College of Further Education in a poor area of Northern England found that many children had bulges in their arterial walls already, because of a high fat diet, little exercise and an obese body. These children would be true candidates for coronary artery disease before they reached 40!

There is only one way that we can take cholesterol into our bodies and that is from animal fats. No berry, nut, pulse, bean, fruit or vegetable contains cholesterol. The American Cancer Society says that 70 per cent of all cancers are diet related.

There is an increase in cancers: in fact never before have we had so many terminal diseases, prostate cancers, breast and cervical cancers, cancers of the brain, spine and kidney. Why? Red meat, plus the high consumption of meat products – i.e. beefburgers, hamburgers and sausages – are responsible for a lot. The cattle industry is deeply involved in feeding cattle with growth hormones to produce a 3,000-pound animal and we are taking these hormones into our bodies daily.

Anything we do to the body in the way of suppressing or interfering with a function, such as a vasectomy, sterilization in a female, the birth pill, or the fertility drug, must have a drastic effect on another part of the body.

Cow's milk is an incredible food for cows. The cow has a remarkable digestive system, four stomachs. We are not cows and are the only species on this planet that drinks milk from another species. The only milk designed for human beings is breast milk. This includes everything the body needs including the genetic material to build a strong immune system.

Artificial feeding is why so many children have glue ear, upper and lower respiratory tract infections and asthma; all this, plus constant immunizations and antibiotics from a very early age against nearly everything.

Why do you think there are such things as childhood illnesses? Measles, mumps, chicken-pox and rubella were all intended in order to give the immune system a kick-start. We need these infections so that the body knows what to do when an invasion of bacteria comes onto the scene. The thymus would then become activated and the body produce millions of white blood cells to fight the illness.

The Chinese and Westernization

The Chinese have a very low incidence of cancer whilst they live in their natural environment. Once they become Westernized, within five years they get the same diseases as we do.

The Chinese do eat meat, mainly beef and pork, but the average amount for a family of four for a week is one pound.

Natural living

I once knew an Italian naturopath who lived in a small village in Italy with his wife and six children. The children led a very free life, mostly out of doors, which was possible because the climate was very reliable. They ran about with bare feet when at home and ate vegetables and fruit which were grown in their large garden.

They never went near a doctor and any health problems were

dealt with in a natural way, with herbs, dietary attention and rest, and the body usually did the rest. They never had a vaccination or a drug.

When I was visiting them one day the youngest, who was a toddler of about 18 months, was running about the garden and came across a bad apple, lying in the earth covered with mud, grit and mould. I hastily took the apple out of the child's hand. 'Don't do that', my friend exclaimed, 'let him eat some rubbish. Bad fruit and some soil is good for him; it will help his immune system to function.' Never be too fussy about all this sterilizing: once they crawl it is all pointless.

These six children grew up fine, healthy specimens. They are adults now with families of their own.

The naturopath and his wife are elderly, very fit, and follow the same rules of living, treating illnesses the natural way and neither has ever been near a doctor or a drug.

Healing really is simple.

It is man who has made it so complicated.

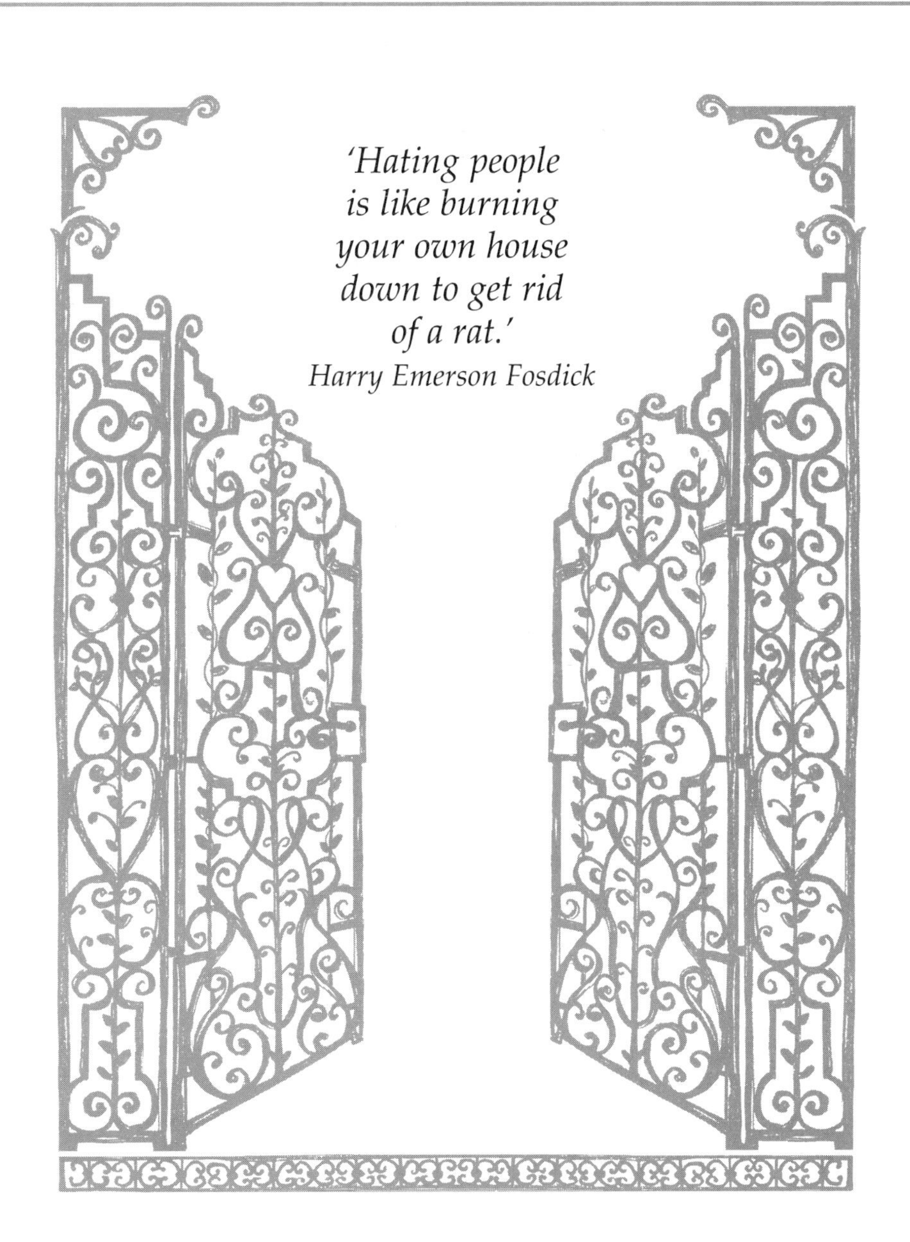

*'Hating people
is like burning
your own house
down to get rid
of a rat.'*
Harry Emerson Fosdick

CHAPTER 3

Energy fields

3 Energy fields

The word 'energy' conjures up much interest in the fields of clairvoyance, spiritualism, precognition, telepathy and the like.

It's amazing how we all very conveniently use all forms of energy in our daily lives without question: television, telephone, radio, the fax machine, radar and so on, and on we could go.

It surely must be hard to perceive that as we walk around a shopping centre, within minutes we could be linked up to our son in Australia, or our next door neighbour 2 miles away. All this from a hand set which has no connecting wires, just a small box which we can hold in the palm of our hand – quite amazing if you consider that just 50 years ago it was a luxury to have a telephone. The progress since the war years is very hard to comprehend.

Individual energies, like the individuality of personality, are impossible to define. No surgeon can, by opening the brain, withdraw personality. And what is personality but our own individuality, our own personal energy?

We talk freely about a soulful person, a warm-hearted friend, a cold-hearted acquaintance in whose presence we prefer not to be.

We have all, at some time in our life, been involved in the time-consuming and often very frustrating job of house hunting. With great enthusiasm we draw up in front of a property whose written description sounds ideal but when we inspect it we are often sadly disillusioned. There again we eventually do find the right house for us and usually we say, 'That's the right one for us, it has a nice feel about it.' What we are actually picking up in this house is a positive energy that is compatible to us. The same often occurs in a garden. Somehow the vibes are just right and give us a very comfortable feeling within.

As the reverse of this we can enter a property or maybe an old stately home which leaves us with a feeling of depression or coldness, and again we say, 'No, that just does not feel right.' We talk about unpleasant atmospheres which are created by individuals, regardless of the fact that not a word has been spoken. What we are picking up are energies which have been emitted from others.

Human beings, in keeping with all other forms of life, emit energies which vary in frequency, amplitude, length and phase. Many different methods have been employed to observe and measure these emissions, including Kirlian photography, a process of identifying 'the aura'.

One of the greatest energies of life is the wind, which again we cannot see, but we are aware of its presence. We can feel its strength, it can be a cool breeze on our face or uproot a city during a tornado and leave death and destruction in its wake.

The power of healing, which is the transference of one energy to another, is known to many. Many gifted healers have an abundance of their own personal energy which can, through the hands, be transferred into the sick. Sick, depressed and ailing people have very limited energy levels. The so-called miracles of the Bible were just these expressions.

Christ was so highly evolved and developed mentally, was so free of all negative thoughts and inhibitions that he had developed his healing energy and was able, by the laying on of hands, to heal the sick.

During this period, the lives of people were very simple and uncomplicated. They planted their grains, ploughed the fields, harvested their foods. Just imagine what a miracle it was when a man just laid his hands over the sick and dying, and they rose up from their beds and walked.

Our personal energy fields are by no means limited to the immediate dimension of the material world. They may be manipulated by the mind and therefore extend their influence into those subtle realms to which the various arcane traditions and psychological disciplines extend.

An instinctive consciousness appears to be slowly emerging from the collective beliefs which accommodate the exchange of energy principle that one must give in order to receive. The psychological consequence of living in a continual state of take is abundantly clear, a fact which many psychiatrists and psychologists will, I am sure, be happy to endorse. People who are essentially takers, who give nothing in return, either spiritually, emotionally or practically, are more prone to neuroses and psychoses than those of a more generous disposition.

It was for this reason that many tribal or early cultures instituted rites, both collective and personal, which involved the act of giving out before one could take in, thus lessening the tendency towards mental and psychosomatic problems and engendering a sense of responsibility to both the community and the environment.

Many early cultures that may appear primitive by our Western standards possessed a knowledge of energy fields far in advance of our own. The shaman, for example, was, and still is in many cases, able to extend his or her aura or influence beyond the human sphere into the animal, plant, mineral and elemental kingdoms.

Of course, human energy fields are not the only ones that influence us and affect our lives and health. Many people suffer from depressions resulting from adverse weather conditions, seasonal changes, sunspot activity and lack of sunlight. The pineal gland has proved to be the culprit in some of these cases. A small, reddish vascular body in the posterior part of the third ventricle of the brain, until recently its functions were uncertain in its relationship to the human form. In other animals it is known to secrete a substance called melatonin. Recent research has come to link it with the effect of light and seasonal variations in the bodily functions. Seasonal depressions are now believed to have pineal origins, while the pigment melatonin appears to be connected with skin colour. One cannot help thinking that the originators of the seasonal rite long, long ago might have been aware of all this, the rite being evocative of energies designed to affect the seasonal adjustment.

Exponents of the new physics are beginning to acknowledge the interaction between all life forms and their associated energy fields and that even the minutest particles are able to communicate with one another regardless of time and space.

There are, however, some hostile energy fields that exist within the environment of our own planet, which pose a considerable threat to our well-being. The damaging effects of nuclear radiation are all too well known. The toxic, polluted place that our planet is becoming causes no end of effect on the health of our nations. Electromagnetic radiation and too close a proximity to electrical force fields can also adversely affect the health of many people.

Nor are all the external cosmic rays that bombard our planet of a beneficial nature. The threatened 'greenhouse effect' hardly encourages hopes for the health of future generations.

Another powerful energy, radionics, like faith healing, has affinities with dowsing, in that it uses forces not fully understood. Water dowsers often had such strong reactions when walking over barren ground with their dowsing rods that they were forced to the ground by the impact of the movement of the rods when they came into contact with water. The explanations of this power are not fully understood. Some believe that what is happening is purely scientific. Others believe that there is some energy that abounds between the dowser and the earth.

In the nineteenth century it was discovered that dowsers could distinguish between pure and impure water by their rod, and could even identify different kinds of impurity. From this it was a short step to using dowsing instruments and in particular the pendulum. The pendulum would have a different reaction when held over a healthy organ from what it had when held over an unhealthy one.

Today this principle is being used for testing allergic reactions to certain foods. The sufferer simply holds a pendulum over a food and by the rotating or swinging action of the pendulum is able to determine whether the food has a positive or negative effect on his body.

At the end of the nineteenth century Abbé Mermet developed diagnosis by the use of a pendulum. As he was highly respected in the Church and had studied the subject very carefully and scientifically, his ideas gained acceptance in his own country and in Italy. Among those who consulted him was the Pope of his day.

Diagnosis by the pendulum was called radiesthesia and owed its development in America to Dr Albert Abrams. Abrams had studied physics as well as medicine and, after completing his studies in Europe, he became a neurologist of international renown.

It was by pure chance, as are many beneficial incidences in life, that Abrams discovered when examining a patient who was suffering from an ulcer on his lip that one small area of the patient's stomach sounded dull when tapped, instead of hollow.

Since this only happened when the patient was facing west, Abrams deduced that the phenomenon had something to do with the earth's magnetic field.

He began examining patients suffering from various diseases and came to the conclusion that atoms in diseased tissue gave off some form of radiation. He was able to relate different sounding points to different diseases.

He argued that if healthy and diseased tissue gave off different radiations, it should be possible to build equipment that would detect those radiations, diagnose and then cure the disease.

Abrams designed a machine that was known as 'the black box'. It produced measured vibrations which he claimed destroyed the infection or imbalanced condition in the patient. His work was scoffed at by some, but when it was tested by the British Medical Association in 1924, his claims for its authenticity in diagnosis were upheld. Unfortunately he really never did reap the rewards for his research and hard labours and died a disappointed man.

Abrams had already found that it was not necessary for a patient to be present in order to arrive at an accurate diagnosis. He could find out what was wrong by a blood spot alone. The blood spot was a microcosm containing within it all the attributes of the macrocosm. Absent diagnosis and healing had become a possibility, since by the use of the blood spot the machine could be tuned in to the distant patient. By focusing on healing vibrations on the blood spot they could be sent forth to the distant patient. These were the striking claims of radionics.

The practitioner uses extrasensory perception rather as a dowser uses his rod. He attunes his mind to the distant patient when he puts the blood spot into the machine. He asks questions but he is more concerned with the causes of the patient's condition rather than their physical manifestation. His aim is to help the patient to realize his full potential in life and thereby find health and happiness. The aim of this treatment is therefore totally holistic.

Faith healing

Faith healing can be divided into various categories. In one form the healing energy can be directed towards a patient by the spirit of a past tribal man, emperor or such-like, who sends his power to the healer: the healer then transmits this power to the patient. This would be classified as spiritual healing. This form of healing is often conducted by the healer in a trance.

The clergy today conduct healing sessions and believe in the laying on of hands and prayers. Hands really were meant for healing. Do you realize what healing you have in your hands? Just rub your two hands briskly together for a few minutes. Feel the heat which builds up in your palms. Now, very slowly separate your hands. Feel the powerful energy between your two palms: it is almost magnetic. Repeat this procedure, each time widening the gap between your hands.

When possible, place your hands on the shoulders of another, preferably somebody who is unwell or very stressed. This is healing. We all have the power to heal in our hands but we need to practise this skill to develop the power of healing.

As we pray, we place our two palms tightly together. What we are really doing is attuning our energy, this time directing it inwards to our own soul. What is our soul? It is the very innermost part of our individuality.

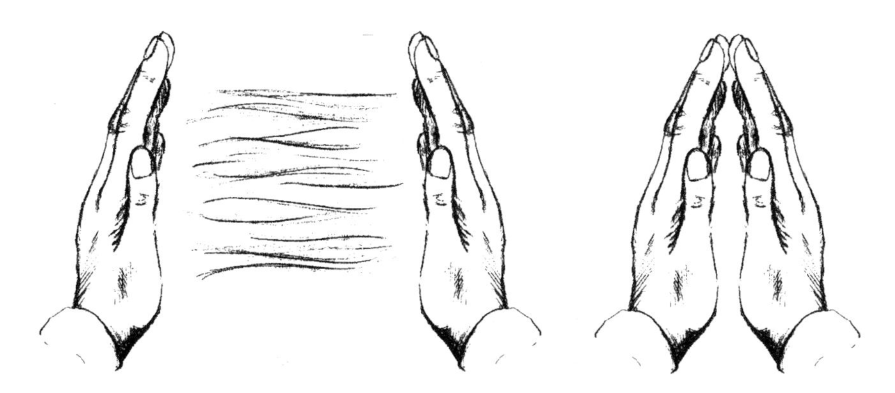

When a church holds a prayer session, as many people as possible are encouraged to attend in order to promote good feelings in the sufferers. What these gatherings really do is to increase the positive flow of energy to the sick.

When we come into this world we enter it in a pure, uncluttered state. We are not born with phobias or fears or inadequacies: they are acquired by the living process – by life itself. As we experience life and all its mysteries, each deed, thought, action, happy, loving experience and sadness is imprinted like the memory bank of a large computer onto our inner self, our soul. Good and bad thoughts and actions are never forgotten. At the end of our life we take these experiences which are contained within a little fluffy ball into our next life. This is our lifeforce, our heaven or hell, our energy which can never be cancelled, lost or forgotten.

Finally there is the healer who recognizes that a power flows through him to the patient but, rather than think of this as being related to supernatural power, he prefers to think of it as a natural power like magnetism or electricity.

Healing has a long history. The Chinese practised its methods 5,000 years ago, and the Egyptians thought that all cures and illness were controlled by the gods.

Common to all groups of healing is the principle that they all work towards the good of the patient and the patient does not necessarily have to believe that what the healer is doing is going to work, although a positive attitude does help.

Faith or spiritual healing has been with us in all civilizations since the dawn of time. It is based on the belief that physical or mental ills can be cured by having a positive faith in some sort of power that may be generated within the patient's own body or drawn from some external supernatural force such as demons or gods.

That an unshakeable belief in the fact that you are going to recover from an illness or injury seems to prompt the body to stimulate its own immune system and heal itself is not disputed. Modern research is hot on the trail of how this works.

Even in this hi-tech age of scientific discoveries and diagnosis the media are full of accounts of people who have recovered from apparently lethal conditions. Other people die rapidly from seemingly uncomplicated conditions. Maybe they had just given up the fight, or had nothing much to live for. Celebrities such as Roy Castle, Marti Cain and Paul Eddington lived for many years after being told by their doctors that there was no hope.

The thousands of people who confound the medical profession come from all walks of life. What they seem to have in common is a determination to live life to the full for as long as possible, plus a faith in their power to survive.

How did such faith originate? Experience must have taught the earth's earliest people that illness or pain simply went away or got worse; if the latter then they would be doomed to die.

As tribal societies developed and people communicated on a more sophisticated level, a sense of the existence of something more powerful than themselves developed.

Through this communication, primitive religions were founded which led to spirits and devils being blamed for illness because an understanding of the real cause of disease, either on a mental or physical level, was beyond man's capabilities. Equally, when a patient made a full recovery, it was thought to be due to the kindness of the gods.

The wisest members of each tribe became doctor-priests who combined the use of healing herbs and potions with magic cures.

The natives of Latin America and Africa still blame the supernatural for their illnesses, and strongly believe that an evil force has invaded their body. A miscarriage would be caused by an evil spirit invading the soul of the baby, thereby making it impossible for that child to have a life on earth.

The sorcery may consist of fantastic rituals involving fire, water, loud drumming, trance states, effigies, relics and magic or surgery, herbal medicine, fasting or eating special foods.

A healer with such power is highly honoured among his people. His charisma and the faith placed in him by his patients form a powerful bond, which may explain why these techniques can work.

In ancient Egypt, thought to be the cradle of rational medical knowledge, belief in the supernatural still dominated. The doctor-priests might have had herbal medicine and surgical skills but they relied on charms, spells and amulets to ward off the evil spirits believed to cause injury or disease. Each body part was thought to be controlled by a specific god who could heal it if enough prayers were said.

Towards the end of the ancient Egyptian civilization all the demons and gods were superseded by a new, super-healing god, Imhotep, a real person who lived around 2900 BC and was the minister of a pharaoh. He instructed patients to fast, say prayers and then sleep the night in a healing temple to be cured.

The ancient Greeks took up this cult, building its first temple, at Epidaurus, in 600 BC. This spawned other temples throughout Egypt. Legend says a plague was raging in Rome and help was sought from Epidaurus. The temple snake slithered onto the waiting ship, sailed to the Tiber, disembarked and the plague ended.

The grander temples had a theatre to divert the ailing and a stadium and gymnasium to encourage exercise and bathing. Hundreds of votive offerings for miraculous cures were left by the temple porticoes and every temple had a round building containing sacred water for purification.

The severely disabled would be lifted down into the sacred waters, and although there is no evidence that any particular substance was added to the waters, instant cures were often witnessed. The atmosphere was so highly charged with energy and the patient so convinced of the healing that was taking place that the patient actually healed himself!

As the sun went down the visitor, having already fasted, would observe the complex rites and rituals with the attendant priests. He would then enter the healing sanctuary, lie down on a pallet and enter a state of relaxed consciousness, perhaps drifting into sleep.

During the night the priest, dressed as Asclepios, the god of healing, and his attendants would treat each patient in turn. The treatment might be a laying on of hands, the dressing of a wound, a minor surgical operation or the placing of a sacred animal on the affected part. Occasionally a volunteer would undergo the experience for someone who was too weak to travel.

Regardless of the type of treatment, the patient usually woke up healed, although sometimes it took longer than one night.

Records show that blindness, lameness, headaches and skin diseases were all cured. The most important factor was that the patient had faith that the treatment would work, and every aspect of the temples was designed to encourage this belief.

The classical Indian art of medicine, the Ayurveda, relies on strong belief in both doctors and deities. Patients still ask for amulets, charms and prayers as well as antibiotics to fight infections.

In some areas of India children's ailments are seen as the work of celestial demons, so astrologers as well as physicians are consulted. Many Indians believe injections give superhuman powers no matter what is injected, and pressure their doctors for jabs of pure water.

The most famous healer of all times was probably Jesus Christ. Many of the miracles related in the Gospels refer to the laying on of hands and the casting out of demons who were thought to possess their victims and drive them mad. This belief persisted in Europe well into the seventeenth century and still exists in parts of Africa and Latin America.

The Gospels say that Jesus raised Lazarus from the dead and made the dumb speak, the deaf hear and the blind see. He caused the crippled and paralysed to take up their bed and walk and he cleansed the leprous who were outcasts from society, by the laying on of hands.

Can you imagine what a tremendous impact Christ made on the very simple people of that time? It would have indeed been regarded as a miracle, so much so that during the mass gatherings that accumulated to hear Christ speak, many were cured by just touching his gown. Whatever the occasion, the healing he effected was always miraculous and instantaneous.

Everyone has the power to heal but few ever develop their potential. With the rush and tear of modern fast living and the increase in the development of sophisticated forms of technology we have forgotten the simple forms of healing, and few of us ever use the natural approaches to heal ourselves.

What generally happens is that we spend our lives abusing our bodies with drinking, smoking and the fight to get more and more material belongings, and when we eventually end up as a mental and physical wreck, we throw ourselves unconditionally into the hands of our doctors for an immediate cure.

Through the centuries, many of the devout gained their sainthoods by founding hospitals and hospices. Physical medicine went hand in hand with prayer, healing rituals, exorcisings, the laying on of hands and the use of sacred relics and amulets.

It may be difficult for most non-Christians to believe the ancient stories of Christ's healing, but Harry Edwards, an English spiritual healer who died in 1976, received literally millions of letters from all over the world asking for the healing help of his spirit guides.

Nowadays Billy Graham, the charismatic American evangelist, claims to use the power of faith in God to heal, and packs out huge venues such as Wembley Stadium with his followers, as does Matthew Manning the young British healer.

There is no doubt that mass healing generates an emotionally charged atmosphere which is exciting and exhilarating, but it is difficult to collate evidence on the permanence of any cures which occur.

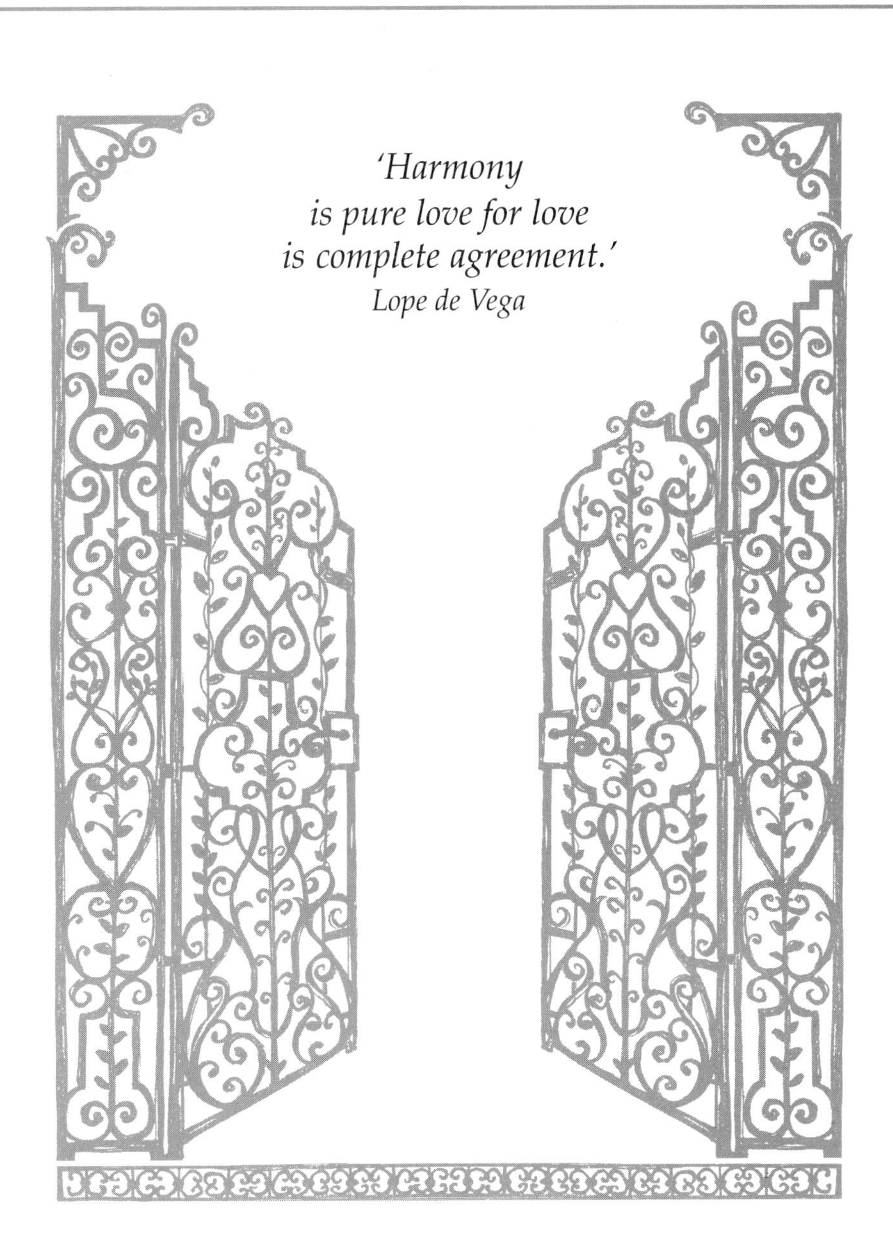

CHAPTER 4

Allergies

4 Allergies

We hear so much about allergic reactions to so many things from cat fur, house dust, perfume, chemical sprays, wheat and cheese, to chocolate and seafood, to name but a few. Why, then, can one person eat as much as he or she likes of any type of food and live quite happily in the environment whilst another suffers continually with allergic reactive symptoms?

An allergy is a hypersensitivity to a foreign substance which produces a violent reaction, taking the form of asthma, hay fever, urticaria, eczema, migraine, catarrh or irritable bowel syndrome. Sensitivity covers a wide range of irritants including animal odours, pollen and insect bites.

All kinds of food may be responsible – milk, eggs, pork, tomatoes, strawberries, coffee, tea and so on – as well as preservatives and artificial colouring.

Substances that cause allergic reactions are known as allergens. Their numbers are limitless. Against these the body produces antibodies to fight off invaders. If we are allergic, such defence mechanisms over-react. The reaction has the effect of releasing various chemicals, such as histamine, which causes irritation and swelling of mucous membranes. Removal of dental amalgam fillings sometimes relieves the condition.

Perhaps the most common allergy is hay fever. It is now known that most sufferers have a family history of the complaint. Asthma is a serious form but with the aid of certain herbs (lobelia, for example) sufferers may lead normal lives.

Premature babies fed on cow's milk are at risk of cow's milk allergy with increased histamine.

Food allergies from shell fish, cereal, grain and fungi are difficult to detect.

A large body of opinion favours garlic (corm, tablets or capsules), it being observed that garlic eaters seldom suffer allergies.

Skin reactions may be severe. Hives, dermatitis and blisters can be the result of allergies triggered off by insect stings or animal bites, drugs, food additives, colouring, monosodium glutamate, chocolate, wines, aspirin, penicillin and other drugs. Cytotoxic tests are made to discover foods to which a person may be allergic.

Heredity predisposes, but forms vary. A 'nettle rash' father may have a 'hay fever' son. Stress is an important factor. While allergy is not a psychosomatic disturbance there is general agreement that emotional distress – fright, fury or fatigue – can be related as our body is already then in 'the red alert state'. An allergy can also be due to a flaw in the immune system, to the body over-reacting to an allergen.

Valerian is an excellent herb to take to reduce nervous hyperactivity.

A diet low in salt and fat but high in fibre is recommended. Eggs and dairy produce are known to cause allergies. Raw salad should be taken once daily. Add more protein cooked and raw vegetables. Rice and pasta are not generally known to cause any allergic reaction unless there is a sensitivity to gluten.

Good general supplements which are recommended are vitamins A, B complex and C, selenium and zinc.

Allergy increases when the body is overloaded with toxins, particularly sugars, so the first remedy is to reduce your sugar intake to nil. Take no refined sugars in any way, and that includes all the sugar-laced drinks. The sugar intake in our diets has increased dramatically since the war years when we were strictly rationed, which was all to the benefit of health, as during the war the health of the nation had never been better.

If you are suffering from an acute episode of allergy, whatever its form, go on a fast. Drink nothing but pints and pints of spring water for two days – give the body a chance to detoxify itself – and the allergy will certainly improve. Very few fruits ever cause an allergy, with the exception perhaps of oranges. Make sure that you soak all fruit in hot water before eating; the sprays used to protect the outer coating of fruits are often a cause of allergy. For the third day of your fast liquidize several fruits, mix with a proportion of spring water and drink as many glassfuls per day as you wish.

Just to confirm my experience in how an acute toxic condition in the body causes allergy I should like to relate a story of a patient of mine who was a sufferer from hay fever and asthma which generally occurred in its worst state between May and July. John had a severe allergy to roses in particular, and to go out into a garden during the rose season was just out of the question, for within an hour or so of being exposed to the pollen he would be suffering from streaming eyes and nose and then within 24 hours a severe attack of asthma would occur.

He was very interested in natural cures, as for years he had been on high doses of various medications for his allergic hay fever and asthma, and all the medication did was to relieve the attacks, but did nothing to help the underlying cause. I recommended that John go and spend his next holiday at a nature cure clinic to see if various detoxifying programmes could help his health problem.

John was dismayed to find that, as he approached the clinic, there was a long drive, on either side of which were masses of roses in full bloom. Within minutes his eyes began to stream and then progressed to a streaming nose. Later that evening things became worse and the clinic doctor was summoned as John had a severe attack which had to be controlled by drugs.

During the next few days John fasted on just spring water for the first two days and then fruit juices seven or eight times a day. He was also treated with coffee enemas to clear his bowel area, and put into a steam cabinet, again to help detoxify his body.

He was given a daily massage and several herbal inhalations to help his asthmatic condition. At the end of this rather severe regime John was feeling very weak and wobbly. However, there was no sign of his hay fever or asthma.

For the second week of his stay his diet was increased to vegetables, rice and still seven or eight glasses of various pure fruit juices, including apple and grape.

John began to feel well, a well-being that was unknown to him. He described it as a lightness of body and mind. He started taking gentle exercise, jogging and swimming, and by the end of the third week was ready to be discharged with instructions on how to eat better, live better and stay well. As John walked down that same tree-lined drive with the roses in abundance, he became nervous of the same situation arising. The doctor who was with him said that as his body was in a cleaned state there was no way in which the allergy could rear its head. 'Bend over the roses and inhale their perfume', he said, 'there is no need to worry now.' John did as he asked and inhaled the perfume from the roses; no reaction occurred because his body was not in the right state for the allergy to manifest. There is truth in the statement that disease flourishes when the soil is right.

From reading this case history it should be obvious now that it is pointless applying hydrocortisone creams to the skin of those individuals suffering from eczema or psoriasis. The skin is the first line of defence in the process of elimination and throws out impurities this way. If we apply creams to the skin all we do is to drive the inflammation back into the body, whereupon nature will find another outlet, such as the ear (ear infections), the throat (tonsillitis), the lungs (asthma and bronchitis), the bowel (diarrhoea), the bladder (urinary infections).

Food sensitivity or allergy can cause asthma, eczema, migraine, arthritis, depressive behaviour and learning problems, diarrhoea, gallstones, tiredness, fluid retention, weight fluctuation, catarrh, epilepsy, mouth ulcers, Crohn's disease and urticaria.

Sometimes it is possible to relate the problem to a particular food or foods, and it is very often the food that you most crave that is the culprit. One problem with tracking down a food sensitivity is that the first symptoms of a reaction can occur within seconds, hours or even days after consumption. There may be vague symptoms after eating the foods, such as flushing, red ears, diarrhoea, irritability or stomach-ache. These will tend to subside. Over a long period of time of ingesting these foods a weakening of the digestive system will occur and an even more severe reaction to the offending foods.

A poor diet, lack of sleep, infections, distress, digestive problems, extreme temperatures, a smoky or polluted atmosphere, certain medical drugs and pollutants in food may together weaken your immune system and cause it to react unusually with a normally innocuous food.

Food sensitivity often rears its head after gastroenteritis, the use of antibiotic drugs, malnutrition or jaundice.

In coeliac disease the bowel cannot absorb gluten. This commonly starts in infancy and can follow gastroenteritis.

The most common culprits in cases of asthma are manufactured fruit squashes and fizzy drinks. Any substance, be it food or liquid, that contains cyclamates or similar artificial sweetening agents, sodium benzoate, milk, eggs, wheat, cheese, yeast, fish and fried foods should be avoided.

Possible culprits with migraine sufferers include oranges, chocolate, sugar, cheese, alcohol (especially red wine), wheat, eggs, coffee, tea, cola, milk or beef. One in ten migraine sufferers is food-sensitive. Try cutting out caffeine, alcohol and added sugars first. If you have migraine your blood may be abnormally sticky.

Other potential dangers are foods containing salicylates or citric acid, which are found in cola drinks and citrus fruit. These foods can cause depression, confusion, hyperactivity, anxiety, clumsiness and tiredness. They have also been linked with schizophrenia.

Diet

Identify culprit foods with an exclusion diet. You may not have to avoid these foods for ever, though coeliac sufferers need professional advice. Sometimes after avoiding the food for several months it is possible to reintroduce it gradually, although you may only be able to eat it every few days.Your symptoms may temporarily worsen after stopping the food but continued avoidance brings relief.

When rearing infants, especially if there is a family history of allergy, ideally breast-feed for at least six months. Avoid cow's milk and all foods produced by the cow. Wheat sometimes has a drastic reaction on a delicate stomach. Citrus fruits, too, are not acceptable, and avoid all foods containing pips until the baby has reached his first birthday.

Lower your risk of developing a food sensitivity by avoiding refined and processed foods. More essential fatty acids may help, and extra fish rich in vitamin A and C may well be useful.

Some food-sensitive people produce insufficient gastric acid. This can lead to poor absorbency of nutrients such as calcium and iron. It may help to eat meat at different times from carbohydrates (different digestive enzymes are needed to digest meat, which causes more stress on the digestive system than other foods, such as vegetables and fish which are of a lighter consistency and far kinder to the stomach). Eat more foods containing niacin.

If you have been eating poorly, because of illness, or maybe you have just been feeling under the weather and your energy levels are low, snacking on quick convenience foods which are usually full of fat and very low in any mineral or vitamin content would have been your routine at this time, as probably you could just 'not be bothered'.

A poor diet means that you are probably short of iron, magnesium, zinc and vitamin B, so eat more foods rich in these nutrients until you feel better.

Cutting down on alcohol may help. Foods rich in vitamin B6 may make asthma less likely and foods rich in selenium may improve eczema. Watercress may help too.

Foods rich in vitamins B6, C and E, garlic and ginger may help migraine. These, along with fatty acids, reduce the stickiness of the blood. Feverfew leaves relieve some migraine headaches; they are certainly well worth trying.

Seventeen years before Pasteur announced his germ theory Florence Nightingale wrote:

> 'It is a continual mistake to look upon diseases, as we do now, as separate entities, which must exist, like cats and dogs, instead of looking at them as conditions, like a dirty and a clean condition, and just as much under our control, or rather as the reactions of a kindly nature, against the conditions in which we have placed ourselves.'

Sometimes allergies can have their foundations in fear – fear of the allergy. So just as soon as a cat, dog or rabbit appears on the scene, which may cause an allergic reaction, a huge amount of adrenalin is released into the bloodstream, which then puts the body into its 'fight or flight' reaction mode. This in turn makes the body over-sensitive. In this state the body immediately reacts to its allergen.

There is an old saying, 'A fear is an unrequited wish', and it is interesting to observe that we frequently attract that which we fear the most. The reason for this is that we tend to visualize the fear. Nor are the results of this visualization process limited to illness and similar disorders. The single man or woman beset by fears of being left on the shelf often experiences great difficulties in finding a partner, and if a new relationship appears on the scene, the feelings of insecurity or inadequacy are so great that the relationship is instantly under great strain, and may be the cause of a breakdown before either party get the opportunity of knowing the other.

If our mental processes can work against us then surely they can be put into reverse so that they will work with us. Doctors tell us that our many aches, pains and allergies are psychosomatic - mentally induced – albeit at an unconscious level. What then is to prevent us mentally inducing a cure and healing ourselves, but at a conscious level? It seems ridiculous that doctors and scientists agree that certain diseases are manifested by stress; for example, a large ulceration of the stomach is caused by the sufferer being in a stressed state, but a large tumorous growth called a cancer is 'cause unknown'! Cancer is often related to the type of personality that tends to feel helpless and repress emotions.

Self-help and self-healing centres are beginning to appear in many towns and cities of Britain. The first and most famous of these is the Cancer Help Centre at Bristol, which was opened in 1980 to offer natural cancer control therapies to patients. The methods designed are not just to treat the symptoms of cancer but to restore the whole person to health.

Disease, in whichever form it takes, be it allergy, cancer or whatever, is the manifestation of chaos in the body. So fear and chaos walk hand in hand. The element of chaos does exist within us whether we like it or not.

We may choose to ignore the symptoms and hope that they will disappear, or bury our head in the sand or look heavenward, but sooner or later our physical body will give way to death and disintegration. You cannot suppress disease; if one part of the body is suppressed then a dysfunction or disease occurs in another.

It is rather like the story of the little Dutch boy who kept his finger in the wall of the dam in order to stop the water flowing out. Sooner or later the finger just had to be removed and then all hell was let loose. Your body works in exactly the same way.

Constant suppression by the use of drugs causes yet more disease and allergy to manifest themselves.

'You can never plan the future by the past.'
Edmund Burke
1729-1797
British politician

CHAPTER 5

Mind, man and medicine

5 Mind, man and medicine

I'm sure we will agree that over the last hundred years mankind has done a great job in destroying this very wonderful planet, with the pollution of our water, frequency of oil leaks from ships that cause such toxicity to our seas and the death of our fish and wildlife.

The thinning of the ozone layer is another complex situation which is causing distress and destruction. We pack too many people onto a very small planet and the destruction of more and more trees in our rain forests leaves a lot to be desired.

There is little chance of the survival of either individuals or the planet unless and until we get it all together swiftly enough to halt the approaching total destruction.

There's nothing negative in having money, only how it is spent or used by those who possess it. Greenpeace, for example, needs the green energy of money to continue its efforts to save the whales, dolphins and seals from cruel slaughter and mindless extinction.

So few of us make enough effort to follow the example of Greenpeace and complain about the plight of the whales, the dolphins and all other forms of marine life. We should all lobby our representatives and make our views known to prevent such unnecessary cruelty from taking place. We must not think it is the responsibility of 'someone else' to do it on our behalf. It is a responsibility we should all share in order to help protect our planet.

Science tells us that a living creature is nothing more than a complex of molecules and electromagnetism which have somehow organized themselves into entities which we call the living body.

In this scenario the mind and body are completely separate. Furthermore, all our daily and life experiences – kindness, affection, generosity, love, intolerance, anger, hatred, jealousy, greed, fear, beauty, the appreciation of nature, the joy of rhythm and self-awareness – arise from the mind, and scientists have very little idea of how exactly that works.

Even mystic, psychic, near-death and out-of-body experiences are all supposed to have arisen from a chaotic state of the mind. Conventional medicine and scientific wisdom has not the slightest idea how all these subjective experiences actually arise.

How amazing it is to accept that the mind, which is the greatest controlling influence of our life, cannot be lifted out of the brain and inspected, so that we can dissect the love emotion into a receiving bowl and place the hatred and jealousy into another.

The mind is the thinking part of man and everything evolved from this planet by a thought: how to create friction from two sticks to produce a fire, the beginning of a powerful energy, the evolvement from thoughts that made man able to invent the wheel. What about wars? They too all started from a single thought: I want to own your land and if you don't let me have it then we will fight for possession.

Everyone acknowledges that the electrical activity of the brain has something to do with brain – mind function, but the electro-magnetic level of energy function is still only physical. It tells us nothing of thought or emotion and of our subjective life as we experience it every day. Scientists do not even know how we waggle our big toe, as they have no idea of what thought is nor of the nature of self or mind.

Looking at the physical, there is no doubt that the body consists of a dynamic integrated wealth of very active cells which move about the body and destroy and rebuild themselves every second.

Like brain and mind function, nobody from a conventional point of view has any idea what on earth is going on.

The power of the mind is such that just the handing over of a bottle of attractive colourful drugs can put the body right, regardless of what the capsules contain.

I remember a drug trial for the treatment of migraine when I worked in a hospital some years ago. A hundred patients were given some very attractive capsules to take for the relief of their chronic migraines. The capsules contained calcium carbonate. A further one hundred patients were given a drug which resembled an aspirin, but was in fact a new drug which had been produced to control migraine.

Three months later the two hundred patients were called back to the migraine clinic.

Of the patients taking the attractive capsules 70 per cent reported a great improvement. Of the patients taking the unattractive tablets 40 per cent said that their condition had improved. The remaining 60 per cent reported no improvement whatsoever. This is known as the placebo effect, and it is part of that area of medicine that is little understood.

The placebo effect and all psychosomatic phenomena indicate that the mind affects body function dramatically. We cannot say that there was nothing wrong with that person anyway, for even pathological and physiological symptoms can disappear when the individual's mind is convinced that they will get better, and the reverse is also true. Therefore if the mind is convinced that health will ensue by swallowing a pill of calcium carbonate then health will ensue, and if the mind is convinced that ill health will continue and there is absolutely no hope, then all the drugs in the world will not help.

The mind therefore is a high-energy field which patterns and administers the function of the human body. A clear-sighted, direct study of the structure of these subtle realms of mind energy is therefore a matter of the greatest importance, which will occupy science for much of the next century.

Let us now consider the large variety of experiences we encounter in our daily lives where the effects of our mind govern our decisions and create in us happiness or despair.

The mind chemistry which we experience when two people become involved emotionally, which we call falling in love, is but one expression. It is a feeling which, after all, is energy arising from two people who know little or nothing about each other, but is dynamic enough to start a relationship.

The despair of grieving for a lost loved one is a shattering experience which can result in the rise of all manner of chaotic emotions: love, anger, loneliness, despair. Not only do the grieving suffer the variety of emotions discussed but they usually exhibit some unpleasant physical symptoms too, palpitations, diarrhoea, aches and pains all over the body, all the manifestation of a painful mind, creating an anatomy of despair.

Illness can in many instances be a very convenient escape from many of the responsibilities in life. After all, if you are sick most of the time you will not be expected to do the housework or shopping, entertain or get a job, so illness is a way of not facing up to living life to the full.

I well remember a friend of mind who was a sufferer from severe migraine, and had been for 20 years. She worked as a part-time medical secretary but had lots of time away from work because of her illness. She always seemed to take an extra week at Christmas, Easter and any other festive occasion because of yet another migraine attack.

Her life was a comparatively easy one, her husband always picked her up from work in the late afternoon, so that she did not have to suffer the stress of queuing up for buses at the end of the day. Her efficient daughters, although very young, seemed to do most of the shopping and a lot of the housework - stress, they said, made Mum's migraine come on. She even had a timer on her desk which reminded her to take her pills at the exact time, just as prescribed by the doctor.

During the period of my meeting this lady I, too, was a medical secretary but also very involved in the study of Reflexology. I was attending a course in London and needed as many feet as possible on which to practise my skills. I offered her the opportunity of having some Reflexology, and suggested that we get together in the lunch hour and use one of the consulting rooms.

Treatments commenced, and after a month an improvement was noticed. The migraines were less frequent, the patient had a brighter look about her and the rather drained, pale complexion took on a rosy hue. So noticeable was the change that many staff in the hospital commented on how much better she was looking. 'You look 10 years younger' was the general statement.

Treatments continued, and within two months medication was reduced to a minimum and I commented that Reflexology was going to give her a freedom from migraine and a much healthier future. Within the next couple of weeks, excuses seemed to appear; she could not manage to have treatment today as she had to go to the shops in her lunch hour, and so on, and so the treatments ceased and the migraines returned.

Upon reflection I realized that my positive attitude to better health for the future for her was the very worst thing I could have said, as it meant a far heavier work load and responsibility, less attention and support from her husband and daughters, and it was a no-go area. Her life with the migraines was easier, she got more attention and this she was reluctant to give up.

A friend of mine who is a very experienced psychologist always says that when a couple come to you for psychotherapy and one of the couple has a chronic illness, the cause of the condition is usually the person sitting next to him or her. How sad it is to accept this, but it is true.

A very dominant person who never allows their partner the freedom of self-expression, who answers all the questions and makes all the decisions, is causing massive stresses in the relationship. Stress causes dis-ease; the more ill at ease your mind is the more imbalances occur in your body. An acid mind creates an acid body, very frequently the cause of arthritis.

A good relationship is where a couple stand side by side, not too close together, or they will be unable to act as individuals. If one leans too heavily on the other, the stresses begin.

'Oh, we have never had a cross word in our marriage,' a husband or wife proclaims, as if that is the ultimate achievement in life, to live without upsetting or not agreeing – impossible.

A relationship could only survive like that if one in the partnership constantly suppressed his feelings and gave in to any situation which arose rather than cause an upset. Suppressed anger causes depression; it also depletes our immune system.

I firmly believe that many victims of cancer are victims of suppression. Maybe they never fulfilled their ambitions, maybe they were creative, but nobody ever recognized it, so rather than force the issue and take up painting, pottery or flower arranging which might have caused changes to be made in their otherwise organized lifestyle, they never bothered and so became members of the 'if only I had' or 'I wish I had taken up this or that years ago' or 'I have always been so miserable in my job, I really hated it' club.

We can look to nature to help us heal ourselves. Trees have great healing energy. Herbalists have always been aware of this, in regard to those properties contained in their leaves, bark and so on.

But contrary to what many may think, the tree, like every other living thing, has a soul or essence which is as enduring as our own. The ancient Greeks called the tree spirits dryads and designated one branch of their kind, the hamadryads, as being responsible for the growth of forests. This knowledge did not die with the ancients, however.

How then can a tree heal? Mike Spring, paralysed from the waist down and in constant pain, sailed to the Azores and back. On his return he confounded his TV interviewer with the statement that the only way he was able to obtain relief from the pain that continually racked his body was to press his back to an oak tree. This would give relief and helped him to carry on with life. When asked for an explanation Mr Spring said that he had none. He had heard of the treatment from an American Indian who had been using the treatment successfully for many years.

Maybe we all need to put the fun back into our lives. Laughter and becoming a child again for a while will help to reduce stress and improve our immunity levels – you know, splashing around in a puddle, climbing a tree, sitting on a swing, throwing stones onto a pond and watching the ever enlarging circles. Reducing stress and relaxing releases endorphins (the body's own chemicals that boost well-being) and may even increase your energy. If this miraculous substance came in pill form, stores would not be able to keep it on the shelves.

Laughing, according to the American Institute of Stress, makes the heart beat faster and the lungs pump more effectively. University of Louisville psychiatrist Joel Elkes, MD, is so impressed by the health benefits of enjoying oneself that he holds workshops for medical students to teach the role it plays in healing.

Fun is a gift, one you should give yourself every day, even a few minutes of pleasure a day can give you the strength to tackle your responsibilities with renewed energy and enthusiasm. Fun comes in many forms. Enjoy a few minutes a day or revel in it for a few weeks at a time.

Jot down every way you can think of having a good time, however impractical it may seem. Your ideas might include getting together with a friend, sneaking off for a day at the beach, getting a massage or facial. Set aside at least one day a week and try out one of the ideas from your list. Decide which people in your life bring you the most joy and spend as much time as possible with them.

Understanding disease

Disease is an integral part of the rich tapestry of life. Unfortunately, the very word evokes, in most of us, fear, and thoughts of disability, pain and eventual death.

A century ago it was taken for granted that disease was an organic physical process caused by pathogens – germs, viruses, toxins and similar constituents. Each specific disease was believed to have its own specific cause, and if that cause could be identified and a cure found for it then so much the better. Medical students were taught that the mind and the emotions played no part in the disease process. A medical prescription was the panacea of all ills; any condition which defied that was viewed as either incurable or a suitable case for the surgeon's skills. Even mental illness, it was assumed, would eventually be traced to some biochemical malfunctioning, and those who were suffering from neurotic or hysterical disorders were seen as not really ill in the strict sense of the word but rather as social misfits who should be pulling themselves together and not wasting the doctor's time. Symptoms are the body's way of crying out for a little help, support or comfort, a signal for attention.

All physical ailments had to be the result of somatic disturbances. Until psychiatry and psychology made inroads into the areas of established medical thought there was no other factor to consider.

Fringe practitioners, such as osteopaths, chiropractors or homoeopaths, were viewed as quacks, charlatans or at best well-intentioned cranks.

In ancient China there were three types of doctors. The first kind merely cured your disease and was the least of the three. The second was an expert in diagnosing an illness, not only after it appeared but earlier, shortly before it appeared. He was higher on the medical ladder. The most skilled and most respected physician was the one who kept his patients so healthy that they never manifested sickness in the first place.

And it went further. A doctor in China was paid only when his patients got well after he had healed them, and in some districts the doctor was under strict obligation to make economic amends should a patient become worse or continue to be ill under his care, because it was considered that if he had not kept his patients healthy then their diseases were fully his responsibility.

Every time a patient died a lantern of a certain shape was hung outside the doctor's office and a doctor with too many of these lanterns swinging at the front door could be assured of a slow business.

The physicians who complain today about the high insurance caused by malpractice suits should be glad they weren't practising in ancient China when the doctors were blamed for everything (unjustly) and the patients given no responsibility for their own mental attitudes, which caused their illnesses to linger.

Why must everything be one extreme or the other? A little of each would be nice, with physicians and patients taking equal responsibility for good health.

Sad though the truth may be, the medical profession would appear to be incapable of imposing the necessary disciplines upon its members, while testing procedures, especially upon animals, cannot always detect dangerous side effects early enough to prevent serious casualties later.

Brian Inglis and Ruth West in their book *The Alternative Health Guide* state categorically that research over the past 20 years has revealed that many of the scientific theories upon which modern medicine has been built are quite simply fallacious. Disease is not an organic process, they insist; germs, viruses and toxins play a part, but it is a relatively minor one. Just how minor a part has been exposed in research into heart disease and cancer in particular, as it has now been made clear that these diseases have no single cause, although there are several contributory factors which are mainly concerned with our lifestyles.

Heavy smoking and the consumption of large amounts of animal fats increase our risk of falling victim to these two potential killers, while it has now been discovered that some personality types are more susceptible than others. People are at most risk when subjected to certain kinds of stress, retirement, redundancy, bereavement and similar traumas. So, our personalities dictate the type of disorders from which we are most likely to suffer, our lifestyles decide the level of the risk, and our stress precipitates the outcome. As recently as 15 years ago a pronouncement of this kind would have met with outright rejection by the medical authorities, but not so today.

For many British people, the thought of visiting a psychiatrist or psychologist for fear of being recorded as unstable, or odd, on some secret records that might exist in the memory bank of a heartless computer, would have been unacceptable. People should stand on their own feet and sort out their own problems, we hear.

These days more and more people are facing up to their problems and trying, through therapy, to change their lot and find a new quality of life. There again therapists often cost money and GPs do not, so for the vast majority of us it is the local surgery or hours spent in the waiting room of a busy hospital.

While it is all too easy to decry the shortcomings of the medical profession, in spite of their drugs, closed minds and disregard for less obvious aspects of human mental sufferings, where technology is concerned they have performed their own special brand of miracles. Enormous strides have been made in surgery, and the use of lasers has helped to alleviate much suffering, to restore sight to many and to give children the chance of a life they might not otherwise have known.

Some of us respond to the red alarm, others try to pretend that symptoms do not exist. They clutch the inevitable bottle of pain killers, antacids or such-like in the hope that the symptom will disappear just as quickly as it appeared. Sometimes it does and sometimes it does not.

The majority of chronic illness is a combination of pre-disposition, inadequate defence (that immune system again!) and repeated challenges in the form of nutrition, radiation, pollution and so on. Our systems are subjected to an excess of pollution due to the so-called progress of this twentieth century, and our immune systems are having to work overtime in coping with this overload of toxins.

Inflammation is the standard response of the body to sudden challenge from heat, light radiation, chemicals and organisms, the symptoms being pain, heat, swelling and redness which is caused by the dilation of blood vessels. Inflammation of one kind or another is seen in the majority of cases of disease and ultimately we must all succumb to the failure of whichever organ has been used or abused the most.

Orthodox medicine looks at the body as a machine, and this is both its success and its failure. The failure of the orthodoxy is its apparent inability to distinguish between the body and the person and in making the assumption that they are identical. This is the inevitable consequence of the approach in medicine to specialize – one doctor to treat the lung, another the heart, yet another the digestive system, and so on. All systems of the body are linked together and cannot be separated, and as you treat one part with drugs or surgery it has an ultimate negative effect on another.

It is becoming evident that the only way forward is to examine the whole ecological framework within which a disease prospers and find ways of adjusting that environment so that the condition simply evaporates within the course of time. Indeed, the model that we are left with is that of the body as a continually changing process kept in dynamic balance by its own internal precision.

Consider the heart, which starts its life as two moving tubes and eventually forms itself into a double pump, approximately the size of its owner's fist, which can go on relentlessly beating billions of times without (a) a new part and (b) never needing a service. No other pump has ever been produced by man that can work so efficiently for so long without attention.

What about the brain, a comparatively small computer, which can store experiences of a lifetime, building on its memory capacity day by day?

The endocrine system is another marvel. Minute hormonal balances are secreted directly into the bloodstream, activating every special need of the body, to drink or procreate, to give immediate action in times of stress, fear or exhilaration, and all controlled by a master gland, the pituitary, just the size of a peanut, which lies between the eyes and behind the nose. Our hormonal secretions give rise to the massive growth spurt in puberty which changes the little girl into a woman and the young boy into a man.

During our maturing years, the powerful sex drive to procreate lessens and the woman's child-bearing years cease as her body decides to rest a little, slow down and enjoy a different life as her offspring leave the nest and she can watch and wonder and enjoy a different stage of her life.

I believe your body feels your mind: if your mind hurts it creates a pain, ache or problem with a function in a part of your body.

I believe that if we suffer a painful attack on our femininity as a woman – like an abortion, still birth, the inability to conceive –

that in turn leaves us wide open for disease to manifest in our sexual organs if all other factors are in place, and that means a toxic body and depleted immune system.

The painful attack could, in many instances, be an emotional attack. This is even more damaging, in many events, than a physical one.

The same theory applies to men; they too need nurturing and can suffer the same physical distresses when an attack occurs to them, say as the result of divorce, lack of open contact with their children, the increased financial responsibility that occurs when the family home has to be divided and each of the couple go their own way. The couple are then involved in an entirely new form of stress.

Would not this be a contributory factor in the ever increasing statistics of prostate and testicular cancer in younger and younger men?

If the body therefore has this marvellous ability to perform so well and variously for so many years, it must have also the ability to repair, rebuild and heal itself given the right opportunities so to do. It can do so with the right input and care and consideration from its owner, and that's YOU.

CHAPTER 6

Focusing on the positive

6 Focusing on the positive

In any given moment there is ample evidence to prove that life is a bed of thorns or a garden of roses. How we feel about life depends on where we place our attention, that is, what we focus upon.

Right now, in this moment, you can prove that life is an arduous, impossible experience, with tragedy around every corner, the weather is not up to much, the road traffic is denser by the day and your overdraft is increasing.

Very few of us ever see the same view from the same window. We can become blinded from our mental chaos from ever enjoying a sunset, a lawn after the rain, a bed of roses, a bird on the wing. Even when these beauties are all around, when in the negative frame of mind all we ever see is that small grey cloud in a sky of brilliant blue.

What is around you that you find aesthetically pleasing – a painting that you have really not looked at for years, a vase, wallpaper or the pleasant colour of your carpet? Some look out of their windows and see that four-leafed clover, others see an old cola can!

If you look for things that are not quite right with your body you will be totally dissatisfied, particularly as you grow older – a lump here, a rough spot there, thinning hair, a few aches and pains in areas where once there were none. With medical conditions, it's good to keep track of symptoms, but it does no good to dwell upon them.

I remember treating a lady who came to see me with a host of various medical conditions, the main one being a very painful left shoulder. Added to that she had irritable bowel syndrome, asthma, painful arthritic knees and migraine. After several treatments I asked her if her health problems had shown any improvement. 'I have still got my irritable bowel trouble, my asthma has been the same and my knees have been really painful.' 'What about your painful shoulder?' I asked. 'That is what you really came to see me about.' 'Oh that,' she replied. 'I had no trouble with my shoulder following the first treatment!'

This lady obviously had to hang onto her health problems. Life without something to complain about would have been unacceptable.

There is a story told of a guru who saw a dead dog decaying in the road. His disciples tried to keep the unsightly animal from him but the guru said, 'What pearly white teeth he has.' So even in the decaying state, something good was discovered.

Don't put off living your life until you are better. We can all say, 'I'll do it when I am older, I'll do it when I have more money or when the children are off my hands.' Regardless of all these things you keep putting off, remember that you are in your 'laters' now.

The only thing that prevents you enjoying your life is where you focus your attention. There are so many simple pastimes and pleasures that cost very little to do, a swim in the local pool, that aerobics class that you meant to join last year or was it the year before? What about tramping about in the forest, flying a kite or visiting an old friend?

If you can't find anything to be pleased about, hold your breath. Within a few minutes you will really feel pleased about being able to breathe freely.

The desire to live can be strengthened. You obviously have some desire to live, or you would not be alive. When people completely lose the desire to live, they fade very fast.

It is a good mental exercise to get two sheets of paper. On one list the bad things about your life, on the other list the good. If the negative list is the longer, then every day add one simple thing that is a positive feeling about you, some of your qualities. Lie for half an hour in some aromatherapy-scented bath oils and at the same time listen to some relaxing music.

List some nice things about yourself; there must be many. Unless you learn to love and nurture yourself, nobody else will ever respect you.

Aim to be the very best you can be, read more, learn more about life and the universe, learn more about people. See if you can give up perhaps an hour once a week to visit a lonely soul in an old people's home – there are many out there who have no one.

If you are in a rut, if you have grown accustomed to tolerating intolerable situations, change may not be comfortable and change may not be easy. It needs courage to take an honest look at one's life, discover what is no longer working and then change it. Mark Twain reminds us, 'Courage is mastery of fear - not the absence of fear.'

Without clear goals in life you will never achieve your full potential. Each goal met increases confidence and spurs you on to your next. Try this exercise. Think of a goal that is important to you, write it down as clearly as possible in one sentence. Give yourself a time limit to achieve a goal, however small it may be, and be sure to complete the challenge before the anticipated date. It may be something simple such as taking up a new sport while away on holiday, planting a herb garden, or decorating a room!

If you want things to be better, you will have to change what you think, feel and do. Life shrinks or expands in proportion to one's courage.

Are you perhaps one of those people who has to say 'yes' to anything or everything, rather than run the risk of becoming unpopular? You know, perhaps you are up to your eyes coping with a busy life, a job, children, running a home and then you are suddenly asked to alter a dress for a friend who needs it in a hurry for a special function in just three days' time.

You know you should smile sweetly and say that with your busy life you just cannot take on any more, but rather than perhaps not be liked, you take on the job sitting up half the night to do it, get up late, which means that the family is in a state of tension because you are so tired, have a bad day at the office and come home and take it out on the whole family, all because of a favour for a friend.

Being with people who are heading in the same direction as you are is stimulating. If you know people who have a positive direction to their lives or who are working on one, you may find them more rewarding to be around. Positive people give off a very positive energy which is quite catching. Negative, gloomy people make most people feel that life is just not worth living.

Responsibilities

Why do we constantly look to the heavens and blame 'God' (whoever we acknowledge Him to be) and ask 'Him' to save the world? We hear it said repeatedly, 'If there is a God then why does He allow these dreadful things to happen? Why does He not save the world and allow peace and harmony to reign?'

The reason why He does not is because it is man who destroys. All that was right, pure and good was given to man as a unique gift, plus eventually a written direction, i.e. the Bible, which gave us a good insight into the correct way to behave, live and think.

As time progressed we have become more and more lost on the wrong road.

Life is a 'chain reaction' and everything we think and do has a direct effect on something else, negative and positive, cause and effect, good and bad.

God is within, not without, and the only way we will change the world is to change ourselves and then the chain reaction will commence.

We are responsible for the atrocious neglect of our planet, our decreasing concern for standards, the vandalism, crime and litter. Why do children enjoy destroying trees, hacking off branches? I was lucky enough to have experienced my childhood years of development after the war when, if a notice at the entrance to a park said, 'Please keep to the footpaths and don't walk on the grass', that is what we did. Not so today.

Muddle and gross untidiness cause mental confusion. Frequently the muddle and lack of care in individuals' homes reflect the muddle and chaos that is within their minds.

Young children have no concern about tidiness or looking after their own possessions, yet alone somebody else's, but somewhere along the line in their development they have to start to learn and the only way they learn is from their parents. It is not the responsibility of the headmistress or schoolteacher to teach them respect, it is up to the parents.

Depressive illness and stress is on the increase. Why, when most of us have so much, when living standards have improved dramatically since the war years and foreign travel is within the reach of most people, not the chosen few? It is because we have lost touch with simplicity and concern for other people.

Depressed people don't care. They don't care about themselves, their environment, or anybody else. Most of us come across stress every day but rarely do we get stress-related illness. Stresses on a personal level are not left behind when we go to work, they play on the mind and create a complex interaction.

Even the state of the political situation can affect our stress levels – the reducing standard of education, chances of employment, the high level of taxation. The way forward is not how stress can be avoided but how it can be coped with to advantage.

What can we do as individuals to improve the quality of our lives, however humble they may be?

First and foremost we can make a deliberate effort to improve the standard of the environment of our home, if this is an area of our life that needs attention.

A tin of paint can give a real face lift to even a bed-sit; a wooden table would come to life if somebody gave it a generous coating of wax polish and a good rub. Wood is a living entity and has the right also to some respect.

A clean window increases our awareness and 'lights up' the world on the outside and you will have a better view of what is going on around you!

What about creating a display, a flower arrangement, with a bit of Oasis and maybe a few flowers and some autumn leaves, so that you have a living, visual beauty which is self-created. Our minds, in order to develop and grow, need colour, harmony and nurture.

Try an aromatherapy candle. Use some lavender oil. Lavender is a great relaxant and your senses become enhanced if you see good things, feel good and inhale good perfumes.

Now let's open our front door and have a walk outside and have a good look around and see what we are doing to our world, our town, city or village. The environment we create here is our responsibility, not the local council's or the government's.

Why do we have to drop every packet, container or wrapping that we use on the floor for somebody else to pick up? The mammoth amount of take-away food containers has increased dramatically in recent years – beefburger boxes, the containers for our chips which are often discarded on the roads and pavements, with a supply of chips which not only transforms our environment into rubbish tips but is a danger. I witnessed an elderly lady slip over on a greasy box of chips and break her hip. A chain reaction here, pain and suffering to the lady, distress to her family and more unnecessary expense to our already overburdened National Health Service.

If you don't let your children chuck their rubbish on the road when they are in their pushchairs they will become the responsible teenagers and adults of tomorrow.

I vividly remember when I was four an incident that has stayed with me for the rest of my life which I will now share with you.

I was sitting in my pushchair with a small bag of wrapped, boiled sweets which a neighbour had given to me as a present. As my mother pushed me home I started unwrapping the sweets and throwing the papers on the pavement. When we got to the end of the road my mother suddenly stopped and turned the pushchair around. In a very nice voice she said, 'Now I want you to get out and we are going back along the pavement and I want you to pick up every piece of paper and then you can put them back into the dustbin when we get home. Do you realize what would happen if every child in the world dropped their rubbish? There would be so much mess that the waste would pile up so high that eventually you would not be able to get out of your front door for rubbish.'

An over-exaggerated example, but an incident that really stuck in my mind, and from that day I did not drop rubbish.

How long does it really take to clean up your kitchen, wash the dishes, put things away, hang up your tea towel and leave a pleasant-smelling, welcoming environment for you, your spouse or other members of your family to walk into in the morning to start another day, a clean slate?

To face a sink full of dirty dishes, swimming around in cold, greasy water with a pile of unwashed saucepans and a bin full of smelly rubbish is a mental 'downer', again a lack of standards, discipline and creating an environment of gloom and despair.

We hear disturbing news of four-year-olds in class being uncontrollable, teachers being 'stoned' by eleven-year-olds and being attacked and threatened with chairs. Is this then the Government's fault? Behaviour so destructive that teachers are having to consider going on strike if certain children are not removed from the class.

Added to this we are not allowed to smack, punish or assert any pressure or discipline on these youngsters.

It is frightening if we stop and think that in certain Middle Eastern countries still, today, people have their hands cut off if they steal a sheep!

All this again should show us that it is the parents who are at fault and nobody else.

For thousands of people the so-called bond of marriage has become a prison. Some force is very busy in breaking marriages up. I wonder what it is? Jung suggests that the strength of women in the Western world who are joining careers in management and professional statuses is partly responsible.

As they grow in their strengths and professional opportunities in many instances this weakens the marriage bond to such an extent that they wonder if marriage is, after all, worth the bondage. More deep seated, I believe, is the growing desire to be free.

Today men and women find themselves without any spiritual goal. Previously attention to the church as a place of worship was used as a retreat or a support structure in times of disharmony and that has vanished.

Woman, still dazzled by the glitter of what they thought would be freedom promised by their new status, often find themselves pressed into the uncomfortable moulds of our commercialized society or swamped by domesticity so that they have no outlet for the talents modern education has stimulated in them.

In any event they become more irritated and frustrated, and close their eyes to what they do not want to accept and break the prison which is nearest to them – their marriage.

Conflict

Emotions operate intensely in any close relationship, especially marriage, and close relationships of parent and child inevitably lead to some measure of conflict, frustration and aggression which is directed against one or other partner.

It has been said that 'An argument a day keeps divorce at bay'. I would say this is a little over-reactive, but emotional outbursts are not necessarily danger signals if the frustration, fury and anger can be expressed in words and people are willing to listen to each other.

Although arguments and quarrels are distressing, they do release tension.

Repressed feelings over a period of time can give rise to physical and psychological symptoms such as insomnia, compulsive behaviour and depression and even lead to situations like shop-lifting and crime.

If the argument, although heated, is always related to trivialities there is usually an underlying big problem maybe going back years: harbouring grudges leads to stress.

If you can, imagine your body as a large plastic tube filled with water, the top representing your head and the base of the tube, the lower pelvic areas of your body. The shoulders would be represented by the upper part of the tube.

Tighten the lid and then apply pressure from the base of the tube. Somewhere along the line, the tube will be submitted to such pressure that there will be a leak from some part, and there is no guarantee from which part of the tube the break will occur. Maybe it will be at the top, around the cap, your stroke; at the sides of the tube, your painful, aching shoulders; the middle of the tube, your heart attack; the lower end, your pelvic and bowel area. Maybe that continuous low back pain, or your irritable bowel symptom has something to do with repressed emotions.

The solution is to loosen the cap on the tube, preferably removing it all together, and then take the first steps in trying to resolve the conflict, first trying to decide what the conflict really is about.

Try to analyse your last argument. Did you direct your anger at the right person? Was it a difficulty at work or a long-hidden conflict with your sister which you took out on your husband?

If we could all keep our 'lids open' and allow free, open communication with all we come into contact with, there would be far less disease, which is all caused by suppressed emotions.

There is very little that you cannot say to anybody about anything when it is said in the right tone, using words of comfort rather than aggression.

If we could all change our attitudes as to how we want our world to be instead of looking to somebody else to be the scapegoat, we could all 'Heal the world, make it a better place, for you and for me and the entire human race' (Michael Jackson).

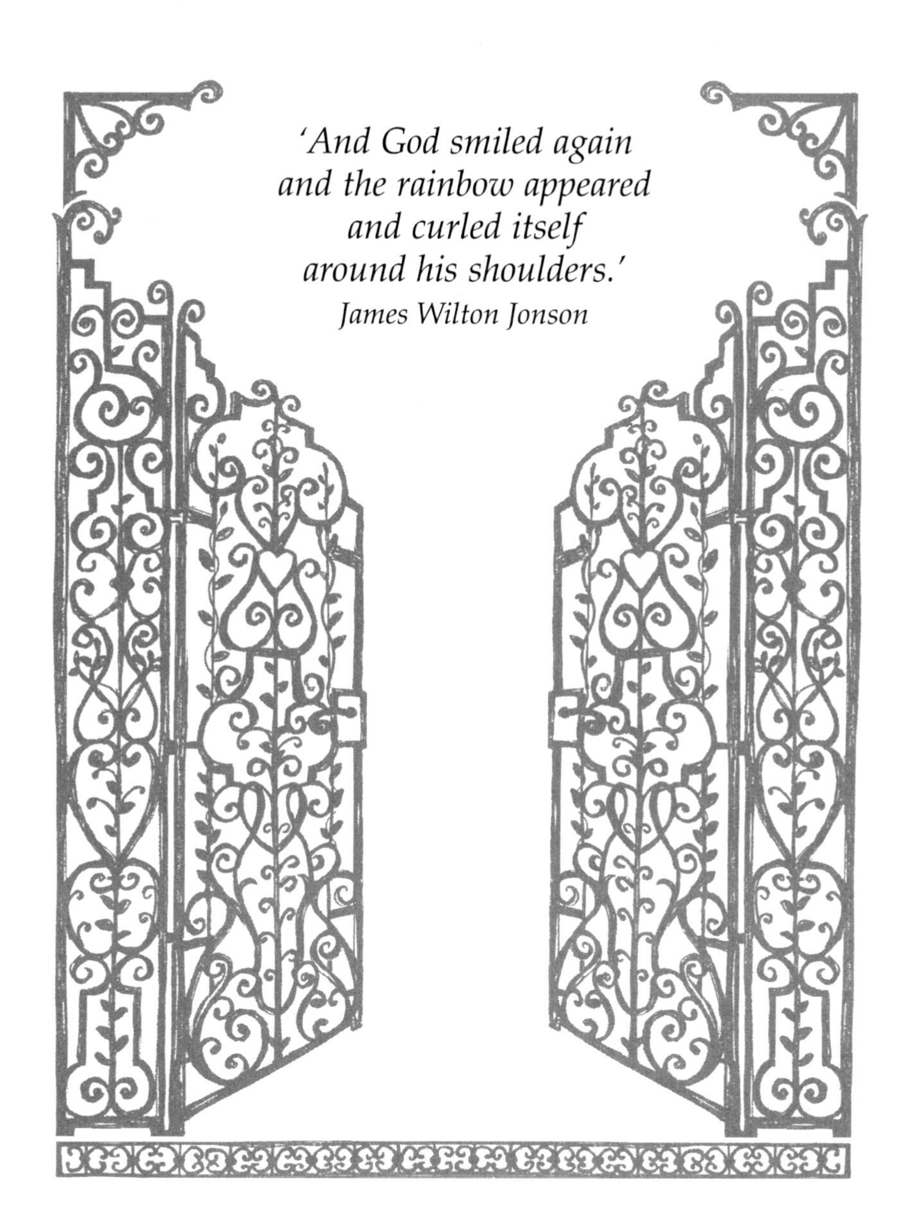

CHAPTER 7

Astrology and your health

7 Astrology and your health

In the ancient Mesopotamian world, as far back as 8000 BC man lived precariously beneath the open sky. His spirit was almost totally dominated by an upper world of apparently infinite resources – thunder, lightning, burning heat, eclipses. The heavens maintained an unpredictable barrage, spectacular and devastating beyond anything man could contrive for himself. The idea of celestial superiority, of looking upward for guidance, became part of everyday life.

In his primitive state man did not make allowances for the possibility of accidents; everything that happened was set in motion by some purposeful force. For everything that seemed to defy explanation within his narrow span of experience, a physical source urgently had to be located and named and a range of behaviour attributed to it. This made him feel less vulnerable.

A star is the ancient Sumerian symbol for divinity. The stars which filled the clear skies in that part of the world were the real founders of astrology. Although their role was and still is seen as essentially a passive one, they provided a highly impressive background to the interaction of other celestial bodies. Even today we are naturally aware that the sun and moon exert a strong physical influence on our lives. For our primitive ancestor this influence must have been a matter of great and mysterious significance. The sun kept him warm or faded in the increasing cold of winter, day alternated with night, the sea rose and fell with the tides.

It is a well-known fact today that many people are influenced by mood swings which link directly to the fullness or otherwise of the moon. The word 'lunatic' describes the sufferers of manic or other disturbing psychiatric symptoms having exaggerated reactions during the fullness of the moon.

Observation of the planets

From a viewpoint on earth the stars turn round us in a pattern that is virtually unchanging from one year to the next. Shifts are of course constantly occurring, but they are so slight as to have conveyed little if anything to the earliest observers. What they did notice was the relatively rapid movement against the starry background of seven major bodies. The sun and moon we have mentioned. The others were the five visible planets referred to as 'wanderers' or 'goats' and which we now call Mercury, Venus, Mars, Jupiter and Saturn.

In the earliest records we find that observations of the planets were being carried out in Babylonia. The pantheon of the gods was well and truly established, each god being allocated power over a particular area of human experience. For example, Mercury, a quick, cunning, bisexual god, was held to have a certain calculating wisdom; Mars was the ruler of violence and war; Jupiter was a king-like ruler of men; Saturn, seen as a distant cooling sun in exile, was quick-tempered and cruel. Gradually, as these associations of the gods with the planets gained in authority, they became accepted as astrological lore.

Recent studies of Ice Age bone markings, for example, suggest that men were aware of lunar periodicity as far back as 32,000 years ago.

Less remote are the fragments of documents surviving from the reign of Sargon of Agade (*c.* 2320 BC), which shows that predictions were made according to positions of the sun, the moon, the five known planets and a mass of other phenomena, including comets and thunder-bolts. Undoubtedly there was a great deal of isolated activity well before the first specific astrological records to reach us were set down in the seventh century BC.

From ancient Egypt, star charts have come down to us which have been reliably dated to around 4200 BC. Although in the latter case some scholars believe that the charts were drawn up for exclusively astronomical purposes, it is hard not to impute astrological significance to them.

For throughout the history of astrology until the outbreak of rationalism less than 300 years ago astronomy and astrology were an identical subject, the role of scientific techniques being to establish or predict the influences of extra-terrestrial life forces.

The importance which early man attached to the movements of the sun, moon, planets and stars is vividly illustrated throughout Western Europe. In recent years there has been an accumulation of evidence to show that one of the principal functions was to compute the yearly movements of celestial bodies.

The erection of the mighty stones at Stonehenge went through 13 main stages of construction, representing a task that Professor G.S. Hawkins has calculated as having taken 1,497,680 man days. These monuments are an impressive sight, and recent research shows that its construction may have begun before 2500 BC, predating the Mycenaean civilization.

The layout of these stones was submitted to the professor, whose interpretation was that the stones were nothing more nor less than a giant megalithic computer. The massive blue stones at Stonehenge were quarried in the Preseli mountains and transported along a 240-mile route.

There lies a ring of 56 holes beyond the outer stones at Stonehenge which are known as the Aubrey Holes after the antiquarian John Aubrey (1627-97), who rediscovered them. Professor Hawkins has shown that by using a system of four movable marker stones, deficits could be corrected and virtually every eclipse of the sun and moon predicted.

Astrology, the pyramids and ancient worlds

The pyramids of Egypt still hold pride of place among ancient astronomical buildings. They are oriented to the north pole of the sky, which now lies close to Polaris, but was in those days nearer to far fainter stars. The pyramids had a dual purpose as burial places for the pharaohs and astrological calculators.

It used to be one of the world's great mysteries whether the pyramids were only elaborate tombs or whether they had a wider purpose as active spiritual or scientific centres. We now know that the sloping corridors leading from the faces into the interior were used as sighting tubes, allowing Egyptian astrologers to make naked-eye observations of the planets with great accuracy, from which astrological calculations were made.

Astrology in ancient America took on a different importance. In fact they possessed two main calendars, one plotting the solar year of 365 days which governed the planting of crops and other domestic matters; the other, of 260 days, had a ritual use. Each was linked to an elaborate astrological system to cover every facet of life.

The Mayan priest-interpreters, as with the Aztecs who later took over the Mayan system, emerged as an all-powerful hierarchy. On the fifth day after the birth of a boy, they would cast his horoscope and say what his profession was to be – soldier, priest, civil servant or sacrificial victim. Under this primitive misapplication of celestial theory, people found themselves dominated by an inaccurate belief in predestiny.

In very ancient times the Egyptians practised a mystical form of astrology which depended on the religious and economic source of their civilization – the Nile. The great river was the source of all life; floods bringing fertility to an otherwise barren region were activated, the Egyptians believed, by the concerted action of the sun and Sirius, a bright star which consequently assumed enormous importance.

A remarkable star map in the shape of a seated man appears on the tomb of Rameses VI, one of the pharaohs who reigned during the twentieth dynasty, 1200-1085 BC. According to Dr Margaret Murray it would have been possible to read from this map the culminations of the stars for each hour of the night throughout the year.

Astrology came relatively late to Greece. But by about 250 BC the Babylonian astrologer Berosus had made a great impact on the classical world with his astrological writings. As a result he was able to set up a school of astrologers on the island of Cos. In the course of the next 400 years the Greeks zealously converted Chaldean astrology to their own traditions, making it steadily more complicated. They also were responsible for popularizing a system of diagnosis which had hitherto been available only to the king; they devised a method of calculating individual destinies based on the moment of birth.

Astrology and medicine

Close bonds have always existed between medicine and astrology. Indeed, until the eighteenth century the two sciences were inextricably mixed, a study of astrology being as a matter of course part of a doctor's training and a vital element in the treatment of disease. A chart was drawn up from the moment a patient took to his bed and served as a guide to when the crisis would come and what medicine to give. The various parts of the body were considered to be under the rulership of specific signs and planets, which were also associated with specific diseases. An individual's health was strongly influenced by his birth chart, and with due care and attention (eating the right food, for example) he could avoid certain illnesses.

The Greek doctor-philosopher Hippocrates (born *c.* 460 BC) proposed that man's character was the result of the balance of four 'humours': blood, phlegm, black bile and yellow bile. These four were loosely linked in astrology with the triplicities, the four groups of signs: fiery, earthy, airy and watery.

These connections have not always been welcome, however, since at times they are wildly wrong. Gemini, for example, is an 'airy' sign and therefore 'sanguine', but the melancholic humour (black bile) is connected with Mercury, the ruler of Gemini, and sorrow, slowness and weakness are scarcely part of the mercurial character.

Sun sign rulerships of the body

Certain individuals suffer from weaknesses in certain parts of the body. These weaknesses are dependent on their sun sign.

ARIES	Tend to suffer from headaches, facial pain, i.e. neuritis, sinusitis, with a tendency to weakness in the cerebral hemispheres of the brain.
TAURUS	Taureans are subject to infections in the throat, larynx, tonsils, carotid arteries and jugular vein.
GEMINI	Often described as 'living on their nerves' and getting on everybody else's. Suffer also with aches and pains in their shoulders, arms, fingers, lungs and upper ribs.

CANCER	Cancerians are known as the 'mother earths' of the zodiac and therefore tend to suffer from discomforts in the breasts, uterus, thoracic duct and lymphatic system.
LEO	Leo and lion-hearted, so they say, and the circulatory system is their weak spot, so the heart, aorta, the back and spinal cord can cause them some suffering.
VIRGO	Problems with elimination and absorption in the large and small intestines and pancreas.
LIBRA	Frequently they have trouble with skin irritations, the kidneys and equilibrium.
SCORPIO	Congestion and inflammation of the genitals, descending colon, rectum,circulatory system and sometimes the back.
SAGITTARIUS	Prone to discomfort and wear and tear in the hips, sacrum, femur bone and the liver.
CAPRICORN	Suffer with the teeth, bones, knees and the skin.
AQUARIUS	Have a tendency to varicose veins and circulatory problems and have a weakness in the lower legs and ankles.
PISCES	Suffer from conditions affecting the bodily fluids, i.e. fluid retention, lymphatic congestion and discomforts of the feet and legs.

Astrology and diet

People with particular signs strong in their charts may tend to be deficient in certain mineral salts. Here is a short list of foods and minerals which will remedy these harmful deficiencies.

ARIANS	A recommended part of their diet would be to include potassium phosphate, which is found in tomatoes. A lack of this causes anxiety and depression.
TAUREANS	Taureans like their food – particularly rich, high-calorie food. Celery can help to clear the system of over-indulgence.
GEMINIANS	A diet rich in the B vitamins is recommended to help their fragile nervous system.
CANCERIANS	Foods rich in calcium are recommended. Deficiency causes cracked skin and poor teeth. Watercress and milk are recommended.
LEOS	To reduce heart strain, plums and all dark berries, i.e. blackberries, blackcurrants and raspberries, will help their circulation.
VIRGOANS	To help skin eruptions and dandruff, lemons are recommended.
LIBRANS	To help maintain a balance between acids and normal body fluids, strawberries, which are high in mineral salts, should be eaten.

SCORPIOS	Scorpios have difficulty in resisting over-rich food. Prunes should be eaten.
SAGITTARIANS	Asparagus and cucumber are high in silicon, which promotes a healthy balance of the skin and hair.
CAPRICORN-IANS	As they are prone to rheumatism, cabbage and kale should form part of their diet.
AQUARIANS	Pomegranates contain an alkaline agent which Aquarians need.
PISCEANS	Pisceans tend to be anaemic. Raisins, dates and cereals help to remedy this and, as they are prone to fluid retention, cucumber would benefit them.

Consider some of that wisdom from Hippocrates. He wrote in his diaries that 'he who practises medicine without the benefit of the movement of the stars and planets is a fool'. Hippocrates further stated firmly this warning, 'Touch not with iron that part of the body ruled by the sun, when the moon is transitting.'

Today, his counsel may need some interpretation for the medical people who, having ignored the astrological wisdom of their founding father for so long, often haven't a clue as to how to translate his words.

Medicine has always treated the disease the patient has. Medical astrology and homoeopathy treat the patient who has the disease - and there's a vast and vital difference.

Your individual birth chart (or horoscope) indicate at the moment of your first breath of life on this earth the weak links in your body's chain reactions. That is why medical astrology is more concerned with the diagnosis and prevention of disease than with the treatment. If it is known at birth that a baby's nativity indicates a strong predisposition to diabetes, for example, the parents can control the diet of this small human early enough to prevent the adult the child will become from ever developing diabetes. An ounce of prevention is worth a pound of cure is a true adage.

Medical astrology provides the medical profession, if they would only accept and recognize it, with the true original cause of the breakdown of certain organs in each individual's body. Every illness, without a single exception, results from certain mental and emotional attitudes.

Here are two examples. The emotional seeding that causes arthritis is resentment, bitterness and frustration held inside, controlled and not allowed to express itself outwardly.

Heart disease and heart attacks are caused by (a) the lonely longing resulting from not being loved, (b) the inability to give or return love, or (c) the inability to love oneself. The emotion of love and the human organ of the heart are inseparable.

CHAPTER 8

What do we know about stress?

8 What do we know about stress?

We hear about it all the time, our stressful, competitive lives which are shortening the lifespan of so many, in our fight to do more, achieve more, work longer, faster, pack every second of every day. But what for? Is this what we call a successful life?

What really happens to us when we are in a stressful state? Let's go into this in more detail, for unless we know what happens we are never going to be able to do anything to combat stress and its ultimate destruction of the body if we are stressed out most of the time.

When we lived in a cave our main purpose in life was to kill to eat, cook our prey and then be satisfied that we had sufficient food to feed our families for another few days. The body performed exactly as it was meant to, the 'flee or fight' reaction. We worked during the light hours and slept away the night, and that was the main purpose and function of our life.

So the caveman decided to seek out a wild boar to secure food for his family. Just thinking about confronting the boar set up a chain reaction of events: his adrenal glands, which are stimulated by fear, excitement and passion, would release adrenalin.

This in turn raises the blood pressure and dilates the arteries, so preparing the body for an extra supply of oxygenated blood to serve the body which would probably be fighting and killing a wild animal. Fats and sugars would be excreted from the liver stores to give more strength to the muscles, the heart in particular. The caveman's hair would stand on end and this would give the appearance of being 'larger than life'. He would even become longer-sighted, so that he could see further. His urinary and digestive systems would 'shut down' as his body would not want to waste its energy on digesting food or dealing with the demands of the urinary system when it had so many more important functions to perform.

The caveman would either confront the boar and kill it, or the boar would kill the caveman and that would be that. Acting on the former event, the next feat of achievement would be to secure the carcass on a length of rope and then drag the animal back to the cave, which could mean walking many miles! The animal would then be placed securely in the back of the cave waiting to be cooked.

The caveman in his exhausted state would sleep for many hours; his store of fats and sugar from the liver would have been burned up, his blood pressure would have returned to its normal level and the over-production of adrenalin would have ceased. The vital circulatory system would have been working to its maximum efficiency, blood coursing through healthy arteries, the heart working overtime, maintaining the strength of this very vital muscle.

Today we get plenty of stress but stress of a very different kind, created by the very rapid progress and constant changes in almost everything. We therefore sit in traffic jams inhaling toxic exhaust fumes (very bad news for our lungs), desperately frustrated at not being able to get to that important interview or meeting on time. As far as our body is concerned, fear and frustration are the same, and the 'flee or fight' reaction kicks in. Fats are released from the liver, adrenalin courses through our circulation, our blood pressure rises, but nothing happens. The body is all geared up to 'run', 'fight' or at least do something which is terribly active, but all that happens is that we sit clutching the steering wheel even more tightly, muttering a selection of not too sociable phrases.

The extra fat and sugar has therefore nowhere to go as it is certainly is not going to be used in physical activity, so it nicely lines our arteries and starts the development of arteriosclerosis which is today's number one killer disease – a disease of affluent living, not poverty. We have never moved less than we do today. Cars, two and sometimes three per family, are not unusual. Children go to school in them and return at night, so walking in the fresh air is an experience of the past.

Escalators and lifts are everywhere, and because of our modern homes and machinery, there is no such thing as heavy housework, so women have never had an easier time either.

So what are we going to do about this sorry state of affairs? We cannot change the world, but we have the choice to change our lifestyle, which will ultimately change life on a much larger scale. Remember, it only takes one small stone to start a landslide.

It is essential to have some physical activity, and the more stress you are subjected to, the more exercise you need. It is far better to swim ten lengths of the pool or have a heavy game of tennis or squash than to curl up in a chair with a pint and a cigarette to combat your stressful day.

Meditation is as old as religious belief and its main therapeutic value is in combating stress. Its religious significance is extensive and it has formed part of the discipline of hermits, monks, priests and lay people of many faiths.

Transcendental meditation became fashionable in the late 1960s when the Beatles took it up, and probably this is the form of meditation most familiar to lay people today. Many have been put off, however, by the yellow-robed, shaven-headed figures who teach meditation in some of our big cities. But you do not have to go to a guru or teacher to practise meditation, nor do you necessarily have to join a group or a new faith.

The principle behind meditation is that you relax and empty your mind of those thoughts that chase each other round and round, those worries, anxieties, fears and even hopes that will not let you alone. When you have stilled your thoughts in this way, you will be led gently into full and effective relaxation and it is believed that this will lay you open to the spiritual powers of the universe.

Since it is difficult to empty one's mind completely, teachers of transcendental meditation and of some other of the Eastern forms suggest that their students chant a mantra. The word 'mantra' literally means 'thought protection'. It is the use of sound, both audible and sometimes inaudible, to protect our minds from our thoughts. It is usually a single, meaningless word, which is repeated over and over again until it drives all extraneous thoughts from our mind.

Followers of Hari Krishna, for example, will chant his name repeatedly. Other teachers will give their pupils a letter of the Sanskrit alphabet, whose mere sound is said to transcend language and to put the person who chants it in touch with universal vibrations. This in turn is said to awaken dormant sections of the brain with beneficial effects, both physiologically and psychologically.

An experiment was tried in India in which young thugs were given the choice between spending a term in prison or studying Sanskrit for one year. Of those who chose to learn Sanskrit many were transformed into good citizens. Teachers would claim that it was the mere speaking of the sound, putting them in touch with the basic sound of the universe, that brought about the transformation.

The mental relaxation that leads to the state of true meditation is helped by physical relaxation. This too has a beneficial effect on the body. Physical relaxation is best achieved by tensing each muscle in turn so that you will know what it feels like when tense, and then slowly relaxing it.

Mental relaxation does not just make you feel good, it has a dramatic effect on the entire functioning of the human body. Blood pressure is reduced, our heart beat slows, respiration too. Our immune responses become active and vibrant, our kidneys deal with impurities in a more efficient way, our liver functions – which are so complex and varied that a further chapter could be written on just that one organ – become super-efficient.

When we are in a stressed state our body is so busy using up all its supplies of energy that there is an insufficient supply to be distributed to major organs, which is exactly why when we are stressed we are so open to the onset of disease.

I have dealt briefly with one type of everyday stress at the beginning of this chapter, but there are so many others which we may hardly realize can contribute to our feeling 'stressed out', a very common term today.

City life with its pollution of air and environment, vandalism, noise, bright lights, high-rise dwellings, overcrowding, muggings, burglary, traffic dangers, the speed at which everything goes, including life itself, the lack of a supportive community, all these are stress-producing factors. Country life too has its drawbacks. Loneliness, isolation and a sense of deprivation may be felt, particularly by the young who compare their lot unfavourably with city dwellers who have amusements to hand, more stylish shops and access to sports, culture and wider job opportunities.

Work is one of the prime causes of stress. There is the struggle for promotion, the disappointment of being passed by, the fear of unemployment, working with incompatible colleagues or supervisors, the lack of fulfilment in repetitive and seemingly meaningless tasks, the failure to achieve any job satisfaction, or at the other end of the scale, responsibilities greater than the capacity of the one who has to bear them.

Do we have the Monday morning feeling, a despair that comes about as we go to our office or shop to survive yet another week, the only glow of hope being that Friday is only five days away? What a terrible waste of life!

Housewives too are under stress. If they have all the latest labour-saving devices they may become bored in the home. If they are struggling with old-fashioned equipment they may feel they are hard done by in comparison with their neighbours who have these devices.

If they can take a job to ease the money situation or because of boredom, they may then become overburdened and resentful if their husband does not take his full share of household tasks to help.

Marriage generally produces stress, particularly if there is fear or suspicion of unfaithfulness or if it has been entered into when the partners were immature, or if love has somehow gone with the passing years. Sex life can produce stress if there is a change in a partner's needs or capabilities. Financial problems, religion, sex or colour all cause stress.

Almost all illnesses are aggravated by stress and people who are subjected to it are more accident-prone.

The child who is living in an environment where he either witnesses abuse of one or other of his parents, or, worse still, may be the subject of abuse himself, may frequently suffer from accidents, a broken leg, concussion, a deep cut or wound. This child is calling desperately for help and is almost inviting disaster in, in an attempt to get some attention.

We all have experienced the expression 'a dog can feel your fear'. A dog is more likely to attack someone who expresses fear when face to face than when one is relaxed about the confrontation. Road accidents often occur when the driver is in an angry frame of mind. His angry expression attracts a similar situation.

Life is all about cause and effect. What we throw at it comes back to us. If we smile in the mirror it will smile back at us; that is the chain reaction and the same applies to many aspects of our life.

Some people escape from their stress by taking alcohol or drugs and then become addicted to one of these. They may find their stress triggers off allergies, heart attacks, strokes, ulcers, backache, migraine, constipation, diarrhoea, indigestion – all these are conditions that can arise from stress. Perhaps even worse is impotence in males, since a man's worry over his lost ability and its effect on his partner creates even more stress.

Two compensations frequently resorted to are over-eating and smoking. The first leads to obesity and the second can lead to lung cancer.

The ingesting of drugs causes unreal stresses to the functioning of the body. Drugs do help many symptoms. The diabetic patient would not be alive without the daily dose of insulin, and drugs used as anaesthetics can make very necessary surgical operations possible, and today they are extremely safe and effective with none of the lasting side effects of the past.

Drugs can harm the patient in various ways. There are side effects; for example, drowsiness from phenobarbitone, vomiting from digoxin or morphine, male sexual difficulties from drugs used to relieve high blood pressure. There are secondary effects, for example, thrush when antibiotics eliminate natural flora in the bowel.

Two killer stress-related diseases in Western society today are cancer and coronary thrombosis. Stress helps to bring on one, poor diet the other. It is worthwhile to consider therefore what are the causes of stress in our individual lives and whether we can do anything about them.

Are we in work that fully uses our talents and yet is not beyond our capabilities? Under-employment of our talent can be as frustrating as over-loading us with responsibilities we cannot cope with. Do we have a right to the balance of work and leisure in our lives? Ambition is very good, but to pursue it at the cost of every other enjoyment is not good for our health. Are our personal relationships with family, friends or colleagues all they should be? Are our working conditions poor, noisy or ill-lit?

All these things can be a cause of stress and it is best to face them honestly and to bring our frustrations into the open. People who have a good row and then forget it are doing their health more good than those who bottle up their feelings.

Emotional sources which can trigger disease

AIDS	Sexual guilt. A poor-self image and often a tendency to reject the ability to find happiness.
ARTHRITIS	'An acid mind can produce an acid body.' Acid feelings towards another can trigger this illness. The inability to change attitude.
ALLERGIES	The foundation of most allergies is stress. What we need to treat is the reason the body has become allergic, not the allergy. Who are you allergic to?
ANOREXIA NERVOSA	A fear of adulthood, therefore a fear of life.
ARTERIO-SCLEROSIS	A resistance to opening the mind; tension and narrow-mindedness.
BACK PROBLEMS	UPPER – Those who carry too many emotional loads. MIDDLE – Guilt; 'get off my back.' LOWER – Back-breaking financial burdens.
BLADDER PROBLEMS	Anxiety. Stress in an emotional sexual relationship.
BLOOD PRESSURE	HIGH – Long-standing emotional problems LOW – Defeatism. Lack of love as a child.

Emotional sources which can trigger disease

BREAST CYSTS	Over-protection. Over-mothering.
BREATHING PROBLEMS	Frustration in certain aspects of life. Being 'puffed up'.
CANCER	Deep hurt. Long-standing resentment. Repressed emotions. Lack of ability to express their real abilities. Usually a restriction caused by another person, partner, parents, etc.
CANDIDA	Frustration. Anger. Demanding. Untrusting.
COLDS	Unshed tears. Mental confusion and a disorder in life.
FIBROID TUMOURS	A blow to a woman's ego. Nursing a hurt from a partner.
HEADACHES	Self-criticism. Fear. Expecting too much from personal abilities.
HYPOGLYCEMIA	Overwhelmed by life's responsibility.
MENOPAUSAL PROBLEMS	Rejection of femininity. Guilt. Fear.

Emotional sources which can trigger disease

MIGRAINES	Sexual fears. Resisting the flow of life.
MISCARRIAGE	Fear of the future. Wrong timing.
MULTIPLE SCLEROSIS	Mental hardness. Iron will. An inflexible attitude to life.
SKIN PROBLEMS	An old buried fear, anxiety, feeling threatened. We all hear it said, 'It gets right under my skin.' Who is irritating you?

CHAPTER 9

Listen to your feelings

9 Listen to your feelings

Talking over problems and sharing one's worries with mature people we can trust is one of the most positive steps forward to lessen stress and get rid of a host of confusing symptoms, from anger, hate, love and joy. Love and hate are very powerful emotions and the dividing line between the two is sometimes hard to define.

We all expect happiness today; in fact we want to be happy most of the time. What is happiness? The absence of sadness maybe! We need to experience both in order to feel joy and pain and distinguish between the two.

Television, with all its advertising, presents happy, smiling faces, hour after hour, and whether they are encouraging you to buy that new shampoo which will transform your hair into luxurious locks, or buy that new car which will transport you to paradise, the latest washing machine or chocolate bar, they are all presented by happy, smiling faces.

We therefore grow up with that thought firmly implanted in our minds, that in order to be happy we first have to have all the material things; they are paramount.

If that were so, then why do so many pop stars who are fabulously wealthy commit suicide, become drug addicts or alcoholics if possessions are all life's secret for happiness.

Years ago, and not so far back, seventy years or so, women had a hard time, often living with a husband who drank heavily and knocked them about, lots of children, impoverished living standards. From early morning until late at night it was heavy household chores with no equipment to ease the load.

There was no way out, no battered wives' refuge, or state system which would house the woman and children and provide the necessities of life. Happiness for a woman then was very limited: she probably did not know what the definition of happiness was. A day away from the home, visiting the country or sea, would have been paradise. Her expectations were small, her lifespan would have been short. She would look an old woman at fifty.

The life of many men was not so comfortable either. Long hours down the mines, working in unsafe, deplorable conditions for next to nothing, or heavy physical engineering work with little free time. There were no unions to protect their rights, or holidays and sickness with pay.

We therefore demand as our right today happiness with a capital H, and if it is not there we rapidly become disillusioned with our partner, job or lifestyle, or seek refuge via the divorce courts to see if life on our own or with another partner will change things.

Usually it means the transference to another series of problems. That new partner has his or her past and his or her emotional baggage which they will bring with them into a new relationship. You then have two people with two ex-partners and two sets of children and no doubt a very strained financial burden also. No wonder second marriages have even less success than the first!

Happiness comes from within, not without. Money can bring happiness but the love of money does not. Giving money to others, if you have a surplus, and seeing the change it can make in a young couple's life or giving benefits to the quality of life to your grandchildren, can bring happiness to the giver as well as to the receiver.

Happiness for the little Indian boy living a primitive existence in, say, Bombay would be his bowl of rice every day. The rice would be a surety of his survival and the bowl in which he carried his supply, his most priceless possession.

Feelings are the tools we need in order to forge relationships with other people. They are the antennae with which we find our way around. As we give our feelings room to communicate and as we learn to listen sensitively to them, we shall discover that they are a living entity. We shall learn to trust and value their wisdom.

Most of us are well aware of having some inner weakness. We may drink too much, eat chocolate in excess or have fits of overspending and then weeks of remorse as we try to cope with a never-ending barrage of credit card debts.

We may find that we just cannot get through the next hour without reaching out for a cigarette. 'Smoking', we say, 'makes us feel relaxed.' It may well do, just for a short period and then we become agitated and depressed and reach out for yet another. We hate ourselves for being so dependent and feel a failure.

The cigarettes may give us coronary artery disease or lung cancer; the alcohol, cirrhosis of the liver; and drugs eventually rob us of all our senses.

Food addiction which leads to obesity is the cause of so many health problems. Why don't we get addicted to celery or carrots? We never do. It is always the sweet, sticky foods that are most appealing, or those with a high fat content.

Another way of smothering uncomfortable, destructive feelings is to fill our lives so heavily with work that there is hardly time to breathe, let alone feel anything.

Food and love are so involved, and at times of emotional loss or confusion the stomach appears as a huge void that needs constantly filling. The food squashes our feelings down, so the more we eat, the less we feel.

Following sexual assault, many women put on an excess weight around the abdomen, hips and thighs. They are subconsciously covering their abused areas: the fatter they become, the more emotional protection they have against men ever abusing them again.

Obesity is misery and nobody is ever fat and happy. In order to lose weight we need a diet, I agree, but first and foremost we need to understand why we need to eat excessively. Perhaps it is fear about our future; our femininity? Do we perhaps wonder how we would cope beng transformed from a fat to a thin person?

Those of us who have experienced rationing during the war years will probably well remember being told to 'eat up all your food. Remember, there are starving masses in China. It is really wicked to waste food, etc., etc.'

Were you fed too much as a child and loved too little?

We, as parents, frequently reward our children with sweets when life is uncomfortable. We are responsible for giving sweets after a fall or injury, giving sweets after a toddler has a screaming tantrum. Too much reward with sweets for suffering can start a chain reaction which the child will find hard to break. Ultimately every hurt and pain, either physical or psychological, will then be dealt with by sweet, high-calorie food.

An increase in appetite usually occurs after a period of deep emotional loss, anxiety and pain.

Sometimes people bury their feelings in a deep void inside

themselves so that they are normally unaware of their existence. The traditional stiff upper lip is a good example of the way we smother our feelings.

The deeper we bury our feelings the more layers of hurt we add to our already overburdened mind.

We all need some defences and boundaries. We cannot afford to be without protection from the assaults of our internal and external world.

Taking time to investigate our feelings is something of a luxury. There was often some merit in plodding on through misfortune. To indulge in feelings was considered self-indulgent. 'Don't cry. You will upset everybody' was a familiar statement.

Nevertheless the psychological research that has taken place in the last century has brought to light the importance of emotions and feelings. We ignore our feelings at our peril.

Doctors are at last actually placing patients into certain categories and acknowledge that certain personality types produce symptoms of heart disease far more readily than others with a different emotional make-up.

It always amazes me how doctors acknowledge that those with a certain nervous disposition, males in particular, are more susceptible to stomach ulcers. So here they acknowledge that emotional distress causes a large, angry ulcer in the stomach or duodenum, but that a cancerous tumour is classified as 'cause unknown'. What is in a name?

Coronary artery disease is caused by an over-production of fatty deposits in the arterial walls; that we know. The elasticity of the arteries is all important too. Arteries and veins transport life-giving oxygen to our bodies. Our blood contains our unique individuality.

Maybe you find difficulty in emotionally sharing and receiving good close communication. Maybe you feel that revealing your innermost feelings is a sign of weakness or emotional dependency on another.

A lack of love in our lives, perhaps from childhood, means that we grow up often with an embarrassment about the display of emotion. What about working towards changing these restrictions and flowing more with the energy of life?

Many of us in the rush and tear of this modern life hardly

know who we are, what we are about and even lose our identity. A mother busy with a young, demanding family hardly has time to know how she feels about anything.

Whether she has a splitting headache, a heavy, disabling period or is suffering from exhaustion from disturbed nights caused by a sick child, she still plays her role as carer to her children. She is bombarded with everlasting pressures from her children and constantly hears the cry, 'I want.' The mother desperately needs to say, 'I need.'

Cancer

Cancer is another major cause of death in the Western world. Despite an increase in pollution and carcinogens in our diet and the very real stresses of life, not all people die from it. It is therefore a combination of emotional and environmental factors that causes it.

You hear it said, 'She was such a nice person, yet she died of cancer.'

Most cancer victims *are* 'very nice people'. They are often the martyrs of the world who expect little or nothing for themselves and spend their lives improving life for others.

They are frequently the uncomplaining doormats – 'Anything will do for me' – as they eat the remnants from a joint of meat whilst the family enjoy the best. They are reluctant to go out and spoil themselves; give themselves a nice hair-do, a new outfit; spend some money on a ticket to a theatre.

Their self-image is often very poor. Very often they have been 'put down' all their life, either by parents, husband or a working colleague. The problem usually goes back to their childhood, where most of our anxieties and insecurities stem from.

Have you not heard it said, 'I was so upset that it got right to my bone marrow'? Deep pains affect our immune systems drastically, and sometimes when life is so restrictive and deplorable we create our own slow suicide as, in the case of lymphatic cancer, we encourage our body to destroy itself.

An accumulation of stresses can cause this state of self-destruction to occur: the death of a loved one, divorce, redundancy, loss of a child.

Denying our own needs and putting others first are common in the cancer sufferer. I believe the cancer victim needs to be able to say, 'I need this, or that, to improve my life quality.' The need can be financial or otherwise.

They really must learn to treat themselves with love, care and respect. Cancer victims frequently become isolated from their own feelings.

Personality types

Personality is a complex aspect of a person's functioning. It is the true identity of self. It is what we remember about a long-lost friend or relative who has passed on to another life; their personality, their kindness, their generosity.

The aggressive individual is full of fear and hostility, with a chip on his or her shoulder. Little understanding is given to other people's feelings and during his lifetime he meets up with a lot of opposition which will be regarded as 'the other person's fault'.

The paranoid individual is guarded and suspicious and sees life as an experience that needs guarding every minute of every day. He or she may become very irritated about the slightest upset, and stresses are usually exaggerated.

Obsessional people are generally preoccupied with their own limited world. Constantly checking that the taps are not dripping, they may be excessively tidy and spend too much time cleaning and re-cleaning the same area every day. Their perception of life is very limited and they look at the world with blinkered vision.

The withdrawn person opts out of stress by going into another world and maybe this is a very safe haven. He or she refuses to let life hurt.

Withdrawn and dreamy individuals are usually very creative – writers, poets, musicians – but they may find it difficult to communicate properly.

The passive individual is one who literally allows the world to walk all over him. They rarely make decisions without the support from other people but also lack drive in taking positive action to solve a situation which is causing great distress to themselves.

We all need to cultivate the ability to stand back and view our lives and accept those difficulties that are of our own making and capable of being improved or fixed situations which are concerned with other people and are unchangeable.

How frequently do we witness a traumatic event in our family or somebody else's – say, a road accident in which a child has suffered serious injuries? When we visit the child in hospital we realize that our petty argument with a relative last week which resulted in our feeling anxious and miserable really was quite ridiculous compared to the trauma we are witnessing at the hospital.

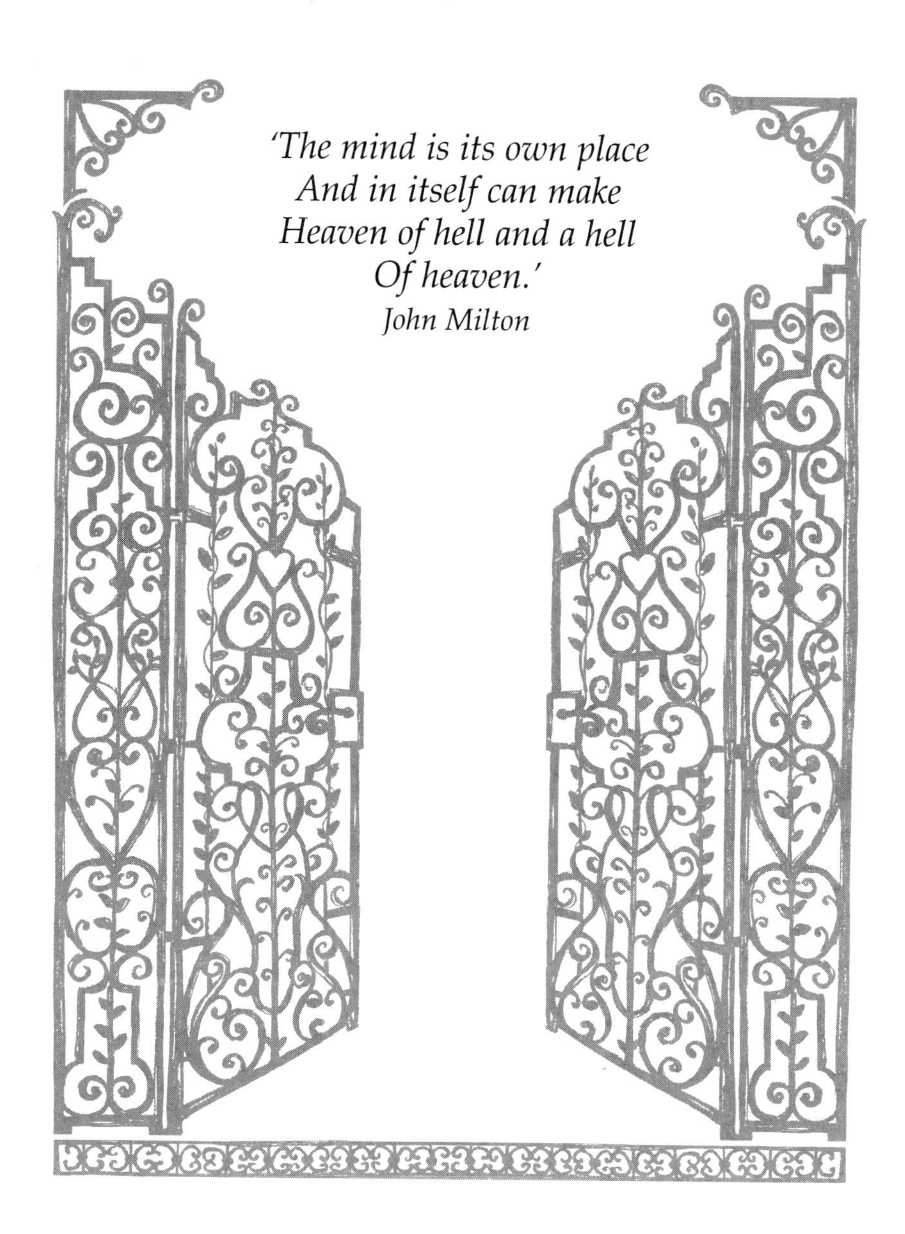

'The mind is its own place
And in itself can make
Heaven of hell and a hell
Of heaven.'
John Milton

CHAPTER 10

Case histories

10 Case histories

I have treated thousands of patients in my 23 years as a Reflexology practitioner – all age groups, all colours, races and religions – and from this wonderful experience I have learnt so much about the human race, about the influence of the mind over the human body and about this very destructive Western condition called 'stress' which is at the seat of so much dis-ease.

I have chosen 24 cases that were outstanding in my experience. Some were very tragic but many of the people described achieved a better quality of life and freedom from chronic health problems.

In several of these cases there was a strong underlying emotional condition that was the very root from which the illness stemmed.

I will explain to you how certain drugs affect the reflexes in the feet and give you detailed explanations in the outline drawings of exactly where in the feet the sensitivity appeared and why.

This information will enhance the work of Reflexology practitioners and will be of interest to patients and all those interested in healing as well.

I will give you some in-depth knowledge of diseases, how stress affects bodily functions and then advice on new directions to follow:

1 Lifestyle changes
2 Dietary advice
3 Beneficial herbal remedies
4 Vitamin supplements.

Let me now share these experiences with you.

Gillian – Anorexia nervosa

ANOREXIA NERVOSA, a neurotic and metabolic condition, occurs mostly in young women who suppress appetite by refusing food in an effort to be thin. Such starvation may result in death.

The patient may start as a food faddist with depressive tendencies. Some gorge huge meals (bulimia) and induce vomiting later. Such women are known to be oestrogen-deficient. Most have a low dietary intake of calcium resulting in reduced bone density (osteoporosis).

Lack of exercise has a worsening influence, often with severe loss of weight.

It is now established that one cause is a deficiency of zinc in the diet. Individuals suffering from the condition, with its depression, may recover when given 15 mg of zinc daily. Starvation causes increased urinary zinc secretion, thus further reducing body levels of the mineral. Most anorectics complain of loss of sense of taste and smell, which is a symptom of zinc deficiency. Loss of these two senses reduces further the desire for food.

Gillian came to me at the young age of 17 with a history of anorexia at the age of 15. She had been under the care of the psychiatric department in a general hospital for this difficult condition and had had several in-patient stays to try and stabilize her weight. When she approached me for treatment I was very newly qualified and had no experience of this distressing condition.

The patient was, in my opinion, extremely thin but she assured me that her weight was not reducing any further and that she was managing to come to terms with her eating disorder. No sensitivity appeared in the feet at all. Her mother had contacted me first, asking me if I thought there would be benefit in treating her daughter, and I thought that maybe the reduction in stress which is always the underlying feature might give a better result all round. This young girl had lots of checks at the hospital on a fortnightly basis to monitor her weight and check her blood levels and so on.

She found the treatment most enjoyable, and said within the first treatment that she felt far less stress and was eating a near normal diet. Her statements on the type of food that she was eating were rather hard to accept as, in my opinion, she was losing weight rapidly. She convinced me that she was attending her out-patient appointments on a regular basis and so I continued treating her.

However, after six weeks she attended for yet a further appointment in a very emaciated state, grey-faced, with sunken eyes and with extremely low energy levels. She assured me that the previous day she had attended for her

Gillian – Anorexia nervosa

fortnightly check at the hospital and all was well.

I felt very uneasy about the situation that confronted me and decided to approach her mother to see if in fact her statements of hospital checks and eating a regular diet were true. Her mother said that in no way was she eating regular meals; she was eating very modestly but how much she was retaining in her system was unknown.

Her mother did in fact approach the hospital the following day to check on her daughter's out-patient appointments and was informed that she had not actually attended the hospital for the last two and a half months. Despite letters of further appointments having been sent through the post, the patient had not responded by making a further visit.

It was one of those situations which could have been extremely dangerous. The daughter was obviously not cooperating in her treatment programme and was looking to Reflexology as some sort of magical cure.

As I felt inadequately trained in the psychosomatic field of anorexia and other food-related diseases and as I felt that the responsibility for this young girl was just too much, I decided to cease the treatments.

Anorectics unfortunately are very dishonest in their approach to their illness and latch onto anything or anybody whom they feel can help them without their having to put in any of the work themselves.

I therefore really feel that anorexia, along with any other phobic disorders, is an area where Reflexology would be very limited in its ability to help.

Reflexes in the feet that revealed sensitivity

ANOREXIA NERVOSA
No sensitivity was found.

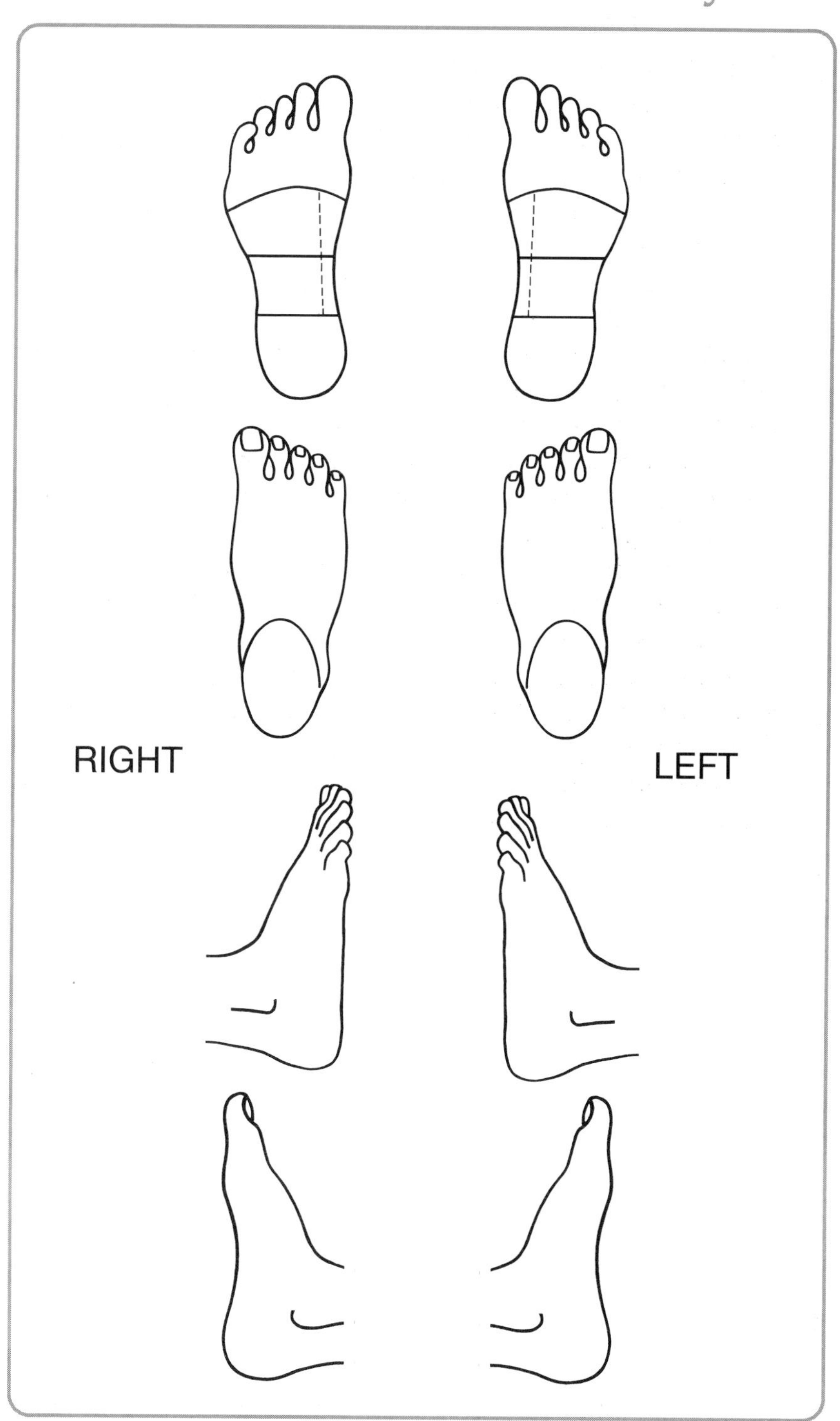

Beneficial herbs, vitamins and dietary advice

ANOREXIA NERVOSA

No special diet was applicable in this instance but generally, in all situations where stress and anxiety are present, the soothing herbs such as chamomile and linden blossom taken as teas are indicated and would be of great use to calm and relax.

Linden blossom
Tilia europea

Chamomile
Anthemis nobilis

Julian – Arthritis, osteo and rheumatoid

OSTEO ARTHRITIS is an erosion of the cartilage of a joint, with pain and stiffness. In the over-fifties it manifests itself as wear and tear affecting hands, knees, spine or hips. Biochemical changes in the cartilage stimulate overgrowth of bone cells (hyperplasia), which is an effort by the body to correct the disturbance.

Common in the elderly and menopausal women. Calcium salts may be laid down in a joint, believed to be due to errors of diet. Small crystals of calcium have been observed to form in cartilage and synovial fluid.

RHEUMATOID ARTHRITIS A systemic inflammatory disease of several joints together where erosive changes occur symmetrically and which may arise from inflammation and thickening of the synovial membrane. Cartilage becomes eroded and fibrous or even bony fusion leads to permanent fixation of a joint or joints. Polyarthritis, an auto-immune disease.

Symptoms are morning stiffness and pain, wearing off later. Easy fatigue and a decline in health. Nodules on surface of bones, elbows, wrists, fingers. Anaemia and muscle wasting call attention to inadequate nutrition possible from faulty food habits for which liver and intestine are at the root of the cause.

Reflexology has been extremely successful in relieving the pain and disability of sufferers from arthritis, whatever its form. Most patients report freedom of movement, reduction in swelling and less pain. I have treated many hundreds of patients during my years as a Reflexologist with very rewarding results. Those with a chronic state of illness are recommended to attend regularly for a 'maintenance' treatment – say, once a month – as this usually keeps the illness under control. However, there is one particular case that stands out in my mind as exceptional.

Julian had suffered from rheumatoid arthritis since his early forties. The disability started in his hands, with very swollen, deformed finger joints and stiffness in his wrists which extended to his cervical spine and shoulders. When he came to me he was having great difficulty in walking.

Julian had been on all types of drugs to try and relieve his condition and he did get some respite from pain but had suffered serious side effects from the medication. As he said to me, 'The side effects to the drugs are nearly as bad as the illness.' He refused to go permanently onto steroidal treatment and this is what made him decide to try Reflexology.

There were very few areas in his feet which were not sensitive. The shoulders

Julian – Arthritis, osteo and rheumatoid

and hips were the worst, which reflected his condition exactly.

He seemed quite contented in his life with a wife and family and did not reveal to me any real reason for the onset of his illness. Sometimes a shock, be it a bereavement, a road accident, or sometimes redundancy, can trigger the onset of the illness.

I gave Julian a good general treatment, concentrating on all the main organs of elimination. He enjoyed the session, said he felt so relaxed and was looking forward to his next visit.

The following day I had a telephone call from his wife to say that Julian was really very unwell, had a high temperature, aches and pains in all his joints and did I think that Reflexology could have made his condition worse. She was very worried and felt rather annoyed.

I knew that this was a healing crisis. The treatment had stimulated all the eliminating organs – the kidneys, liver, bowel and skin – to rid themselves of all those impurities. Much of this was due to the huge amount of medication he had been on for the past five years, and the rest, a build-up of toxins in the lymphatic system which comes about when a patient is unable to move freely and stagnation of the lymph occurs. The lymphatic system is controlled by movement, gravity. It is not pumped through the body as the blood is by the heart.

I reassured his wife and said that if he could weather this reaction, which is what it was, I am sure there would be a good result. I recommended absolutely no food, drinking plenty of fluids (fruit juices preferably, diluted grape juice is best – the grape is a healing fruit) and to keep on this regime for a couple of days.

I telephoned them on the following morning. Julian's temperature was going down but now he had come out in a rash all over his body. 'Excellent,' I said, 'another sign of elimination.' That day he had frequent bowel actions, eight in all, which was most unusual as he usually suffered from chronic constipation mainly due to all the pain-killing drugs he had to take.

On the third day he was much better and was able to come to my surgery for a further treatment.

He took off his shoes and socks and got up on to my treatment couch with far less effort than at his first appointment. 'You certainly got up there with less difficulty,' I said. 'Yes,' he replied, 'and I have hardly any pain in my shoulders today, I can't believe it.'

(A temperature is a healing crisis, produced by the body to burn up toxins.

Julian – Arthritis, osteo and rheumatoid

It is not an illness to be feared, it is a symptom of a condition and until the body burns up all the junk it can never heal itself.)

After the second treatment a similar reaction occurred, although less severe, and again Julian took my advice, a fruit fast, rest, letting the body heal itself.

He attended for his third treatment. His swollen, painful fingers were half the size and he could move them, his shoulders were markedly improved and he was able to walk with little pain.

'Reflexology is just a miracle,' he said. 'I have had more relief in three weeks than in all the years I have been under the hospital taking more and more medication with no positive result. I feel better in myself, I have more energy.'

Julian did not look back from that day. He continued with his treatments for a further eight sessions, on a weekly basis, and then came monthly for his maintenance.

That was 10 years ago and he still comes. He has hardly any disability from the arthritis and pain killers are a thing of the past. He swims regularly and has taken up golf since his retirement.

However, it must be remembered that he accepted the reactions to treatment and went on a few days of fruit juices (incidentally, he still continues with this routine for a day every week).

Julian put in the effort and with the help of Reflexology his body healed itself, which is exactly what it was meant to do.

Reflexes in the feet that revealed sensitivity

ARTHRITIS, OSTEO AND RHEUMATOID
There were very few areas of the feet that were not sensitive.

All the digestive and eliminating organs gave a reaction that was proof enough of the poor eliminating and digesting processes in the body.

The shoulder and hip areas were the most reactive.

Julian experienced a strong reaction in his cervical spine.

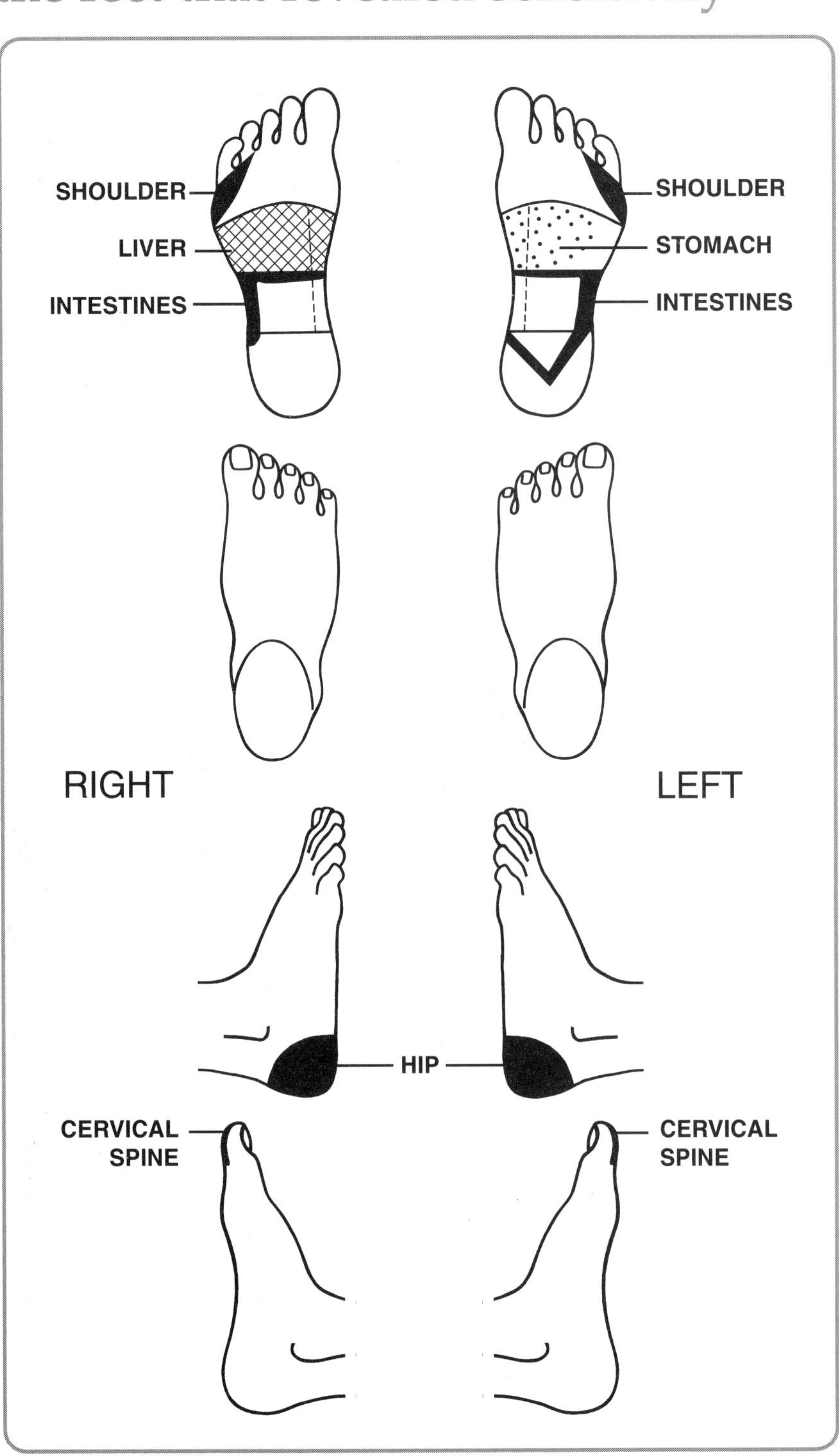

Beneficial herbs, vitamins and dietary advice

ARTHRITIS, OSTEO AND RHEUMATOID
A balanced diet can greatly help both forms of arthritis. Emphasis should be placed on vegetarian foods; oily fish such as herring, mackerel and tuna, eggs and low-fat cheese should be the main source of protein. Red meat is best avoided as it is known to promote inflammation. Avoid dairy products that are high in lactic acid, salty or pickled foods, acid fruits such as berries, citrus fruits and fried foods. Avoid tea, coffee, sugar-based drinks and alcoholic 'spirits'. Grapes from the vine, a healing herb, are particularly recommended. Their juice should be taken diluted.

B5 (pantothenic acid): 250 mg taken two–four times a day may help alleviate painful symptoms.
Vitamin C: 1–2 g daily. Vitamin C is a major part of the substance collagen, a tough, fibrous protein which is an intergral part of tendons and bones.
Vitamin E has anti-inflammatory properties.

Vine
Vitis vinifera

Bill – Asthma

ASTHMA manifests with spasmodic contraction of the bronchi following exercise, emotional tension, infections, allergens, colds and exposure to pollens or house dust. Symptoms are obstruction of airways with a wheezing or whistling sound, and with a sense of constriction.

It is often related to eczema. Infantile eczema treated with suppressive ointments may drive the condition inwards and worsen asthma. Causes – hypersensitivity to domestic animals, horses and pet birds, red or white wine allergy.

An older generation of practitioners recognize a renal, bronchial asthma encouraged by faulty kidney function.

Bill was only five when he came to me with a long history of asthma. In fact, the symptoms started once he stopped being breast-fed and started having milk powder formulas at the age of four months. There was quite a history of asthma in his family: his father and grandfather had both suffered from the condition as youngsters but luckily outgrew it in their teens.

Bill was a very sickly-looking little boy, extremely underweight, grey-faced, dark under the eyes, who, it was quite obvious, was frequently labouring in his breathing. His mother reported him as having attacks most weeks and although the medication, the inhalers and drugs controlled the symptoms, he had a lot of unpleasant side effects to the drugs and in fact some of them made him extremely hyperactive so that he could not sleep at night. Others caused him chronic constipation and he was generally quite tense and anxious.

Bill used an asthmatic inhaler four to six times a day, which was really rather excessive, and was unable to join in any of the sporting activities in his infant class.

He was particularly susceptible to even more frequent attacks during the spring and summer.

The principle of Reflexology in treating asthma is to try and improve the areas of digestion and immunity. Therefore we work to treat the reason the body has become allergic, and not the allergy itself.

As I began to work on his feet the child was rather anxious about what was going to happen and I found extreme sensitivity in the ileo-cecal valve, intestine, kidney area and also the heart and lung, which confirmed the pattern of the illness. In other words, the digestive weakness had been there from infancy and the commencement of dairy products in his diet at the age of four and a half months was the stimulation to the onset of the illness.

Bill – Asthma

The drugs, many of which affect the nervous system, had encouraged his rather anxious, over-active state, and also the asthma attacks caused a lot of anxiety, as obviously at the first sign of an attack impending the child becomes extremely tense and anxious, which made the whole condition even worse. I asked his mother to cooperate with dietary support and remove the child from all dairy products, which she did.

Bill's progress was very rapid. Within the first month of regular weekly treatments his asthma attacks became far less severe. He was able to use only two inhalers per day, one in the morning and one at night.

In the second month he lost his grey pallor and seemed to have far more confidence in himself. His mother reported no attacks that month at all.

They attended for a further two months of treatment, at the end of which he had put on 8 pounds in weight, was able to join in the activities at school and, as his mother said, was a changed child.

The real proof of the success of the treatment was when he went back to the chest specialist at the local hospital where his usual peak flow was monitored. Much to the amazement of the specialist, his output had increased by 50 per cent.

That was 20 years ago and I saw his mother recently in our town. She reported that Bill was now married with a son of his own, and that never again did he suffer from asthma.

Reflexes in the feet that revealed sensitivity

ASTHMA
There was extreme sensitivity in the liver, stomach, ileo-cecal valve and intestinal area which all confirmed digestive weakness.

The kidney reflexes were sensitive, as were the adrenal glands. The cause of this reaction was related to the drugs Bill had taken over a long period of time.

The lungs were sensitive.

The heart reflexes reacted due to the amount of stress placed on this vital organ during the asthma attacks.

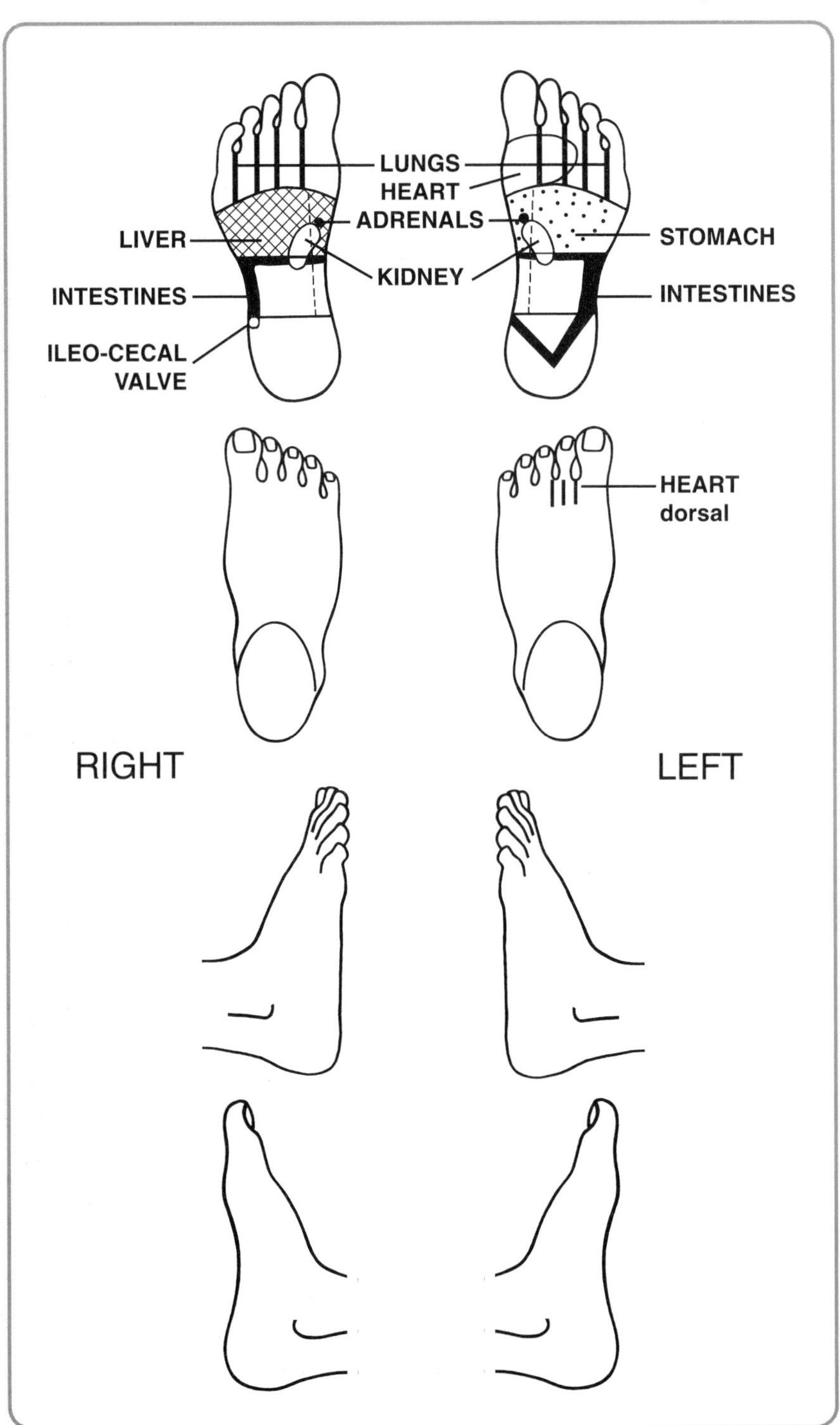

Beneficial herbs, vitamins and dietary advice

ASTHMA

Meadowsweet and dandelion root will help calm any food reactive tendency. Chamomile is a soothing anti-inflammatory herb which will calm down any reaction internally or locally. A diet free from dairy products is to be recommended. Take care that the diet is free from additives. Colourings in particular cause irritation to the membranes in the respiratory system. A diet low in salt is essential as it reduces sensitivity to histamine.

A high dose multivitamin supplement, with B6: 50 mg and B12: 50 ug, will help support the body's immune system. Vitamin C: 1000 mg daily, time released, preferably with bio-flavonoids. High potency fish oil: 3 g daily.

Encourage swimming as this helps to expand the lung capacity. It is a sport that is good for the asthmatic as there is no contact with dust or grass pollen which are present in most field sports.

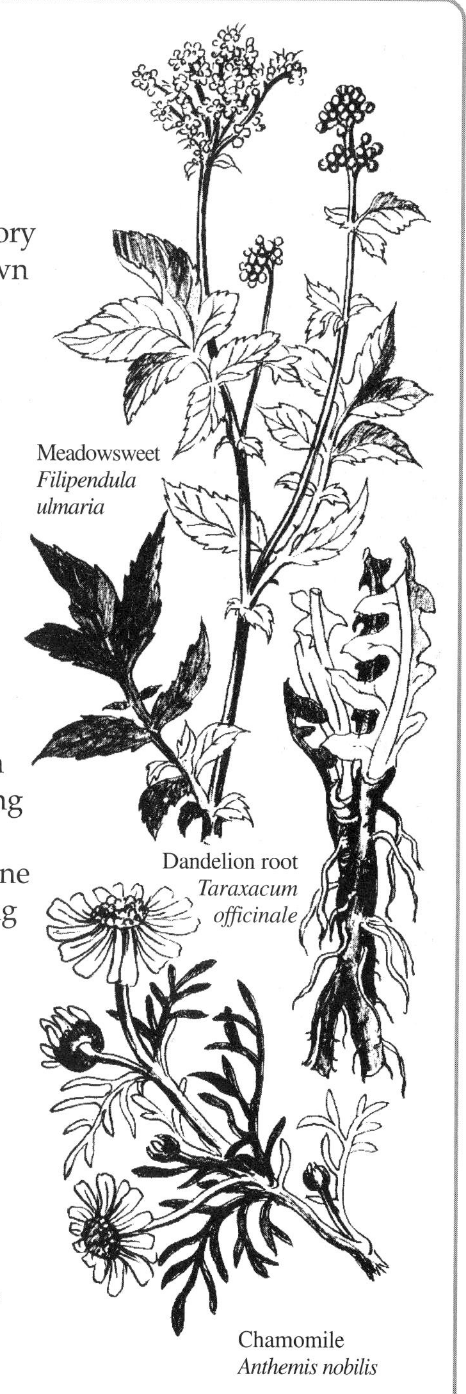

George – Back pain

BACK CONDITIONS take more people from their working environment than any other illness, even more so than the common cold. They are frequently caused by lack of exercise, too much sitting, too much driving and often too much lifting badly. Reflexology is extremely efficient in helping all forms of back pain.

The following case was an unusual one. Although I was not able to help the patient for the condition for which he came, Reflexology was able to bring to light a very serious underlying illness.

I had a telephone call one morning from a very agitated lady who told me that her husband had been suffering from extreme back pain for over a year and was treated with no end of pain killers with very little relief. The condition was now worsening and he was losing the use of his legs.

The doctors had mentioned that in their opinion it was an arthritic condition setting into his spine and apart from pain-killing, anti-inflammatory drugs there was very little they could do for George, who was then in his late fifties. He was brought to me by his wife who had heard from a neighbour that Reflexology was admirable in relieving back pain.

When I was first introduced to George I was quite amazed at how very flushed and red his upper body was, from his waist to his head.

The area from his trunk to his feet was clammy, cold and clay-like in colour. He mentioned that not only did he have this acute back pain which had worsened over the past year, he was now also getting some interference with his urinary output, sometimes retention and sometimes incontinence.

He had not reported this finding to his doctor, which was paramount in the conclusion of the treatment.

As I worked over his feet the reflex areas from the waist and above his waistline area were all quite reactive on contact and seemed completely normal. However, when I worked on the area of his lumbar spine and intestinal areas there was hardly any reaction at all, which was strange because the patient was suffering such pain and discomfort in his low back that he constantly resorted to pain killers in the day.

On working his bladder reflex area I did get quite a sensitive reaction, but the whole of the lumbar spine, pelvic and sciatic area was almost dead in character.

I was confused and could not understand what I was finding in this patient's feet because still he had this very flushed area of the upper trunk and head,

George – Back pain

profuse perspiration on his forehead and clammy, red hands.

As I had worked in a neurological clinic for a couple of years I felt sure that there was some neurological damage in the lumbar area causing these symptoms and that something was quite seriously wrong with this man.

I advised his wife to go back immediately to the GP and insist on an emergency appointment with a neurological consultant and to mention that he had this urinary and bowel retention on occasions which might refer to some obstruction in the low spinal area.

His wife was rather disappointed and a little angry when I said that I would not want to treat George again until he had had investigations into this condition, which did not seem to have been brought to the attention of the medics for the last year, which was far too long. I asked if she would please get an appointment with her doctor if possible that day and that I would ring in the morning to see what arrangements had been made.

Both George and his wife went to their GP the very next morning. He confirmed the urgency of the situation and arranged a domiciliary visit from a neurologist.

George was admitted to hospital that night, and a very large lumbar spinal tumour was discovered, which resulted in his having major surgery and losing a large section of his bladder and bowel.

Although Reflexology could not possibly help in this case, his wife did in fact telephone me and thank me so much for guiding them both in the right direction.

The feet told a true story of the condition that was in front of me: absolute desensitizing of the lumbar and pelvic area, which linked to the obstruction in that part of the body.

Here was a situation that gave me even more confidence in the stories the feet can tell.

Reflexes in the feet that revealed sensitivity

BACK PAIN
George had a very light sensitivity in the liver and stomach areas which I felt were due to the heavy doses of the painkillers he had been taking for a considerable time.

Other than in those two areas there was very little sensitivity in any part of his feet. This was strange, as he had been diagnosed as having arthritis in his low spine and hip areas.

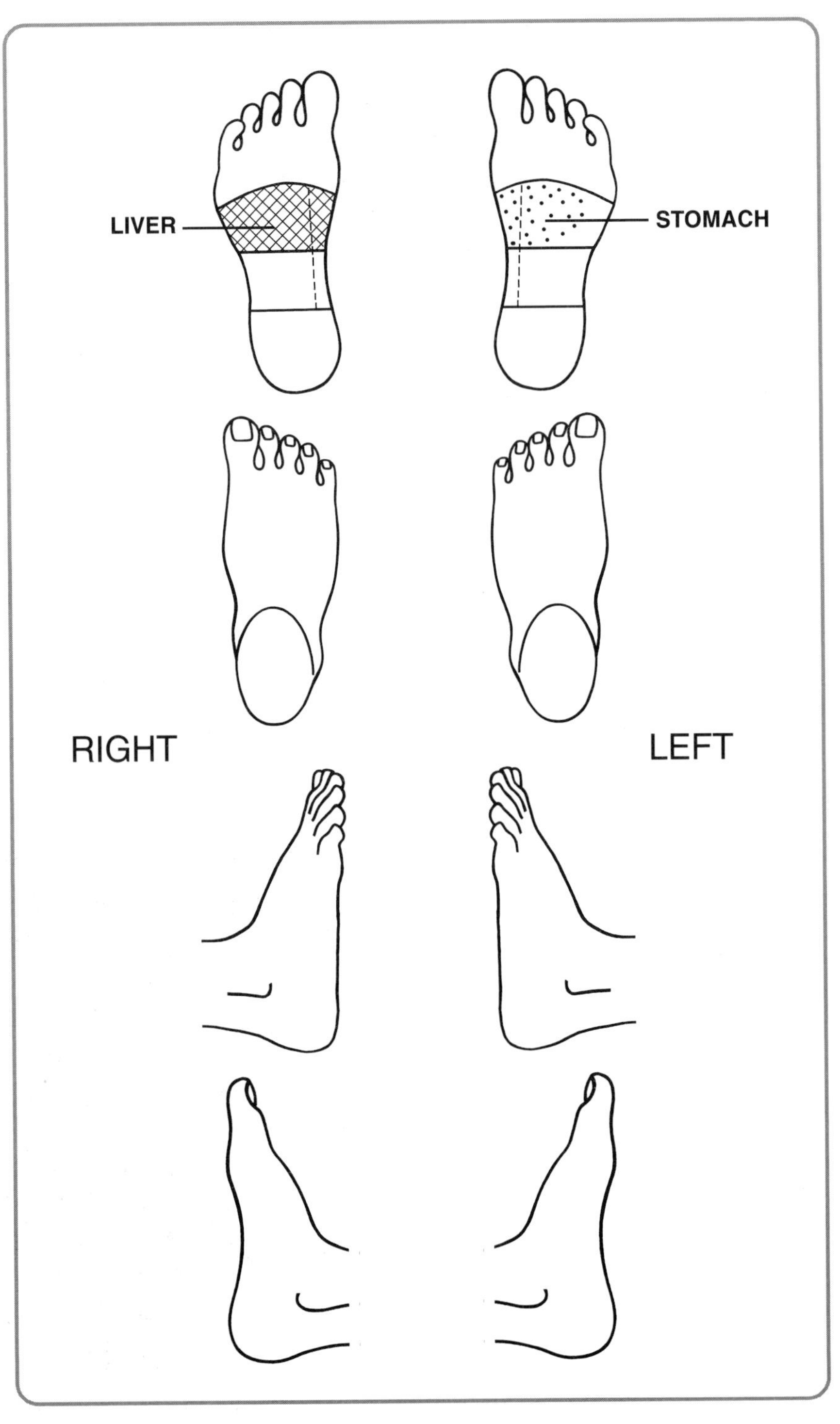

Beneficial herbs, vitamins and dietary advice

BACK PAIN

No special diet was indicated in George's case, but it is generally recommended that the soothing herbs are beneficial for relaxation and as a general aid towards better health.

Chamomile is particularly recommended, taken as a herbal tea.

Chamomile
Anthemis nobilis

Nicola – Cancer

CANCER The body reacts to malignant tumours in its tissues in the same way as it does towards grafts, by rejecting them. It is able to do so because the healthy immune system recognizes cancer cells by the abnormal antigens which they carry (called 'tumour-specific antigens'), which mark them out for destruction. The process of cancer formation appears to be happening all the time as the mutating cells throw up primitive forms at periodic intervals, but this is of little consequence as long as they are swiftly discovered and destroyed. It is only when a defect in the immune system allows one of these potentially independent tissues to escape control that the disease of cancer is said to be present. So it is obvious that cancer cannot be transmitted from one person to another by injecting them with malignant cells.

Indeed, there are those who consider that the immune system in mammals developed primarily as a safeguard against these internal dangers rather than against threats from the environment in the form of micro organisms.

Nicola was in her forties and her health had been good for the major part of her life. She was married with two sons. Her husband seemed pleasant enough and quite supportive of her generally.

Her whole outlook on life and general health deteriorated very rapidly when an unexpected pregnancy appeared on the scene. Their lives had, she said, been very strained financially for many years and, just as the two boys began to feel their feet and were less dependent on their parents, Nicola discovered that she was pregnant. She had quite an interesting, well-paid part-time job. There was now some money in the bank and a foreign holiday, the first they had ever had, was planned later that year. Her husband was quite adamant that this baby would spoil everything that they had struggled for and insisted that his wife have an abortion.

'My head told me that this was the right and proper thing to do, it would be madness to have another child, the boys were ten and twelve now, life was getting easier. What on earth do I want to start all over again for?' But her heart told her otherwise: 'I am pregnant, there is a life within me, even if I am only three months pregnant. Maybe it would be a little girl.' She had always hoped for a daughter.

Their marriage started to be full of stress, her husband insisting that she go to a doctor and arrange to have an abortion and there was no way he would change his mind. Nicola went and the doctor agreed, all sensible reasoning pointed to not having another baby. To save the unpleasantness and stress plus the complete lack of communication between her husband and her over these last three months, Nicola went into hospital with a very heavy heart and had the abortion.

Nicola – Cancer

She became my patient just three months later. Depressed, guilty and full of grief, she sought out Reflexology for an answer. She really did not like her husband any more and thought constantly about the little girl she felt sure she had carried for those 14 short weeks. She was obsessed about the situation, and could, she confessed, think about nothing else. 'She haunts me from day to night, I dream about little girls and wake even more depressed the next day.'

The solar plexus area in her foot told the whole story without her adding any verbal expressions: acute sensitivity. The solar plexus is the centre of deep feelings and emotions. I treated Nicola for another few weeks, the talking helped, the treatment relaxed her well but that was that.

Eighteen months later Nicola telephoned me. I recognized her voice immediately, it was low and sad, lacking any vitality. 'I have just had my breast removed. It was cancer,' she said. 'I am feeling quite ill and want some treatment.' Back she came and the same sensitivity appeared: the solar plexus. 'Don't touch that spot', she cried, 'it's unbearable.' Her breast area too was sensitive, to be expected after surgery, but still she held such pain in her soul.

Nicola came to me regularly. She blamed her husband for not welcoming the unplanned baby, hated herself for not standing up for her rights as a woman and insisting that her pregnancy be accepted. 'I know exactly why I have cancer,' she said. 'It's the abortion. I am punishing myself for what I did.' Despite all attempts at getting her to come to terms with the situation, forgiving herself and her husband and building the rest of their lives on what they had rather than what might have been, no change in attitude occurred.

I was worried when later in the second year of her monthly visits acute sensitivity appeared in the reflexes to the hip, coccyx and lumbar spine. I feared that Nicola had secondaries in the spine. My fears were confirmed at her next hospital visit where a scan revealed the worst. Major surgery to the spine was performed. Nicola did walk again; she came to my surgery on crutches after having extensive radiotherapy. Six months later she lost the use of her legs and shortly after that I visited her in the hospice, where she spent her last few weeks.

'The cancer', she whispered, 'it was all caused by the abortion, you know. I just can't live with myself and I hate my husband.'

I was privileged to be with her on the day she died. We had become such good friends over the four years since we first met.

Such a sad story, but one which proves just how powerful is the mind in its effect on the body, and showing how the immune system is so depleted by stress, hatred and guilt, the three diseases which Nicola died from. The cancer was just an expression of the three emotions.

Reflexes in the feet that revealed sensitivity

CANCER
An acute sensitivity revealed itself in the solar plexus area in the left foot, a sure indication of stress and deep emotional hurt.

The breast area was sensitive. This was the area where the tumour was excised.

Later in the second year Nicola returned. Acute sensitivity was evident in the hip and pelvic areas.

The lumbar spine was sensitive in both feet.

Secondary cancer was later diagnosed in all these areas.

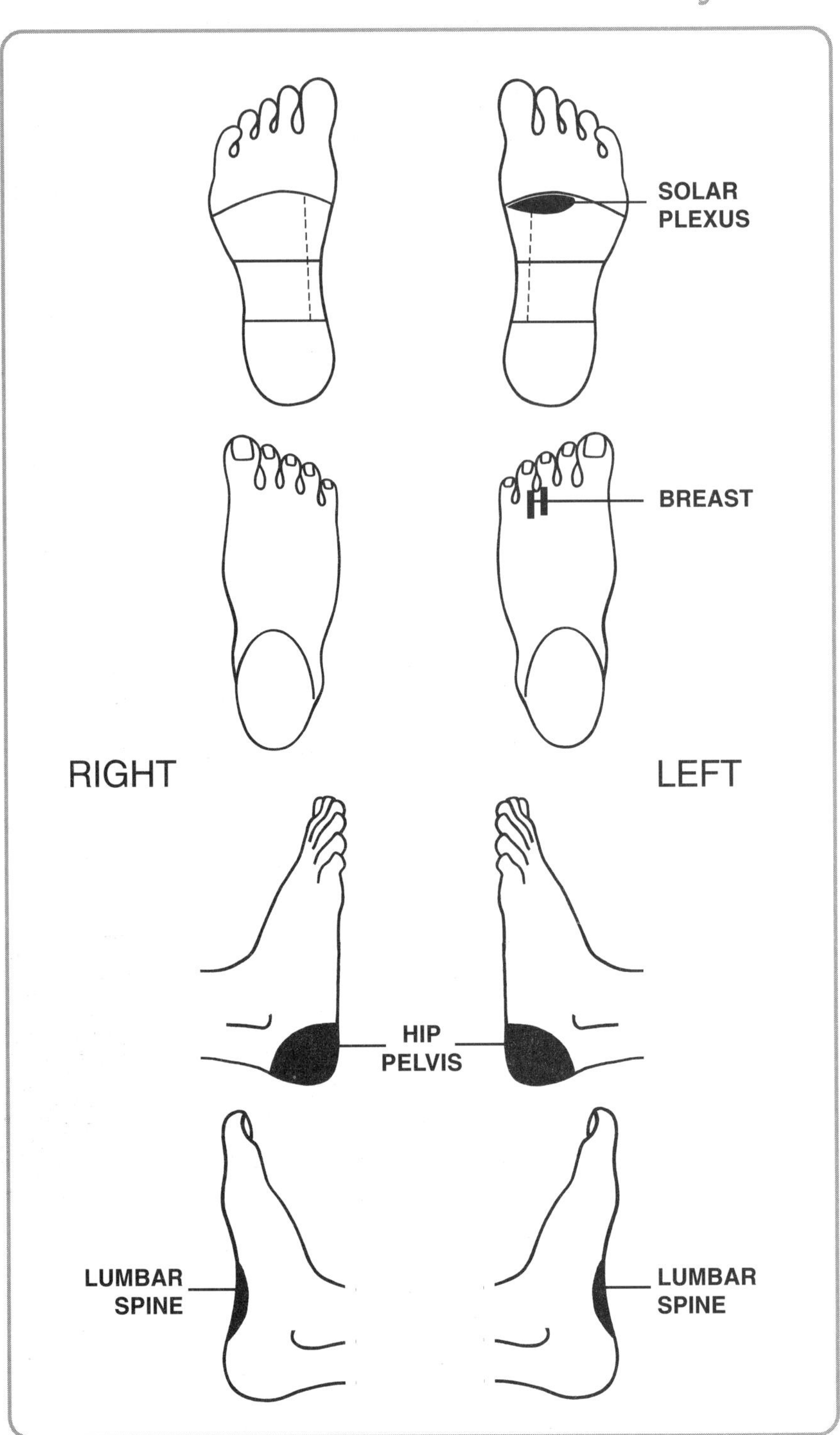

Beneficial herbs, vitamins and dietary advice

CANCER

In treating cancer Echinacea is a good immune stimulant which can be obtained from any herbal chemist or medical herbalist. Echinacea is excellent and its benefits are explained in chapter one – Herbs and healing.

The patient should start taking at least three 8 oz glasses of pure fruit or vegetable juices per day. Any combination of vegetable juices can be mixed. Carrot mixes well with any other vegetable.

Do not mix fruit and vegetable juices together.

Try and purchase a juicer yourself; this will make the whole exercise much easier. Just scrub the outer skin of the fruit or vegetable and place a combination into the juicer. Carrots, small broccoli florets and avocado blend well. The avocado needs to be peeled first!

Juices are great detoxifiers and are beneficial for all health conditions.

A diet high in the anti-

Echinacea
Echinacea angustifolia

Beneficial herbs, vitamins and dietary advice

oxidant nutrients beta carotene, vitamin C, vitamin E and selenium are now recognized as one of the most important factors in the prevention and treatment of cancer. It is important to maintain a good intake of fibre, fruits, vegetables and grains and eat as much raw or lightly cooked food as possible. Strictly reduce the intake of animal protein; instead choose pulses and soya. Avoid tea, coffee and alcohol, take instead herbal teas. Avoid smoking like the plague.

Anthocyanidins, e.g. Grape seed and bilberry extract. Bilberry is a very powerful anti-oxidant.

Vitamin C: 1 g daily. Vitamin C is a free radical scavenger known for its benefit in helping the immune system.
Natural beta carotene: 15 mg daily.
Vitamin E: 400–600 iu daily.
Selenium: 200 ug daily.

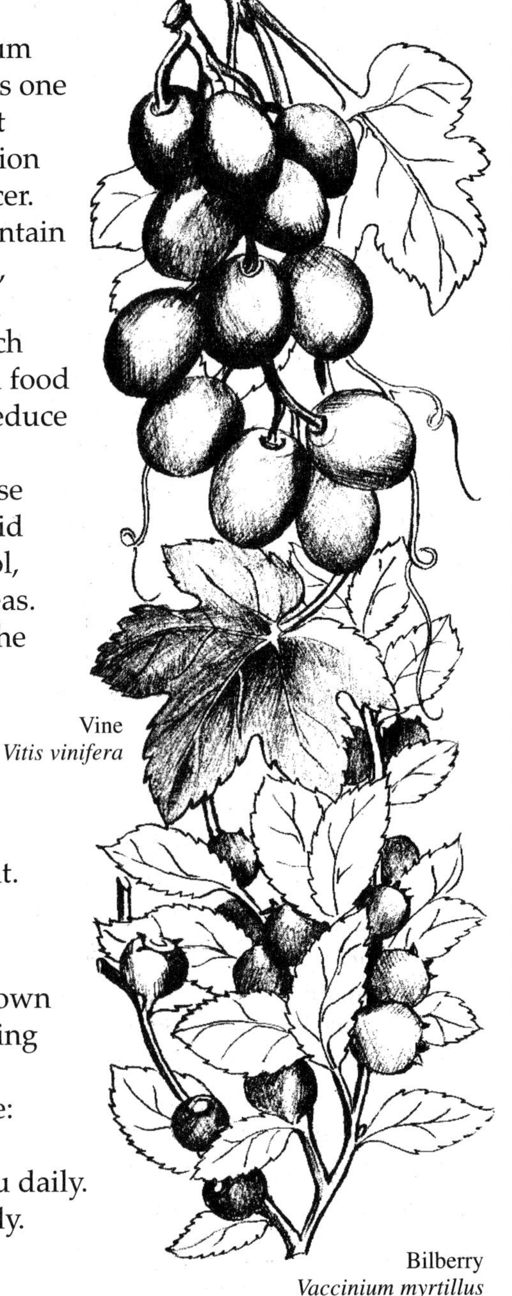

Vine
Vitis vinifera

Bilberry
Vaccinium myrtillus

Mandy – Cystitis

CYSTITIS is the inflammation of the bladder, and is usually acute, with scalding pain on the passing of water. It has a rapid onset. The patient feels off-colour. There is pain in the centre, low in the abdomen, which is worse when urine is passed. There is frequently passing of small amounts or merely the sensation of wanting to. Most cases resolve themselves without the need for deep-acting agents.

Bacteria invade when there has been continued irritation such as that of sand or gravel in the urine. *Bacillus coli* resides in the rectum but may invade the bladder. Urine is often turbid and evil smelling. By travelling down the ureters kidney infection may be conveyed to the lining of the bladder.

A common cause is diuretic indiscretion, such as too much spicy food, curries, peppers, vinegar, coffee, alcohol, tea, too much and too strong cola and other stimulants. Too much meat concentrates urine, as do other high purine foods.

Plenty of fluids should be drunk, either in the form of herbal teas, alfalfa, or bottled waters rather than coffee or tea. These dilute the irritating effect of uric acid in the urine.

Mandy was a very attractive 24-year-old and came to me with a history of chronic cystitis which had occurred during the last 12 months. The infections caused a lot of low pelvic and back pain. She often had a raised temperature and frequent episodes of passing small amounts of urine during the night, which gave her a very disturbed sleeping pattern.

She seemed an anxious young woman, although on the initial consultation there was no real evidence of the reason for her emotionally stressed state. During the treatment sessions the area of the bladder and pelvic areas were extremely sensitive to pressure; in fact, the slightest pressure gave rise to extreme discomfort in her feet and made the general pressure unacceptable to her.

Mandy also reported that during the attacks of cystitis she was quite sure that her eyes became affected as they were normally sore, irritating and watery. She had reported this fact to her GP who said that there was no link between cystitis and eye conditions whatsoever. However, when she was introduced to the benefits and understanding of Reflexology, I explained to her how the kidney and eye areas are in the same related areas and it is very common to find when people have bladder inflammations that their corresponding area, the eye, is extremely sensitive and can cause the symptoms of soreness, watering and sensitivity that she described.

Mandy – Cystitis

Mandy used to bring her three-year-old son with her, so the treatment sessions were not as relaxed as I would have liked them to be, but she explained that she had nobody to leave her young son with and so it was necessary for him to accompany her in order that she could continue regular Reflexology treatments.

We worked out a rota for a weekly treatment session. I said that in normal situations six sessions should give good, satisfactory relieving results, then maybe the occasional treatment on a monthly basis would be advisable for her.

There was very little improvement until the third session, when she said that she had noticed that she felt generally much calmer and very relaxed after treatment, and in fact the night following the treatment session would give her uninterrupted sleep for eight or nine hours, which was most unusual.

She still suffered a lot of low pelvic discomfort, however, and frequency in her urinary output during the daytime. I asked her to return to her GP for yet another urine check just to make sure that there was nothing underlying. There is sometimes the problem of another associated illness linked to urinary frequency and low pelvic pain. However, after her visit to her GP, who gave her a further examination and tested her urine, he confirmed that she was in fact still suffering from chronic cystitis and recommended yet another course of antibiotics, which she declined. The antibiotics always gave her an intense attack of thrush, therefore she had a dual problem to cope with.

Over the next few weeks there appeared to be a great improvement in her urinary condition but it was not until the eighth treatment that she confided in me that her husband had left her and their young son just a year before for another woman, and it was from this period of time that her first attack of cystitis had occurred.

It often happens that when we have emotional hurts which are very close to our heart our reproductive or urinary areas are most commonly affected, almost as a hurt to our very femininity.

Reflexes in the feet that revealed sensitivity

CYSTITIS

Mandy was quite sure that her eyes were sensitive and watery during her bouts of cystitis.

I explained to her that the kidney and eye areas are in the same related areas and it is quite common to find an eye problem during bouts of urinary tract disorders.

The kidneys were sensitive, but the bladder was acutely sensitive even when the slightest pressure was applied.

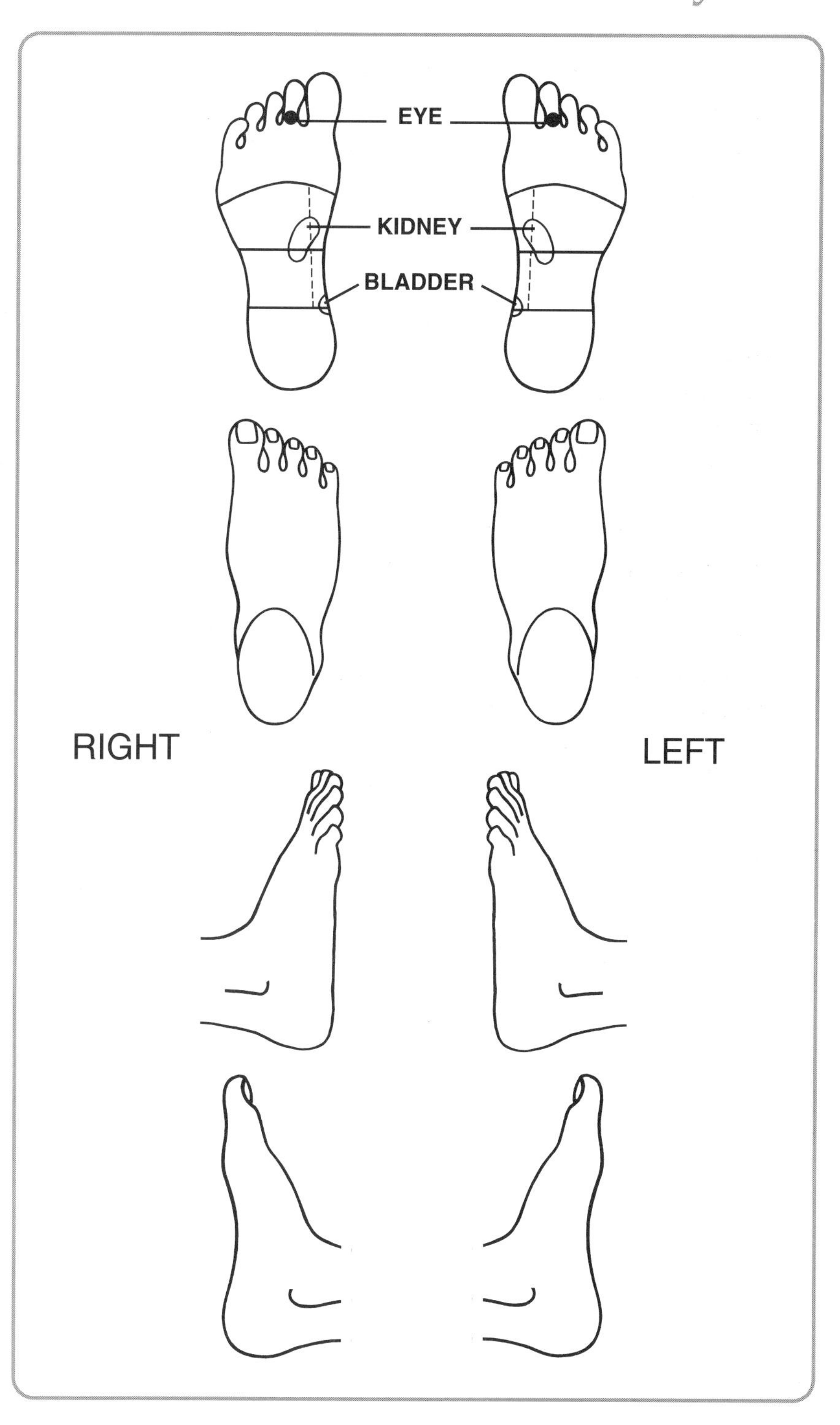

Beneficial herbs, vitamins and dietary advice

CYSTITIS

Tea, coffee, alcohol and any caffeine-type drinks, such as cola, should be avoided.

Echinacea is a good immune stimulant and excellent for cystitis as it also acts as an anti-inflammatory.

Dandelion leaf and horsetail are recommended.

Plenty of fluids are advisable and those with a barley base are especially beneficial, lemon barley in particular.

Cranberry helps to prevent the bacteria from adhering to the bladder.

Vitamin C: 1–3 g daily. Vitamin C helps boost the immune system to fight infection.

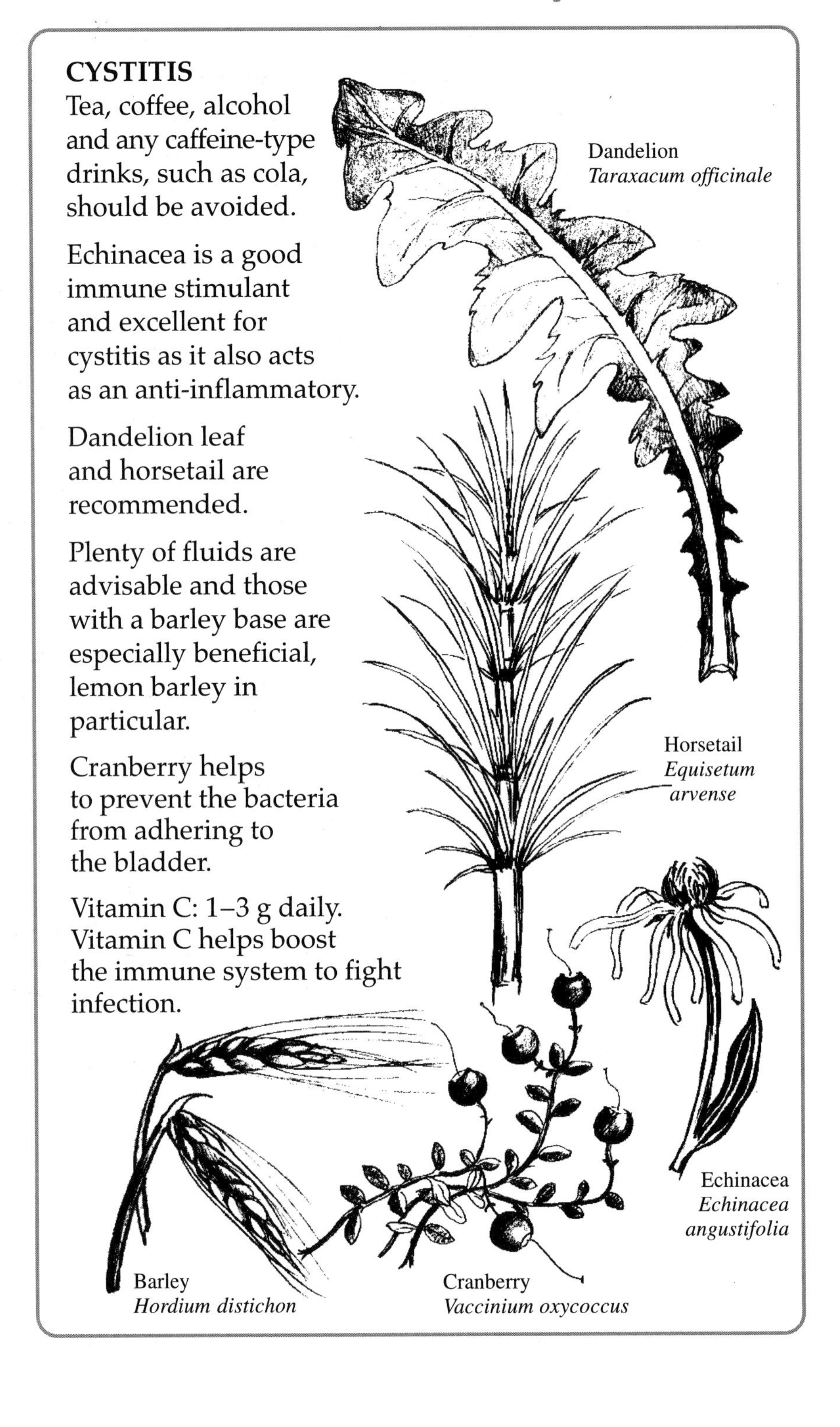

Basha – Detached retina

DETACHED RETINA Basha had flown over from Iran to have retina grafts at a London hospital. Following surgery on his right eye he suffered a lot of pain and bruising and swelling of the area. By coincidence, the ward sister to whom he was introduced had been a patient of mine many years ago and advised Basha to seek out Reflexology while he waited for his second retina graft which was to be performed the following week.

Basha came to see me, and his right eye was extremely bruised and swollen. 'I've only come to see you to see if you can relieve the discomfort following surgery until I return for my second eye operation next week,' he said.

As I worked on his eye reflex on his right foot he explained that he was quite sure that I was working on this point with 'red hot glass', as he described it. He said that the experience is quite excruciating and I would never have believed that one could get that sort of reaction from the feet. I explained that the feet were mirroring the body and his eye had been surgically treated and a lot of bruising and swelling had occurred and therefore the reflex in his foot would confirm that state.

I very gently worked out the sinuses, eye and ear area and, to my amazement, just 10 minutes after the commencement of the treatment, his right eye began to stream with water. It was completely uncontrollable and he had to use a large handkerchief to mop up the fluid output. He too was amazed that working on a small spot in your foot could give this result. He had had little experience, or knowledge, of Reflexology prior to coming to me.

The following day he telephoned to say that the swelling had reduced remarkably and the pain was almost gone, and that he would return to me the following week to see if we could achieve the same result when the second eye was operated upon. We did. He had the surgery on the second eye and exactly the same results occurred. As soon as pressure was applied to the sinuses, the eye and then the ear area, his left eye began to stream uncontrollably, but again the swelling and pain disappeared.

Here was yet another incidence of how accurate the feet are in mirroring the state of the body.

Reflexes in the feet that revealed sensitivity

DETACHED RETINA

The reflexes in the right and left eye were acutely sensitive following surgery.

Just 10 minutes after commencing work on these areas the eyes began to stream with water. This release helped the pain and bruising subside following surgery.

I am sure that it was also conducive to the rapid healing Basha experienced. This was also acknowledged by the surgeon.

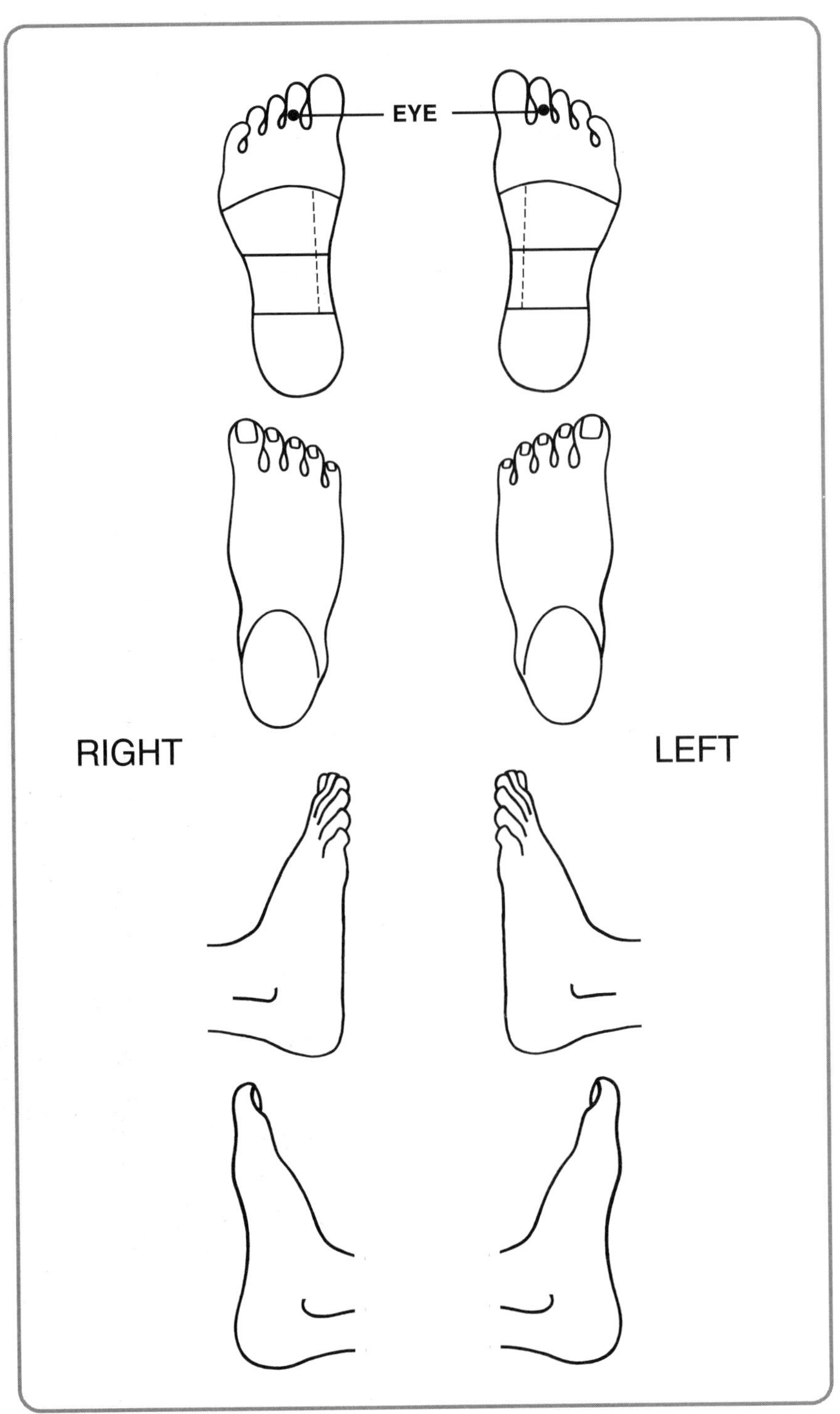

Beneficial herbs, vitamins and dietary advice

DETACHED RETINA
This condition did not require any special herbal or dietary advice but for general eye discomfort an infusion of eyebright applied to the eyes is soothing and cleansing.

Eyebright
Euphrasia officinalis

Chris – Diabetes

DIABETES MELLITIS (Mellis means sweet: Greek) occurs as a result of diminution or absence of insulin supplied by the beta cells of the Islets of Langerhans.

Chris was in his sixties when he came to me having suffered from diabetes for many years. His diabetes had been very difficult to control all his life, and he had suffered as a result arterial corrosion of the eyes and the kidneys. He had also had two mild heart attacks. At the time of coming to see me his main problem was an inability to walk any great distance because of intermittent claudication in his legs, which meant that after very short periods of walking he had cramp-like seizures in his calf muscles which made him have to stop whatever he was doing. The main sensitivities which appeared in the feet were in the eyes, kidneys, heart and groin areas. This indicated the arteriosclerosis that he suffered due to the diabetes.

He was constantly exhausted and had a very restricted lifestyle, although he did take quite an interest in his engineering company, which he had built up over 30 years. He was treated very regularly over a period of eight weeks with hardly any results, which made me feel that perhaps this treatment was going to be of little support for him. However, he was insistent on continuing, and I am so pleased that he did because on the ninth treatment he suffered quite a severe reaction to the treatment.

An angry rash appeared all over his body. He had excessive bowel actions, which was most unusual for him as normally he suffered from constipation and had to rely on laxatives to help any bowel action. After this rather major cleansing of the system he began to make great strides. The main benefit he achieved was the ability to walk distances; the breathless condition which resulted from his mild heart attacks improved considerably; and he was able to take an interest in jobs in the garden which previously had been completely out of the question. Chris was very impressed by the benefits of Reflexology and after three months (12 treatments carried out consistently on a weekly basis) his improvement was so marked that he suggested that he would like to come to have a regular Reflexology treatment every fortnight. This he did and he lived for another nine years, constantly having Reflexology; he described it as his life support.

During the nine years of treatment from me he hardly ever had a problem with maintaining his insulin (blood sugar) levels, which was very encouraging as previously he had had no end of increases and then decreases in his insulin injections in an attempt to try to control his very difficult condition.

Chris was a fine man. He was over-generous to all who came his way, was loved by all members of his staff and family, and when he died (he did in fact die of kidney failure), he left a large sum of money to the Diabetic Trust.

Reflexes in the feet that revealed sensitivity

DIABETES

The eye reflexes were sensitive in both feet.

The kidneys were also very painful.

The damage to the heart was apparent from the reaction in the heart reflex area.

Congestion in the groin area revealed the congestion in the arteries which caused the cramp-like seizures in his legs (intermittent claudication).

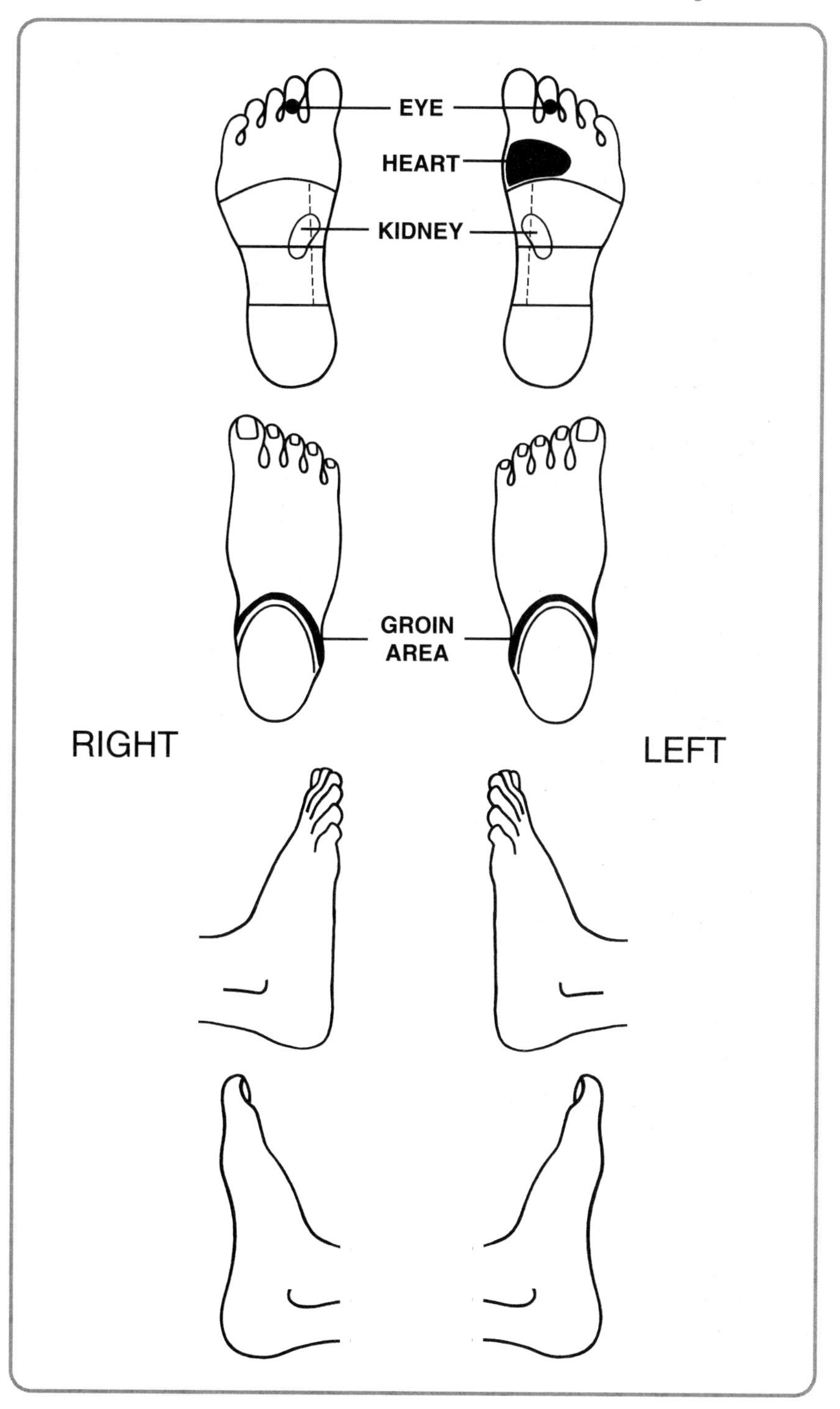

Beneficial herbs, vitamins and dietary advice

DIABETES

The diet suitable for diabetics would have been discussed by the doctor or dietitian in charge of the case.

The dosage of insulin and the number of units of carbohydrate is all-important.

However, a good, basic, nutritious diet, free from junk foods and refined sugar, provides a positive direction for any health condition.

The use of garlic is advised for the general health of the arteries.

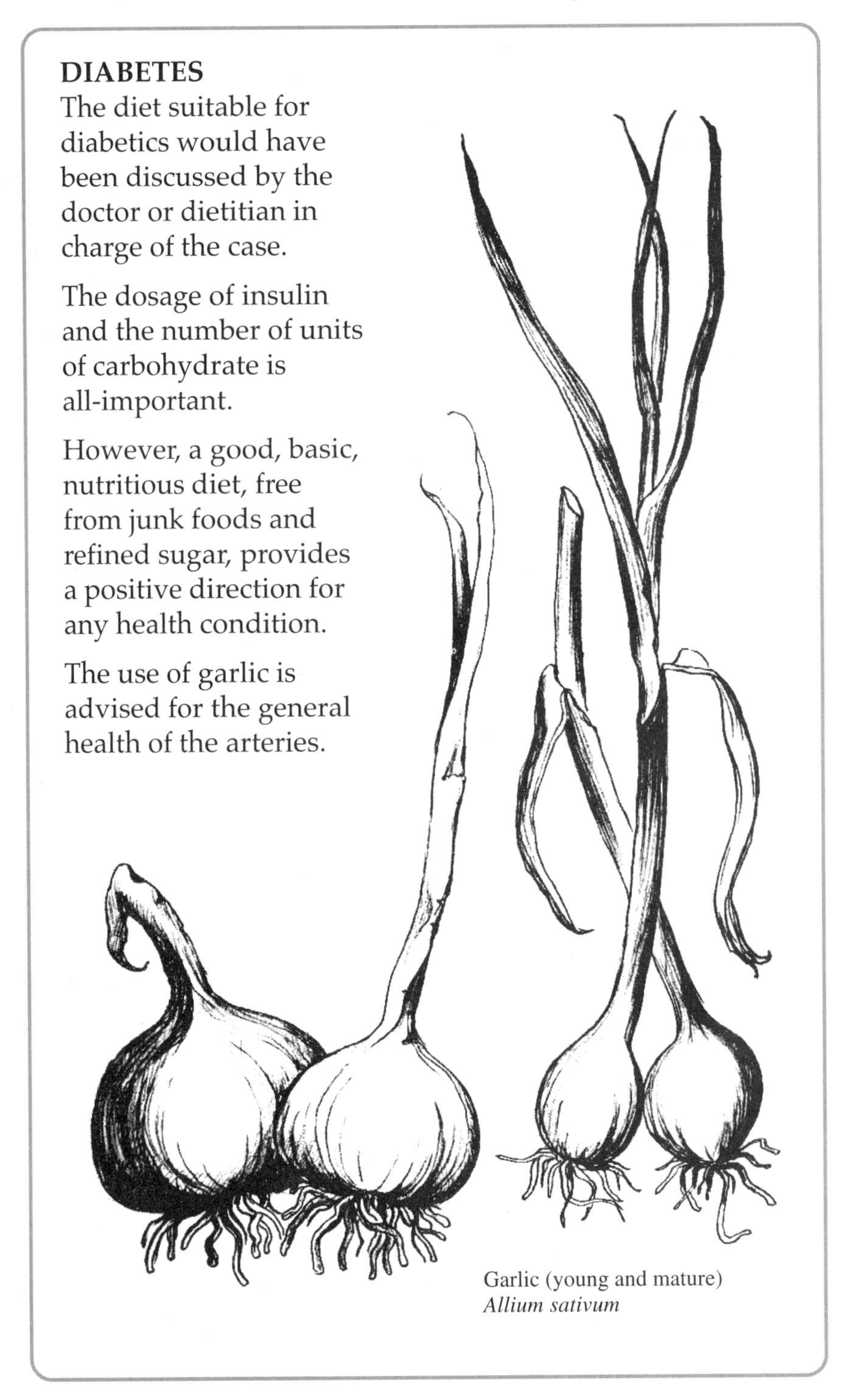

Garlic (young and mature)
Allium sativum

James – Emphysema

EMPHYSEMA is a chronic lung condition which causes destruction of the walls of the alveoli and hence loss of the surface area of the lungs across which oxygen and carbon dioxide are transferred.

Either the bronchitis with its cough, wheeze and occasional haemoptysis, or else emphysema with its breathlessness, is eventually likely to predominate in different individuals. In the bronchitic the carbon dioxide cannot escape (it is more difficult to exhale and to inhale completely) and so is retained in the blood and causes central cyanosis which leads to drowsiness and a characteristic sluggishness. If emphysema predominates, then ventilation (the movement of gas to and from the alveoli) is not a problem, but in order to transfer sufficient oxygen across the reduced alveolar area, the patient must breath more rapidly and puffs rather than wheezes, usually blowing out his cheeks and holding his chest over-inflated, like a barrel.

One of my patients brought her elderly father, James, to see me as a last resort in an attempt to do something to make the end of his life as comfortable as possible. James had been a smoker, as he said, 'for as long as I can possibly remember', and by the time he was in his twenties, suffered frequent bouts of bronchitis.

Despite further warnings from the medical profession he continued with the habit and by the time he was in his forties he suffered chronic bronchitis and relied on a Becotide inhaler to get him through most days. He had several admissions to hospital with acute attacks of bronchitis and on two occasions had near heart failure. However, the habit still continued.

James came to me, age 72, and at that time was reliant on oxygen to get him through his days and nights. It was most distressing to see such a pleasant old man perform even the simplest physical tasks with such difficulty. Just taking off his shoes and socks produced gasping attacks and he became very ashen-faced and collapsed back onto the couch gasping for breath. I had warned his daughter that there was very little I, or anybody else, could do for a case as severe as his but at least we would try to make his remaining months of life as pleasant as possible.

James enjoyed the treatment and said he felt much eased in the chest area. He said, 'The tightness went almost as soon as you started the treatment.'

I was very careful not to overwork any area of his body which had suffered harm due to years and years of medication and obvious damage to his lung area. The patient got off the couch and put on his shoes with much less effort than he did when he got onto it. This pleased his daughter, who said that she was at a loss to know what else to give her father for some respite from all his

James – Emphysema

sufferings. He had been forced to give up the smoking habit as soon as the oxygen cylinder appeared in his home and, as he said, he was about 60 years too late. James had taken antibiotics almost constantly over the previous 10 years to try to control his frequent lung infections. He was also on various bronchial dilating inhalers, and a small dose of steroids was provided to keep the inflammation of the lungs reduced.

Despite all the warnings he had received, James confided to me that he had never thought that anything drastic would ever happen to his lungs. 'We all believe don't we, that nothing will ever happen to us.'

The day after his first treatment I telephoned to enquire how he had been that night, and was pleased to hear that he had a good night's sleep and amazed at how such a frail, weakened body could still produce such an active reaction inasmuch as James said he was constantly bringing up large quantities of mucus from his lungs, which previously he did not do.

The power of the human body to heal itself never fails to amaze me. Even near the end of life, these recuperative powers of self-healing still go into action in an attempt to try and repair the damage.

James came to me for treatment twice weekly, and the most marked change was his improvement in breathing and his ability, so his daughter said, to do simple household tasks. Previously even filling a kettle to make himself a cup of tea was nearly impossible, as any physical action like this would bring on an attack of breathlessness so severe that he would be forced to stop what he was doing. The same reactions occurred after each treatment session. A large amount of mucus was produced from his lungs, which gave him far more ease in breathing, enabling him to use his oxygen less frequently and to be more independent.

We all knew that James had a very limited lifespan and his daughter had quite accepted that Reflexology was not going to be able to perform any miracles. What she was after was a freedom from total dependency, which James hated, and also the contented feeling that she had done everything possible to help her father's condition and had not left any stone unturned.

The prognosis from the hospital when we started the treatment was that James had maybe just a few weeks to live and that was being very optimistic. In fact, he did survive for another 15 months with regular treatments of Reflexology and died of heart failure, very quickly, with very little suffering.

So here was a case where Reflexology could not have restored the body to good health but it did give a patient a much better quality of life and a more peaceful end.

Reflexes in the feet that revealed sensitivity

EMPHYSEMA
Sensitivity occurred in the entire lung area on both the right and left feet.

The liver reflexes were reactive due to the heavy doses of drugs that he had been on.

The intestinal areas were sensitive due in the main to the constant use of antibiotics, which controlled the infections.

Antibiotics destroy the flora in the bowel and the feet revealed this sensitivity.

None of the areas in his feet were as sensitive as would be expected in lung conditions. This would be due to the regular taking of steroids.

Steroids destroy the vitality in the body and tend to 'mask' sensitivity.

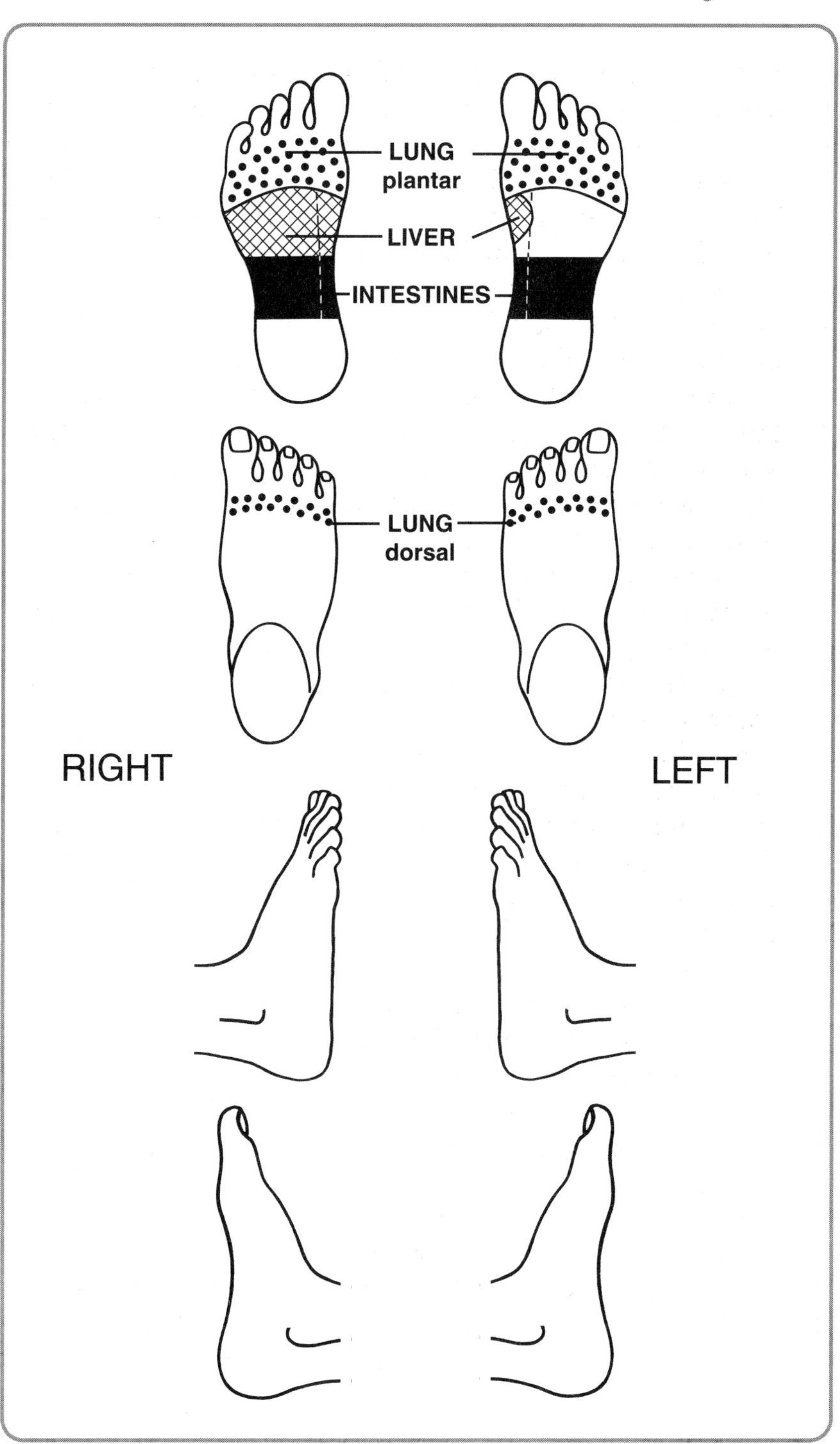

Beneficial herbs, vitamins and dietary advice

EMPHYSEMA

Balm of Gilead has a strong antiseptic and expectorant action and is to be recommended for all chest infections.

Use the herb as a tincture: two teaspoonfuls can be added to boiling water and inhaled.

Liquorice has a strong action on the adrenal glands. An increase in adrenal steroid hormones results in an anti-inflammatory action and again is recommended for chest infections.

A diet rich in garlic and onion would be recommended.

Edward – Frozen shoulder

FROZEN SHOULDER Edward contacted me. He needed an urgent appointment, as the pain and disability in his shoulders was so intense that he was not able to sleep at night. Although only 38 years old, he said that he walked about like an old man of 80.

There seemed to be little reason for his shoulder restriction. He had been married for a couple of years and had just had his first child and his work did not involve any heavy physical lifting. His job was demanding. As a computer programmer for a large company he sat for hours in front of a screen and the more he worked throughout the day, the more his pain and discomfort increased.

His doctor had treated the problem initially with pain-killing tablets, and because the condition failed to improve he then had two cortisone injections. He described the pain of these injections as 'agonizing' and initially had some relief but six months later he was back to square one. The sensitivity in his shoulder reflexes were extreme, his thoracic spine and neck also revealed a lot of tension and inflammation.

After his first treatment he reported that in fact the condition seemed worse. I reassured him that this was not unusual; often the condition gets a little worse before it gets much better following a treatment of Reflexology, particularly the first one.

Edward attended for his weekly appointments and very gradually an improvement began. First and foremost, his pain levels decreased and then gradually he was able to raise his arms a little more each week.

As we got to know each other he said that he had found the responsibilities of marriage, a mortgage and a new baby rather a strain and he did constantly worry about his job security and so on.

I explained that the shoulders are traditionally where we 'shoulder our responsibilities'. Tense shoulders often mean that we are carrying too many burdens. Our shoulders get painful and rigid when we are not expressing our real needs, when perhaps we are doing something that we would rather not be doing.

He said he was scared of sharing these insecurities with his wife in case she felt that he was a bit weak and watery.

Maybe the acceptance of the cause of his condition helped admirably but after eight sessions of Reflexology his shoulder condition became a thing of the past. Edward still comes back from time to time. He says that when he feels like 'the milkmaid carrying her yoke' he rings for another appointment.

Reflexes in the feet that revealed sensitivity

FROZEN SHOULDER

Acute sensitivities appeared in his shoulders, neck and thoracic spine.

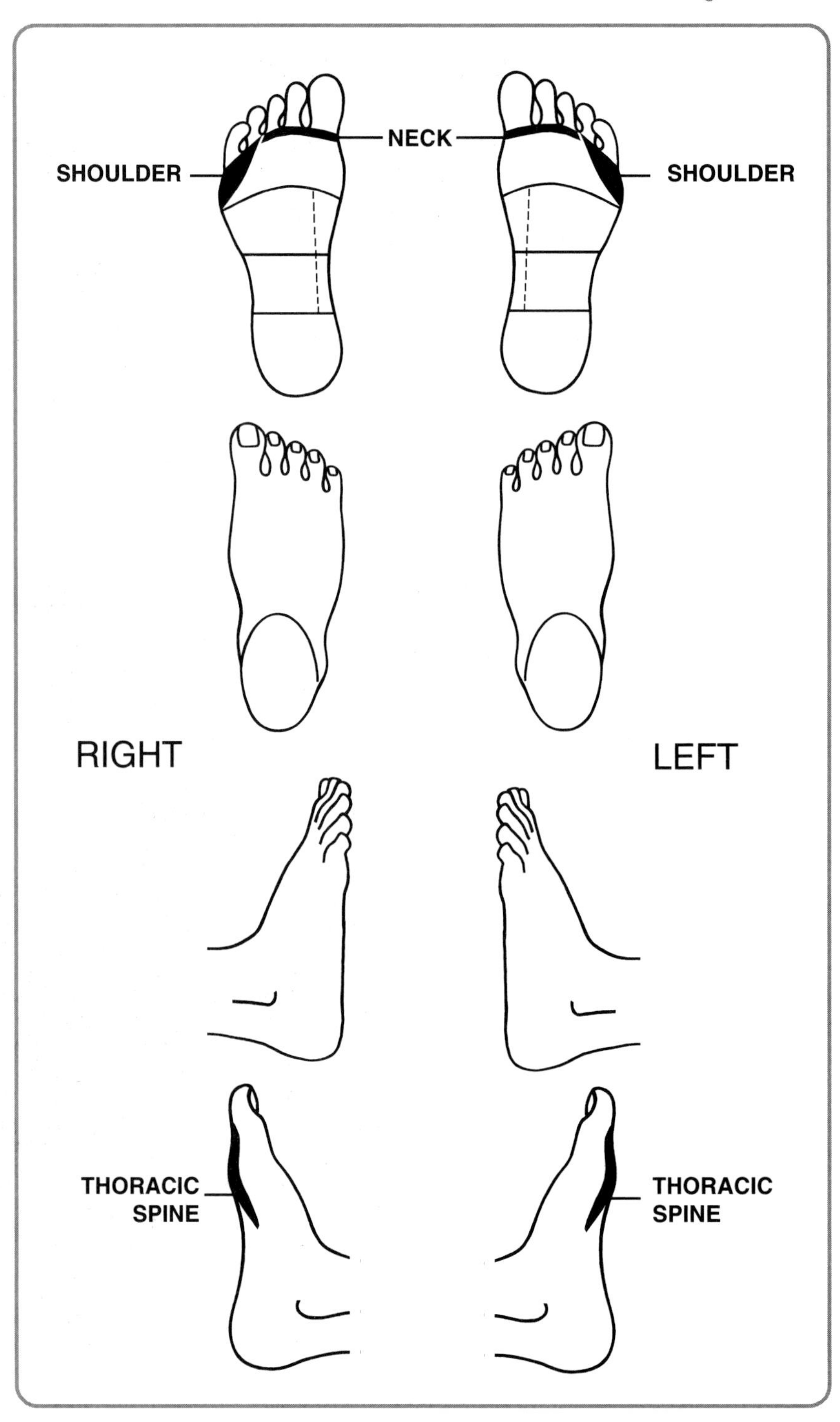

Beneficial herbs, vitamins and dietary advice

FROZEN SHOULDER

Soothing herbal teas such as chamomile are indicated to help towards relaxation in tense and stressful situations.

B5 (pantothenic acid): 250 mg 2–4 times daily may help to alleviate painful symptoms. Vitamin C: 1–2 g daily helps tendons and bones. Vitamin E is known for its certain anti-inflammatory properties.

Chamomile
Anthemis nobilis

Terence – Heart attack

HEART ATTACK When a heart attack occurs, the pain usually starts at rest without warning, often during sleep, and is similar in distribution to angina but more severe, causing sweating, nausea, vomiting and extreme fear. In general, the greater the amount of myocardial damage, the more severe are the symptoms.

The cause of the attack is a sudden cessation in blood flow as the coronary artery supplying one of the ventricles, usually the left, becomes thrombosed with blood or platelets which collects on the ulcerated plaque. This denies the muscle any nutrition and it promptly dies, becoming filled with coagulated blood, turns red and comes to resemble a piece of salami. This is why a heart attack has been endowed with the fanciful name of 'infarction', from the Latin 'infarcere' (stuffing).

Terence came to me following a very severe heart attack, his first, which came completely out of the blue and caused great shock to both him and his entire family. Terence was a typical heart-attack victim: working in a competitive advertising marketing firm with lots of deadlines to meet, driving all over the country at any time of the day or night, and with an urge to gain more and more material possessions.

He said that, apart from being extremely tired for the month preceding the heart attack, he had not had any of the warning chest pains or history of angina which many patients do have. He came to my surgery just three weeks after his discharge from hospital, feeling extremely weak and debilitated. Walking any distance was almost impossible, and he said that by midday his energy levels were absolutely nil and he had to sleep most of the afternoon in order to be able to remain up in the evening.

He had been prescribed beta blockers and had been given advice on dietary needs and what to do and not to do, but he confessed that he felt very insecure away from the hospital environment. He had never smoked, but indulged in quite a lot of alcohol, mainly in social and business meetings. Other than that his main problem was the rush and tear and demands of this very pressurized job. He expected to be away from work for another three months, and he said that he felt that Reflexology surely would be able to help him regain his health and strength.

We talked a lot about his personal lifestyle, which seemed almost as demanding as his job. Reading between the lines, I felt that his wife expected a lot of material benefits in order that she be 'kept happy', which included two

Terence – Heart attack

expensive holidays every year. The year before the heart attack had been one of a lot of emotional trauma.

One of his daughters, who was only 16 and not married, had become pregnant and decided to give birth to this baby which he and his wife were now bringing up. Both his elderly parents had been in very poor states of health, needing much physical and financial help, which Terence had given.

One of his sons was at university and financial demands from him were pretty high, and an elder son had been in a lot of trouble with the police over various problems. So all in all Terence had been the support structure for a lot of weak cogs in the wheel of a rather demanding family. This accumulation of problems plus his business pressures were just sufficient to tip the balance and, as often happens, illness comes along to make the 'supporter' stop and have a look at his life and understand that the demands on him or her are just becoming too much to bear.

Terence admitted that he had always been regarded as a very strong person who would put up with almost anything, so maybe the demands that were upon his shoulders were just normal to the family. However, he did admit that he had had several sleepless nights thinking of all the problems that were confronting him and sometimes not knowing which way to turn.

Terence came to me for six months. He came every single week without fail and made a very rapid recovery from his heart condition. His beta blockers were reduced and he started learning to delegate work in his business concern. As he said, for the first time in his life he realized that other people were able to do many of the jobs which he insisted were his responsibility. He therefore cut down on a lot of the long journeys, attended to far more matters by fax machines and telephone calls than by flying to the Continent to deal with business problems there.

He talked to his family at length about how he felt about his life in general, which is something he had never been able to do before. He made it quite clear that the pressures he had been under were the cause of his heart condition and that unless a repeat performance was going to occur, then a lot of changes would have to be made within the family and fewer demands, both financially and physically, would be necessary.

His wife and children were amazed at how this very strong person, whom they always believed could carry the weight of the world on his shoulders, could confess his weaknesses so readily. They felt bad about the way they had made such demands on him without any questioning the effect that these were

Terence – Heart attack

having on him. 'We never knew how you felt' was the general reply from his children and wife. What a shame that his family communication levels were so low that nobody knew how anybody else felt about anything.

Terence was eventually forced to move from his rather grand, large house into something a little more basic, which reduced his mortgage considerably, and therefore the financial demands on him were considerably lessened. Within the six-month period, as he said, this was a regrowth process both emotionally and physically. He felt that the benefits of Reflexology were responsible in getting him back to his former good health.

At his second visit to the hospital following the heart attack, which was in fact six months later, the stress test results which were performed by the hospital concluded that the damage to his heart was minimal. His blood pressure and weight were within normal limits, his alcohol consumption was down to a very modest one glass of wine per day, he had taken up walking with his wife, and he said not only was it good for his health but it was good for their relationship because it was an hour spent together getting some good physical exercise and being able to share something.

When I first saw Terence in my surgery, his heart reflex area was extremely sensitive, as was his liver, and both kidneys seemed to be under excessive stress. At the end of the six-month term of treatment the sensitivity in the heart was very minimal, just a little damage around the myocardium which one would expect following a heart attack. The sensitivity in his liver was completely gone and both kidneys seemed to be performing normally.

Terence kept up the good work in maintaining his good health and he came to me once a month for a couple of years, during which time there was no further heart attack.

Sometimes when our life is completely unstable and we are going down the wrong road some illness comes along as a means of making us stop and look at what we are and where we are. Terence felt sure that there was a good reason why this had to happen to him. As he said, at least he was fortunate enough to get a warning. Many people have a fatal heart attack and then there is no way of turning the clock back to do away with the reason the heart attack occurred in the first place.

Reflexes in the feet that revealed sensitivity

HEART ATTACK
The heart reflex was sensitive, particularly in the myocardium, which denoted the damage to the heart muscle.

The liver reflexes were sensitive, the liver being a very vascular organ and having associations with heart function.

Cholesterol is produced in the liver, and a fatty liver with poor elimination will show as a sensitivity in the foot.

Patients on long-term medication will usually have a sensitivity in the liver also.

The kidneys had also undergone a change in their functioning due to the disturbance in the heart function.

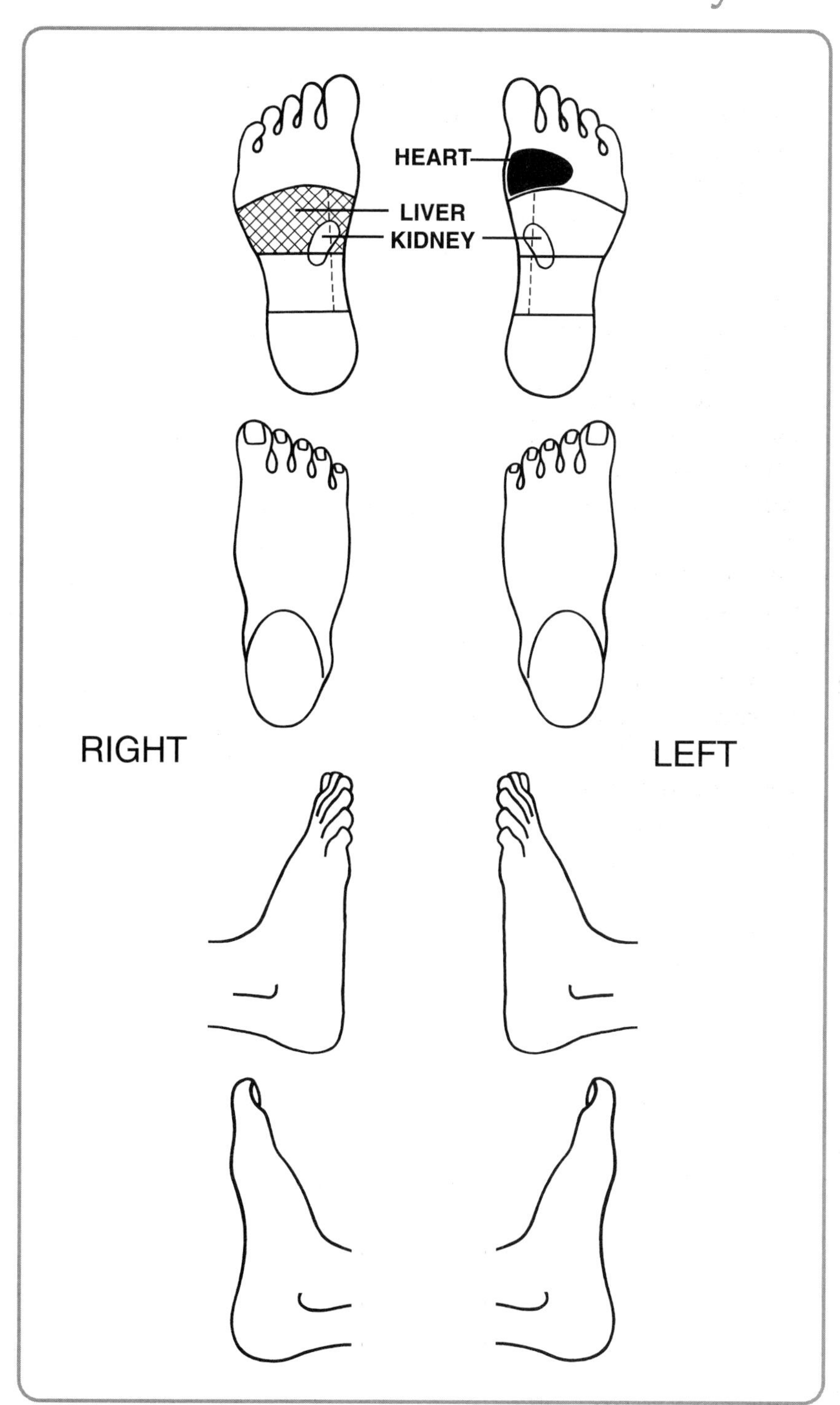

Beneficial herbs, vitamins and dietary advice

HEART ATTACK

Elder contains a bioflavonoid that helps to strengthen the walls of the damaged blood vessels. The main action of the herb is therefore on circulation.

Garlic is an excellent herb to use. Up to one clove of fresh, raw garlic should be taken daily in divided doses. Garlic oil capsules can be substituted.

Garlic contains a healing mineral called germanium and a group of substances which help to control the fat levels in the bloodstream. This is most important as fat deposition is responsible for causing hardening of the arteries, angina and many cases of high blood pressure. Garlic also helps to prevent thrombosis by counteracting the tendency of clot-forming cells to adhere to the artery walls.

Most of us know from constant publicity that a low fat diet is highly recommended for those suffering from heart conditions. It is also

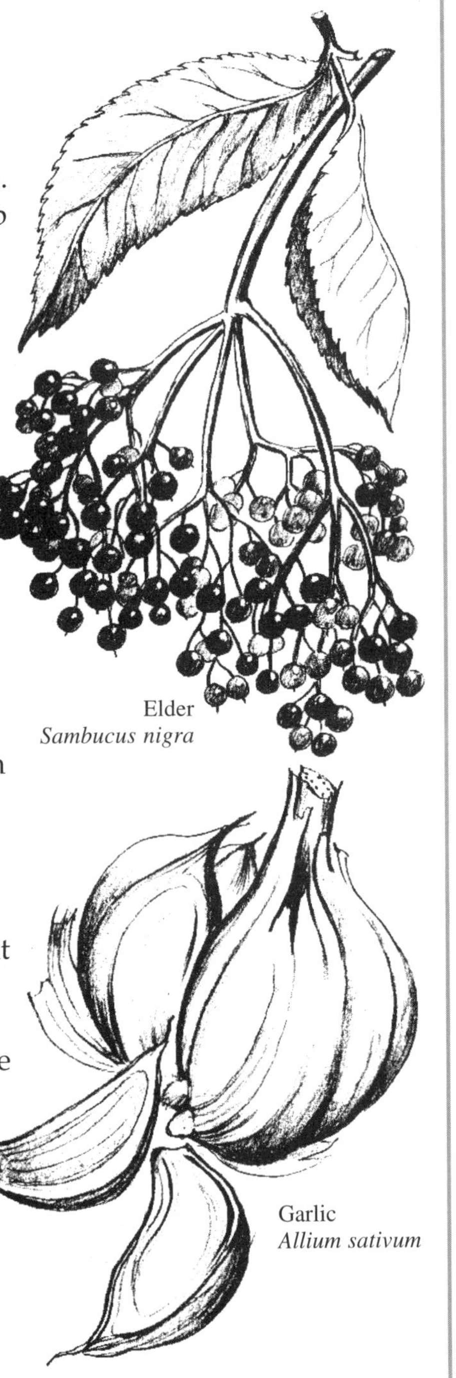

Elder
Sambucus nigra

Garlic
Allium sativum

Beneficial herbs, vitamins and dietary advice

beneficial in avoiding cancer as 70 per cent of cancers are diet related. Limit alcohol intake, red meats, cheese and all dairy products. Make sure that you do not take more than three cups of coffee or tea in a day. Caffeine speeds the heart rate. Eat as much fresh fruit, vegetables, rice, brown bread and pasta as possible. Toss your salads in olive oil.

Learn to relax. Move more! Never before have we had so little exercise. The heart is a muscle and wants to work hard, so take up some form of exercise such as swimming, brisk walking or cycling.

If you can stick to these simple, common-sense rules you will probably live to be 100! Remember it takes a lot of dedicated hard work to become ill and some simple, self-help disciplines to build your body back to vitality.

ANGINA ATHEROSCLEROSIS
Atherosclerosis is caused by an accumulation of fats (largely cholesterol) on the artery walls. The characteristic symptoms associated with this condition include high blood pressure, weak pulse, narrowing of the arteries, leg cramps and mental deterioration.

Consume a diet high in fibre and complex carbohydrates and low in saturated fats. It is well accepted that this condition is a disease of affluence. Avoid stress as far as possible and introduce some gentle exercise. Walking or swimming is recommended. The following are useful supplements to reduce cholesterol levels.

Fibre supplements: psyllium, pectin. Guar gum contains a high amount of soluble and insoluble fibre. Fibre has cholesterol-lowering properties.

Vitamin C: 500 mg twice daily. Vitamin E: 400 iu daily. Fish oil. Lecithin: 3500 mg daily. Lecithin is involved in fat metabolism. High potency garlic capsules prevent platelet aggregation (stickiness).

Brian – Hypertension

HYPERTENSION (high blood pressure). The World Health Organization defines high blood pressure as that with a persistent sphygomanometer reading of 160/90 and over. Average blood pressure is 120/80 for men but lower in women. The diastolic pressure (lower figure) represents pressure to which the arterial walls are subject and is the more important figure.

Main causes of raised pressure include an increase in blood thickness, kidney disorder or loss of elasticity in the arteries by hardening or calcification.

Well-defined problems occur with 10 per cent of high blood pressure cases. By the age of 60 a third of the people of the West are hypertensive.

Other causes are genetic predisposition, endocrine disorders such as hyperactive thyroid and adrenal glands, lead and other chemical poisoning, brain tumour, heart disorder, anxiety, stress and emotional instability.

Food allergies may be other causes. By taking one's pulse after eating a certain food one can see if the food raises the pulse. If so, that food should be avoided. Most cases of high blood pressure are related to lifestyle – how people think, act and care for themselves.

When a person is under constant stress the blood presssure goes up. It temporarily increases on drinking stimulants, alcohol, strong tea, coffee, cola and caffeine drinks generally.

Symptoms include morning headache (back of the head), possible palpitations, visual disturbances, dizziness, angina-like pains, inability to concentrate, breathlessness (left ventricular failure).

Dr Wm Castelli (Director of the Framlingham Heart Study in Massachusetts, USA) records, 'The greatest risk is for coronary heart disease. Hypertensives have more than double the risk of people with normal blood pressure and seven times the risk of strokes.'

In countries where salt intake is restricted, a rise in blood pressure with age is not seen.

Simple hypotensive herbs may achieve effective control without the side effects of sleep disturbance, adverse metabolic effects, lethargy and impaired peripheral circulation.

Brian was a typical hypertensive candidate. He had a very high-powered job in advertising, was overweight, took virtually no exercise, drank quite heavily on occasions and lived on strong black coffee during the day as he described it 'to keep himself going'.

Brian – Hypertension

His usual lunch was a beefburger and chips, and his life, if he continued along that path, so his doctor had advised, was going to be a very short one. He was 46 when he first approached me to see if Reflexology could help reduce his blood pressure.

The medication he was on gave him some very unpleasant side effects. The most troublesome of all was impotence, which created yet more stresses in another direction.

Brian really thought that by just applying pressure to certain reflexes in his feet all would be well, and that was exactly what he wanted, a complete cure with no effort from himself whatsoever.

I made it very clear from the start that it would be pointless to have Reflexology or any other form of treatment unless he changed the reason why he had the condition in the first place.

His condition was very bad – extreme sensitivity in the heart, brain and kidney area – and I was sure that the arteries in these areas were very corroded.

He had three treatments and no improvement was reported, as, apart from not having his beefburger and chip lunch, he really was not helping himself. I suggested that he stop having treatment as it was really a complete waste of time.

I had a telephone call from him three months later. His younger brother had just died at the age of 40 with a massive heart attack. He too had suffered from hypertension for many years, as had his father. It took this event to make him realize that he was killing himself by his lifestyle, and back he came for treatment, this time a very reformed character.

I would not say that he was the easiest patient or that he followed a healthy lifestyle, but he did try, and reduced his weight by 2 stone the following year, reduced the alcohol and coffee and found time at week-ends to take up some activity.

By the end of the first six months the acute sensitivities in his feet lessened dramatically and his blood pressure dropped to acceptable limits.

How often do people leave it all too late, and have their heart attack or stroke before they listen to any warning?

Reflexes in the feet that revealed sensitivity

HYPERTENSION
It was disturbing to find such acute sensitivity in the heart, brain and kidney areas.

Brian was a typical candidate for a stroke or a heart attack.

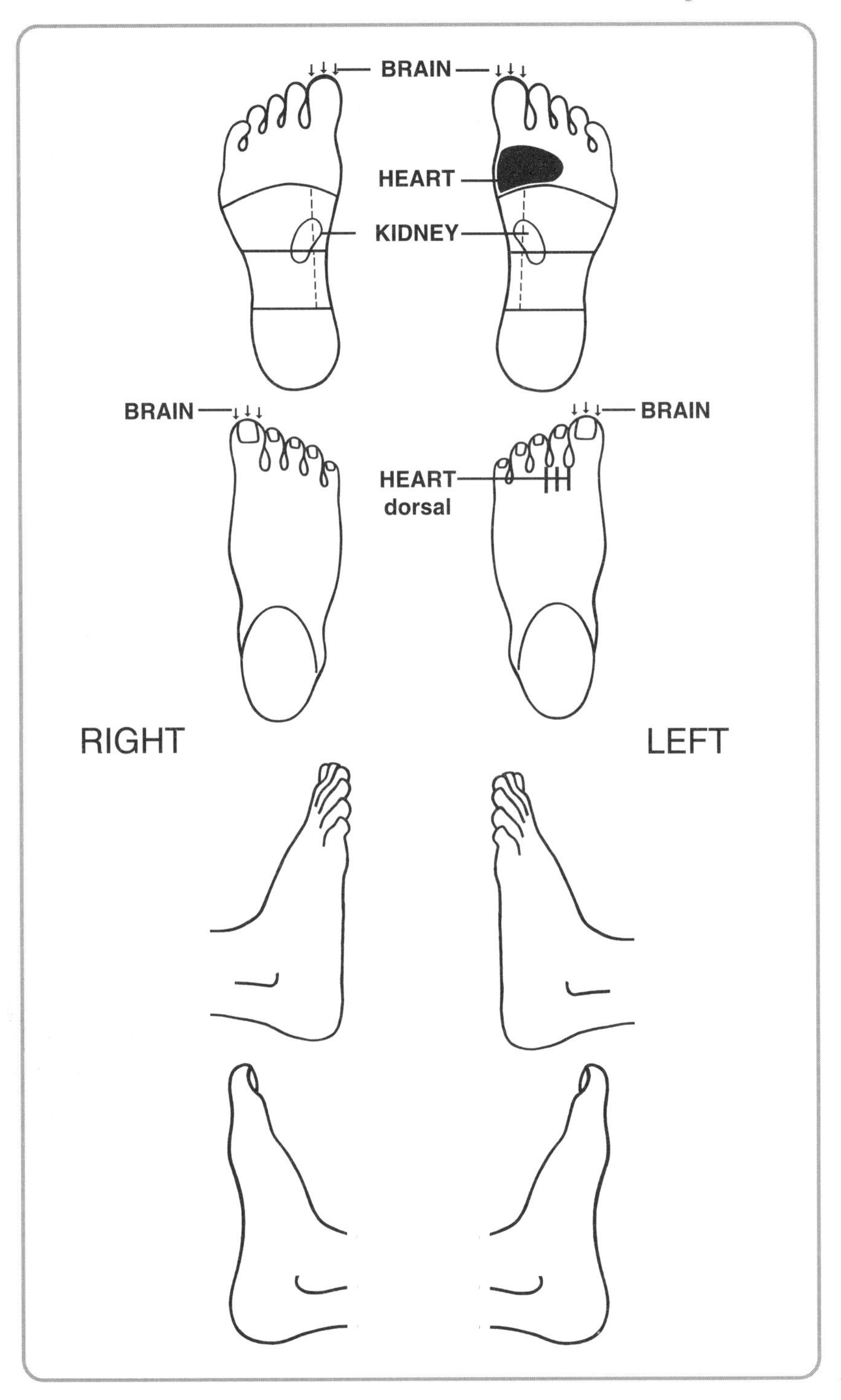

Beneficial herbs, vitamins and dietary advice

HYPERTENSION

High blood pressure is generally believed to be linked to dietary and life-style factors. High intakes of sodium and sugar are known to be important causes of elevated blood pressure. Tea and coffee consumption, alcohol, saturated fats, lack of exercise and obesity can all contribute to high blood pressure. Avoid smoking and aim to lose excess weight. Follow an exercise programme and take in to account overall health.

Change to a whole-food diet which places emphasis on potassium-rich foods such as fruit and vegetables, poly-unsaturated fats and fibre. Studies have indicated that among vegetarians there is a lower incidence of hyper-tension. Hawthorn helps to normalise blood pressure.

Vitamin C with bioflavonoids: 1–2 g daily or high potency anti-oxidant including beta carotene, vitamin C, vitamin E and selenium. Vitamin E: 400 iu daily. Fish oils (EPA/DHA): 1–2 g daily. Magnesium: 150–450 mg daily. Low magnesium status is common in hypertensives.

Hawthorn
Crataegus oxyacantha

Jane and Tom – Infertility

INFERTILITY A young couple contacted me because they were unable to conceive. They had been married for eight years, and over the last five years had hoped that a baby would arrive on the scene but so far there had been no success.

Numerous extensive tests had been carried out and no hormonal defects had been found. Jane had a very normal regular menstrual cycle and Tom's sperm count was within normal limits. No abnormal structural defects had been found in Jane.

Not wanting to embark on any further invasive treatment, they preferred to try some form of complementary medicine.

They had a healthy lifestyle, were non-smokers, only drank socially and followed a healthy vegetarian diet. They were very interested in herbalism and had contacted a medical herbalist who had prescribed some herbs to help fertility.

They certainly seemed a happy, relaxed couple so I did not think that stress was causing the problem.

The feet revealed very little sensitivity in both Jane and Tom, so here was a case where the feet really did not tell a story. I was mystified. However, they were both keen to have treatment and enjoyed the session immensely.

We decided to treat Jane one week and Tom the other, and both agreed to come for a three-month period, in order to work through three menstrual cycles. On the tenth treatment, Jane telephoned excitedly to report that she had missed her period and a month later pregnancy was confirmed.

We shall never know exactly how Reflexology worked here, as nothing appeared in the feet. Maybe the herbal preparation did the trick. However, most important of all, a happy result was achieved.

Jane had a trouble-free pregnancy and a very easy labour. She came to me for further treatment four weeks before her baby was born. So convinced was she that Reflexology had put her body back into the correct balance to conceive that she called her little girl Ann!

Reflexes in the feet that revealed sensitivity

INFERTILITY
The feet revealed very little sensitivity in both Jane and Tom.

Maybe there was some allergic reaction between the couple that Reflexology was able to help by improving the balance in the body and helping the immune system.

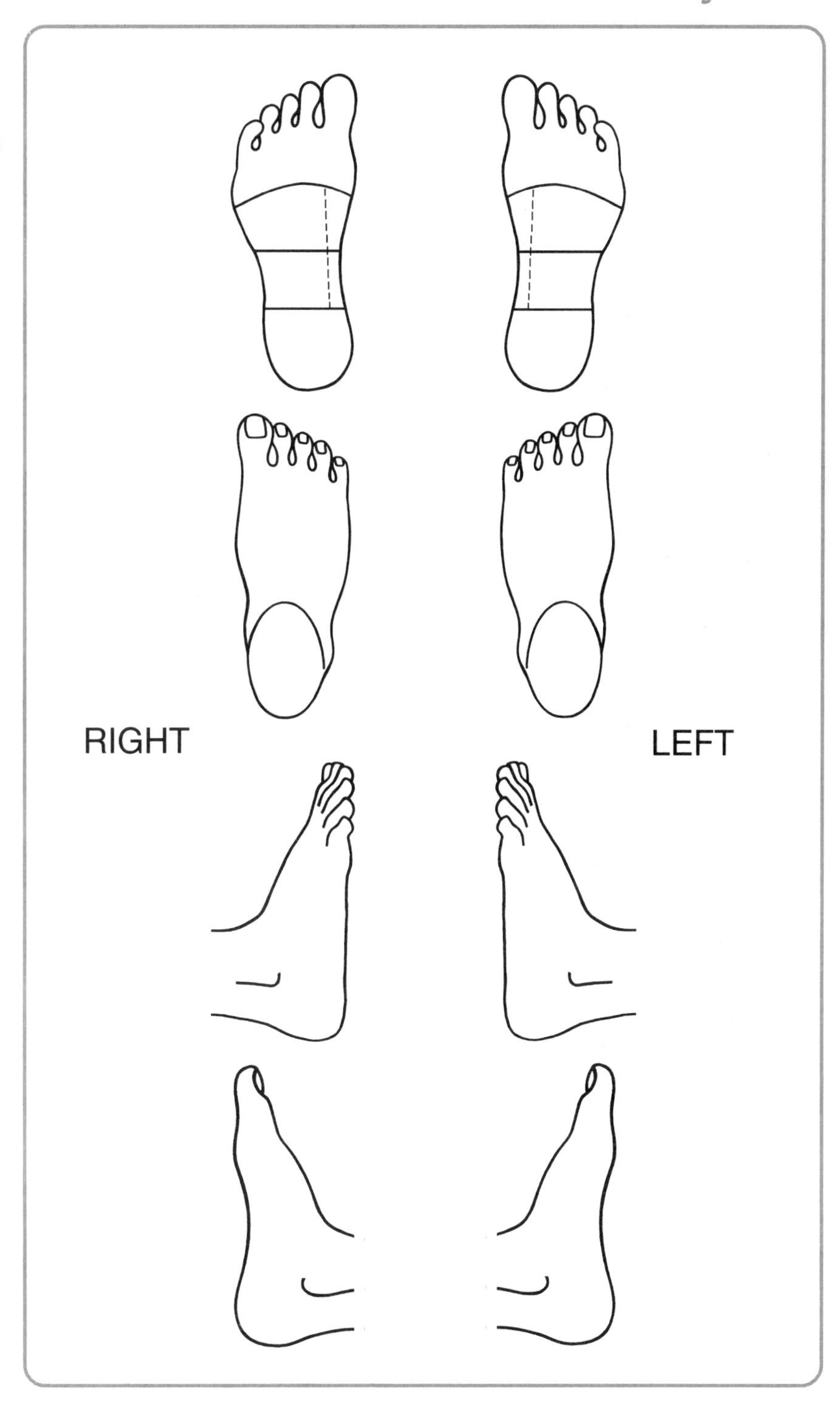

Beneficial herbs, vitamins and dietary advice

INFERTILITY

Infertility has been shown to link with severe malnutrition.

Avoid refined carbohydrates and additives. Cut out smoking and alcohol.

Motherwort, although not recommended in this instance, has been used traditionally to restore and regulate menstruation. *Warning: Motherwort is not to be taken during a pregnancy.*

A broad-spectrum multi-formula vitamin containing vitamin E and the B complex vitamins is to be recommended.
Vitamin C: 500–1000 mg daily is an important anti-oxidant. Researchers found that an intake of below 250 mg of vitamin C daily resulted in excessive free radical damage to the DNA in sperm.
Zinc: 15 mg daily.
Zinc is implicated in fertility / infertility.

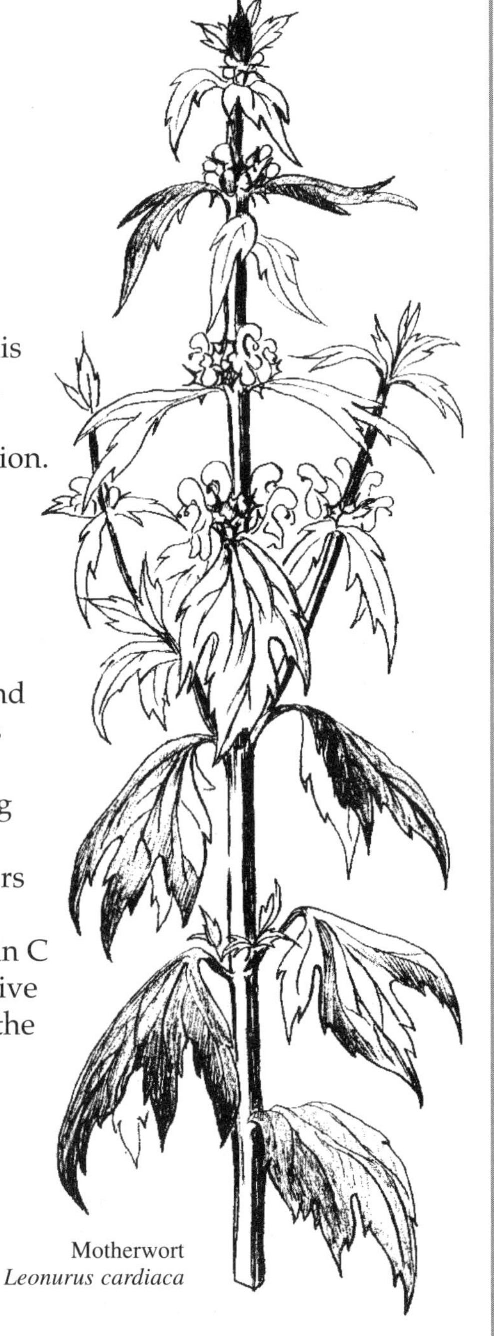

Motherwort
Leonurus cardiaca

Pauline – Irritable bowel syndrome

IRRITABLE BOWEL SYNDROME (IBS) This condition was previously known as 'mucous colitis' or 'spastic colon', and was believed to be associated with psychosomatic rather than allergic causes.

Food is said to be responsible for one-third of cases, but X-ray fails to reveal evidence. Prostaglandins are implicated. Females are far more susceptible than males. Cow's milk and antigens in beef can precipitate the condition.

The two main symptoms are abdominal pain and altered bowel habit. Pain is usually relieved on opening the bowels or on passing wind. Diarrhoea with watery stools may alternate with constipation and a sensation that the bowel is incompletely emptied. There is flatulence and passing of mucous between stools.

The chronic condition may cause weight loss and poor health, calling for treatment of the underlying condition. Sufferers are usually hard-striving perfectionists who find it difficult to relax.

It is said that men express their dis-ease by experiencing duodenal or stomach ulceration which is common in mentalities as described above.

Pauline came to me in a very stressed state. She was only 42 but looked far older. Her life had been very complicated and sad for the previous four years. Her marriage had failed, resulting in a divorce, and she was having quite a time in trying to hold down a job as a sister-in-charge of the accident and emergency department at her local hospital.

She had two children in her care, a boy of thirteen and a daughter of ten. Her son in particular was very difficult to manage following her divorce and seemed to blame her for the breakdown of the marriage.

Finances were strained, as Pauline was trying to maintain the family home and had a mortgage to pay and all the usual expenses of running a home, car and family. She frequently worked extra shifts at the hospital when money became short, and now, just to add to these problems, she had irritable bowel syndrome. It had become so bad that the attacks of diarrhoea in the morning, when they were at their worst, were embarrassing, to say the least.

She experienced quite excruciating pain on her left side, which was the descending part of the colon. The frequent bowel actions had caused haemorrhoids, so now sitting was painful and she was nearly at the end of her tether.

She had had numerous bowel function tests at the hospital and various

Pauline – Irritable bowel syndrome

medications from the doctor, so I knew that nothing sinister was underlying. It is always essential when a patient presents with alarming symptoms such as she had that all possibilities of a severe disease are eliminated. Remember, doctors have access to all forms of X-ray screening devices whereas Reflexologists do not.

Pauline's feet certainly did tell the tale. The intestinal area was so sensitive that she could hardly bear any pressure on the reflexes, particular in the descending and sigmoid colon on the left foot. Her stomach and liver reflexes were over-sensitive too, and that poor old solar plexus area again, the great seat of emotions and feelings. Locked in there I am sure were all the hurts and pains of her divorce, the heavy responsibilities of being a single parent, and uncertainty regarding her future.

Apart from her irritable bowel, Pauline had such severe pains in her neck, shoulders and the tops of her arms that at times she could hardly hold a shopping bag.

People who have a lot of responsibilities and take the problems of the world on their shoulders frequently suffer arm and shoulder pains – you know, rather like the milkmaid carrying a yoke, heavy weights across the shoulders!

Always remember, the arms and hands are the wings of the heart, they encircle your heart, so heavy emotional burdens affecting your innermost feelings affect your arms and hands – your wings!

It was quite hard to know where to start. You can't say, 'Why don't you change your job, let somebody else have your children for a while, have a break?' All those things were impossible.

Having somebody to talk to who understood helped immensely. Reflexology did the rest.

I gave Pauline a light general treatment, and also some body massage, which she said was a luxury. 'Do you realize, nobody has touched me for three years,' she said.

I asked her to telephone me the next day to report any reaction. She said that she slept very well, the best night's sleep she had had for many months. Her bowel actions had been the same, but she felt less stressed and her shoulders and arms were definitely less painful.

Very, very slowly over the next few weeks her diarrhoea improved, the daily morning routine of eight or nine visits to the toilet reduced to two or three. Her energy levels started to improve, and that consequently gave her more emotional strength to cope with her son, who blamed her for his lack of a father.

Pauline – Irritable bowel syndrome

I have suggested to Tony (her son) that he go and live with his father – just to see if he is happier there. He obviously does not like what I have to offer him, she said. Perhaps a few months there will help us all.

After the sixth treatment I noticed a marked reduction in sensitivity in the colon, and to me this reflected that the inflamed colon had begun to heal. Pauline's symptoms were greatly improving now, and some days she was not troubled by her bowel condition at all. She stuck rigidly to the dietary advice.

There was little she could do to reduce her work load at the hospital. She had a responsible, demanding job and there was very little she could delegate. However, as she put it, 'If I can get rid of some of my health problems I will be able to cope more confidently with my job.'

I suggested to Pauline that she take Slippery Elm Food after a busy shift at the hospital instead of trying to eat a rushed meal often at odd times. The bark of the elm is well known for its healing process, particularly of the digestive system.

I worked hard with Reflexology and Pauline put in her 50 per cent, which is so essential in achieving a good result.

Pauline had ten treatments in all, and then a further three on a monthly basis. Her bowel condition improved dramatically. She looked 10 years younger and life took on a better meaning.

Tony, who left to live with his father, returned home after four months with a much improved disposition, realizing that it takes two parents to create a situation that culminates in divorce and there is always another side to the story.

Reflexes in the feet that revealed sensitivity

IRRITABLE BOWEL SYNDROME

The stomach and liver reflexes were sensitive. This was mainly due to the digestive system being out of balance.

The intestinal areas on both feet were so sensitive that even the lightest pressure on her feet was hardly bearable.

The sigmoid colon and rectum on the left foot were acutely sensitive. The inflammation in this part of the colon was at its worst and the rectum was painful because of the haemorrhoids.

The solar plexus is easily upset by emotional disturbance. This was another area that caused a strong reaction to the treatment session.

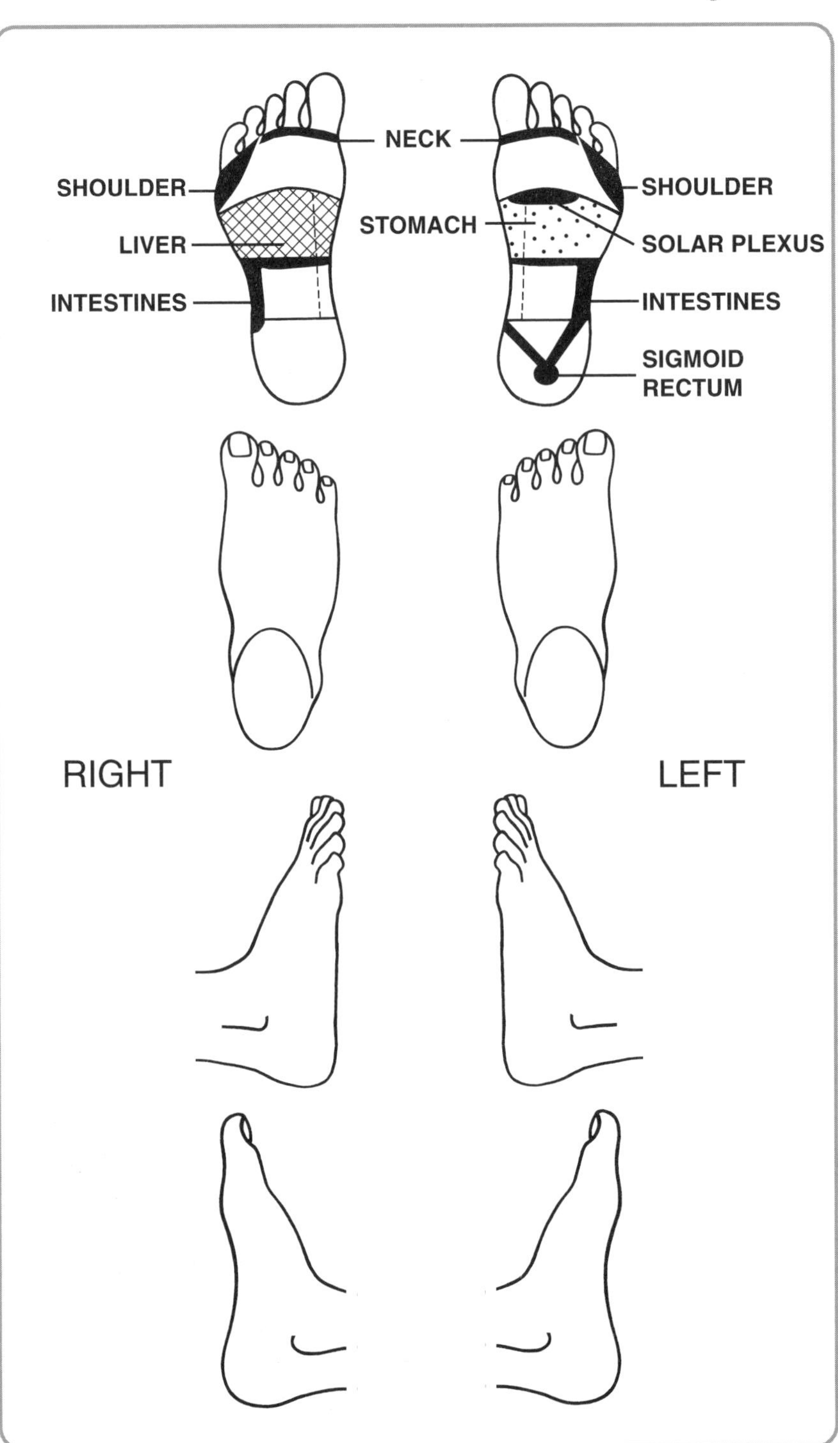

Beneficial herbs, vitamins and dietary advice

IRRITABLE BOWEL SYNDROME

When there is such an acutely inflamed condition in the digestive system it is recommended that you choose perhaps a week-end when you can take life easy and go on a two-day grape fast. Eat nothing but grapes, as many as you like, chew the kernel and swallow. Also drink pints and pints of pure spring water. The grape is a healing fruit; that is why for many centuries it has been taken to the sick as a luxury; the luxury being the fruit, not the cost. Today, grapes are very reasonable in price.

Slippery Elm Food is available in powder form and can be made up in milk as a drink. It is quite pleasant and should be taken first thing in the morning and always last thing at night. Slippery elm is soothing and healing to the entire digestive system.

Coffee and alcohol must be avoided. For the first few weeks, or until you get an improvement, eat fish, chicken, root vegetables,

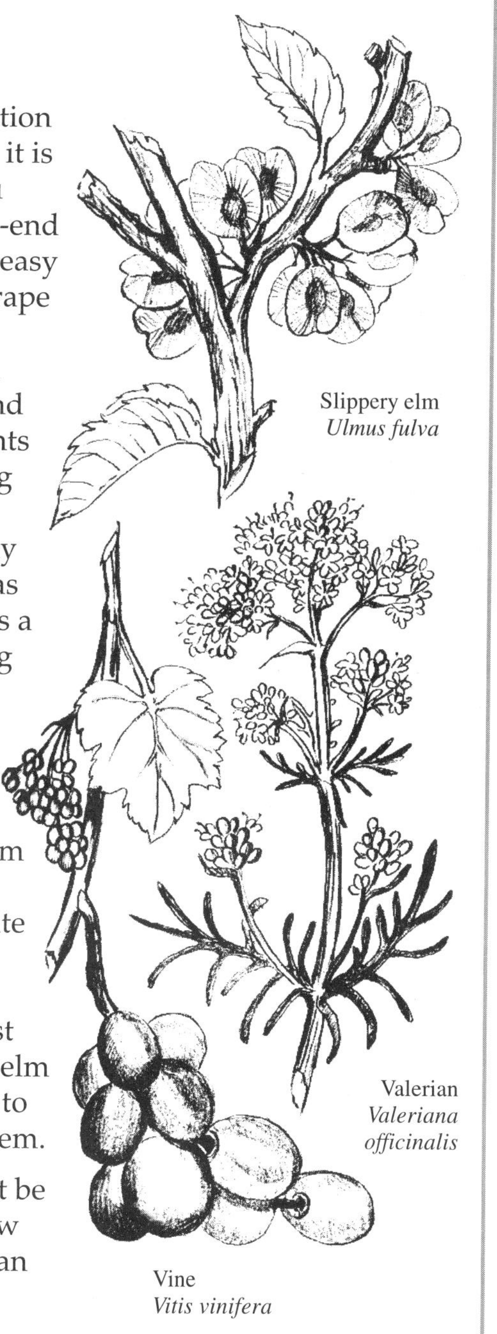

Slippery elm
Ulmus fulva

Valerian
Valeriana officinalis

Vine
Vitis vinifera

Beneficial herbs, vitamins and dietary advice

rice, pasta, potato, pears and stewed apples and avoid a lot of roughage.

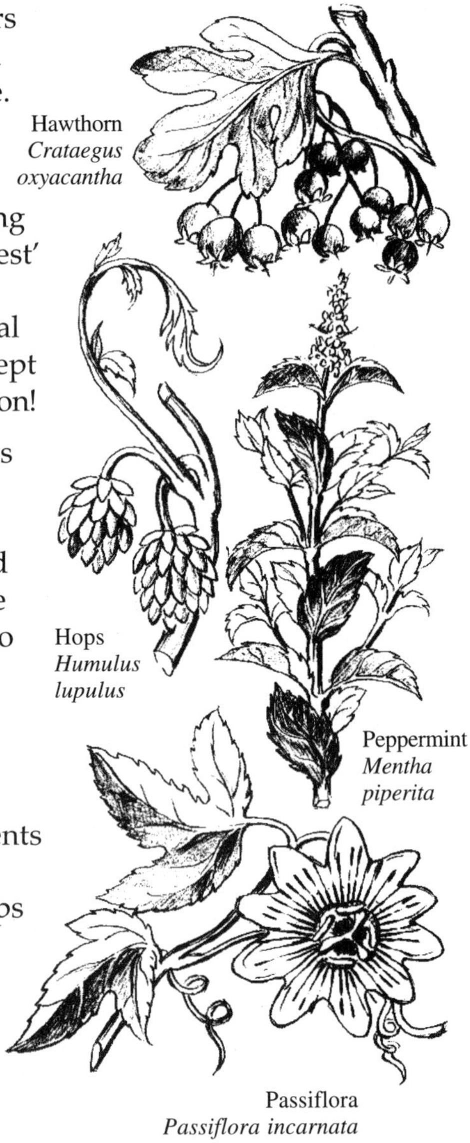

There is usually a problem in the emotional field, a feeling of being unable 'to digest' a certain situation or irritation in the personal life. An inability to accept an inflammatory situation!

The physical symptoms of irritable bowel are often accompanied by fatigue, depression and anxiety. Gentle exercise such as curl-ups help to strengthen abdominal muscles and promote normal intestinal contractions.

Acidophilus supplements contain lactobacillus-acidophilus which helps to repopulate the intestinal flora with beneficial bacteria. Pantothenic acid is essential for proper functioning of the gastrointestinal tract.
Herbal antispasmodic complex such as valerian, hop, hawthorn and passiflora are known to have soothing properties. Peppermint oil capsules can be taken, as peppermint oil has a well-proven antispasmodic effect on the stomach and intestines.

Hawthorn *Crataegus oxyacantha*

Hops *Humulus lupulus*

Peppermint *Mentha piperita*

Passiflora *Passiflora incarnata*

Jennifer – Kidney stones

KIDNEY STONES are caused because the amount of uric acid forming in the joints, blood and other places becomes excessive. Uric acid is made from DNA and RNA, the constituents of the nuclei of the cells, and these are broken down in the liver and passed to the blood for excretion. The amount which the kidney can excrete is limited and if this level is exceeded the pool builds up. If uric acid crystals are formed rapidly they may occur as stones in the kidney and can lead to renal failure, although this is very rare.

Jennifer was in her forties when she came to me with a very unusual complaint. Her telephone call enquiring whether I could help 'foot conditions' was a little vague and I hastened to explain that Reflexology was not about treating foot conditions but by treating the feet as a contact for the human body. Nevertheless, she said that she would like to see me to find out if I could iron out the mystery of why she had this sore, scaly area on just one small part of the sole of her foot; it had been there for 18 months, causing her extreme irritation and discomfort both day and night.

At her first appointment with me I found that the description she had given over the phone was completely accurate. There was an area on her right foot, under the instep, about the size of the thumb nail, which was red, scaly and angry and which was the cause of her constant scratching and irritation, particularly at night when her feet became warm. She said she spent a lot of time each night putting her feet in ice-cold water, and she had applied all forms of lotions and creams to no permanent good. She had already been to a skin specialist who had diagnosed eczema, but why it should be just on that one isolated area he had no idea and prescribed hydrocortisone skin cream which kept the condition under control temporarily – but as soon as one tube was finished and a few days elapsed, back would come the skin irritation and the red, scaly area.

I worked over both Jennifer's feet, applying a pad of lint to the reddened area as any direct pressure on that point would be extremely painful for her, and could find no real basic cause for her condition other than the localized sensitivity in the sore area. I was not sure whether the sensitivity in the area was just through the eczema or whether there was an underlying problem. When I took a full case history Jennifer disclosed to me that the only real health problem she had had in the last six or seven years was a kidney stone in the right kidney.

This, I was sure, had a good reflection on what we were finding, as it was no coincidence that the reddened area on the foot was exactly on the kidney reflex

Jennifer – Kidney stones

point on that right side. I felt that here was a very unusual reaction but it was in fact the reflex area in the feet showing its sensitivity to congestion and inflammation by expressing itself in an eczema-type skin reaction. These findings I related to the patient, who felt sure that it all made good sense.

The big problem was how to work on that kidney area without causing a lot of pain and discomfort to the patient. I needed to be able to apply sufficient pressure to get a good result.

However, after the third treatment the patient remarked that the sensitive area was definitely smaller and it looked that way to me, so we removed the pad of lint which had been placed upon the foot during the treatment sessions and I started with a very gentle pressure to work directly onto that kidney spot. She felt quite a lot of reaction as I did this, and also mentioned that over the previous few months she had frequently felt sharp, stabbing pains in her body, in her kidney area, which I then knew was related to the reaction we were finding in her feet.

Over the next few weeks I continued to work extensively on the urinary system on both the right and left feet, and week by week this little reddened, scaly area became smaller and smaller. At the end of nine sessions the eczema, redness and scaling had disappeared altogether, much to the patient's amazement and relief, and there was no real sensitivity as pressure was applied to this point. I suggested that we leave the situation alone and just see if the eczema reappeared in the same area.

The patient came back to me just six weeks later reporting that she had had no further pain and irritation in the foot and, most remarkable of all, she had stopped having this sharp, dragging pain in her kidney.

As there were no other health problems we both decided that we would cease the treatment and, should the condition return, Jennifer would contact me immediately.

However, the problem did not return and I saw this lady in our local town just a year later who happily approached me, smilingly saying that she was fit and well with no return of the sensitive spot in her foot or pains in her kidney area.

Reflexes in the feet that revealed sensitivity

KIDNEY STONES
There was an acute sensitivity in the right kidney area.

The kidney area in the foot revealed a sore, scaly, itchy patch exactly in line with the kidney reflex area.

Other than that one sensitive spot, the feet revealed no other sensitivity.

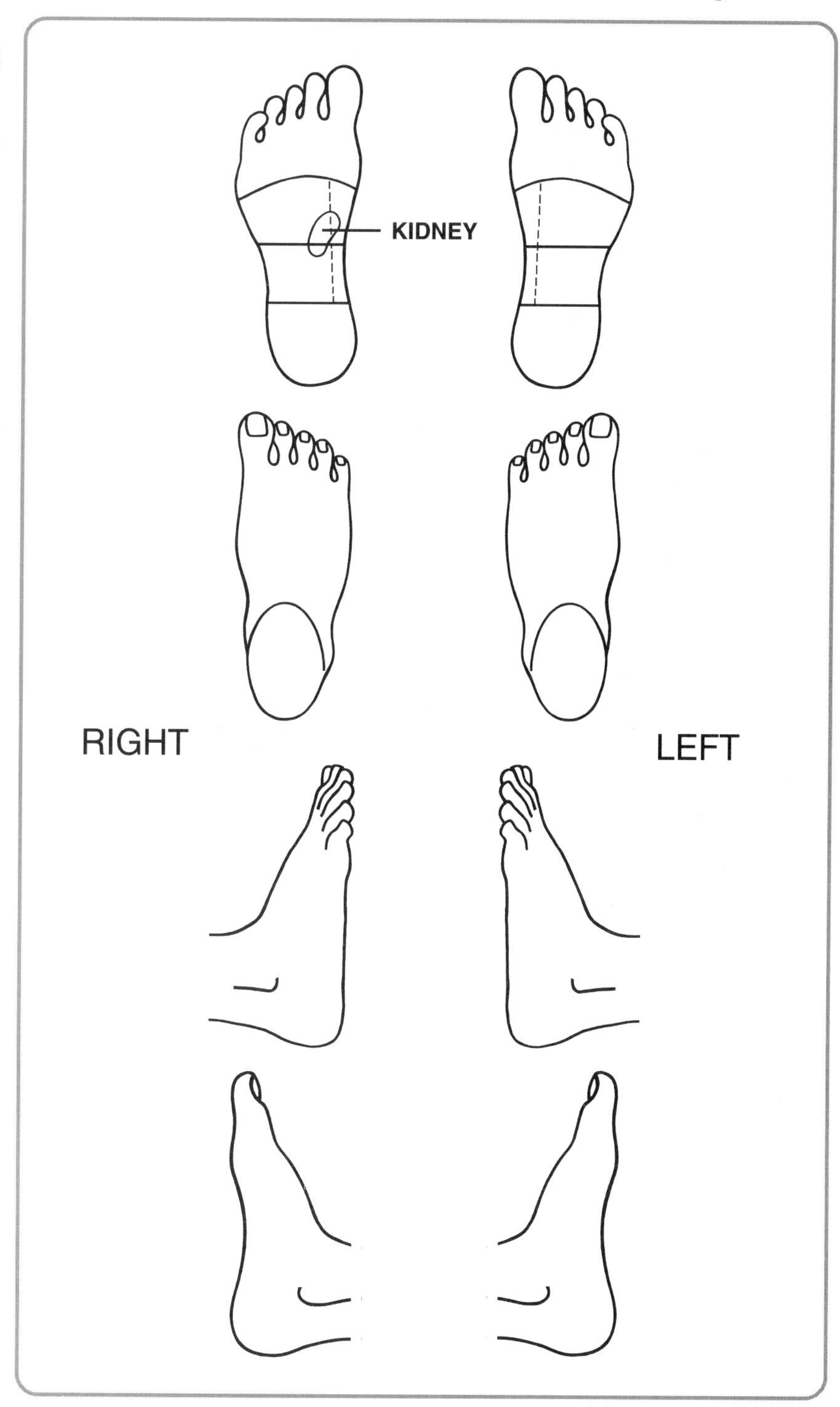

Beneficial herbs, vitamins and dietary advice

KIDNEY STONES

Only the most straightforward of urinary disorders should be treated without professional attention.

The cleansing action of the kidneys is essential to good health and life itself.

Diuretic remedies to flush through the urinary system, such as Dandelion leaf and horsetail, will help.

Echinacea and golden seal will strengthen the body's general resistance to infection.

Warning: Golden seal is not to be taken during a pregnancy.

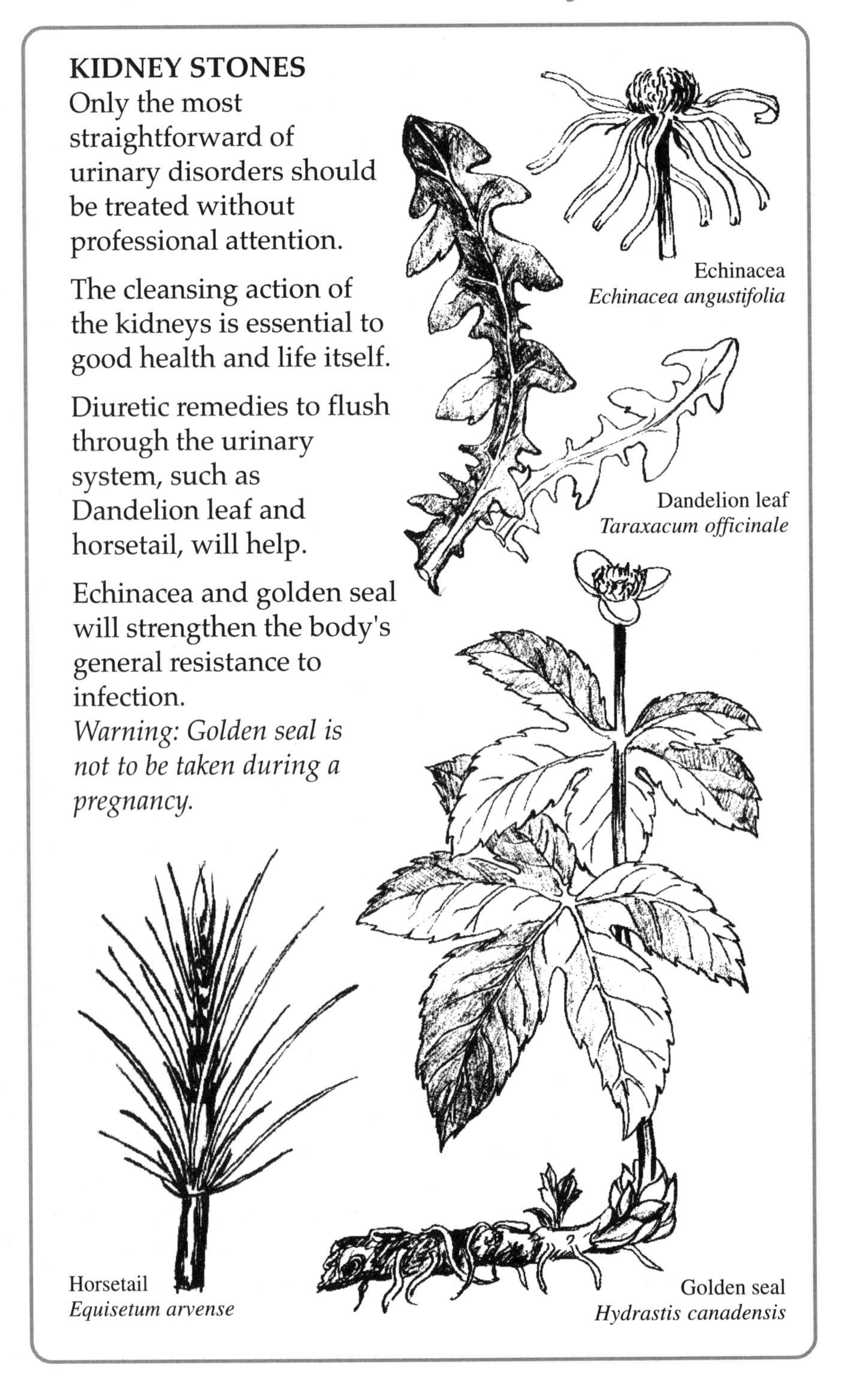

Simon – Laryngitis

LARYNGITIS is an acute infectious illness of the larynx which often spreads to other parts of the throat and sometimes the ear. The infection causes hoarseness, swelling and pain in the throat and often results in a complete loss of voice.

Simon was a dental surgeon who, for the last two and a half years, had repeated episodes of laryngitis which often lasted for several weeks. He said he had suffered many throat infections as a child. There was no real pattern to these attacks apart from the fact that his voice was reasonably normal, although a little husky in the mornings and became increasingly huskier and weaker as the day progressed. He was a very conscientious man, a perfectionist in his work and had worked very hard to build up his successful practice.

He had gone through the usual routine examinations with an ear, nose and throat specialist but nothing abnormal had been discovered.

The courses of antibiotics, which he had resorted to in a desperate attempt to improve his condition, gave him very little relief. His doctor had referred him for allergy testing wondering if there was something he was using in his work that was affecting his throat, particularly in view of the fact that the condition improved once he was away from his practice. The only time his voice returned to near normal was when he took his twice-yearly holiday.

There was considerable sensitivity in his throat and neck area; in fact the whole shoulder, thoracic spine and head areas were acutely sensitive to even the lightest pressure, and the diaphragm and solar plexus revealed a strong reaction. The most acutely sensitive areas however were his adrenal glands. 'What on earth have my adrenal glands got to do with my throat condition?' he asked.

A very accurate picture was emerging of a sensitive, conscientious, hard-working dentist who was under considerable pressure, and his body was indeed in a tense condition, which was why his adrenal glands were so sensitive. His shoulder, neck and thoracic spine were reacting and this, in the main, would have been due to hours of standing over patients in rather fixed position.

His body was reacting to stress by a loss of voice. After explaining the situation to Simon, he tended to agree with my findings. He attended for treatments on a twice-weekly basis, although he was reluctant at first to agree to two treatments a week because of his heavy workload. However he did agree that really his health came first and if Reflexology could sort out his repeated laryngitis then he would be overjoyed. Simon attended for two months and had eight treatments in all. There was a remarkable change in his condition within the first three treatments and after two months his voice was nearly back to normal.

Reflexes in the feet that revealed sensitivity

LARYNGITIS
There was considerable sensitivity in the throat, neck and head.

The area of the thoracic spine and shoulder also reacted to pressure.

The adrenal glands were acutely sensitive, also the diaphragm and solar plexus.

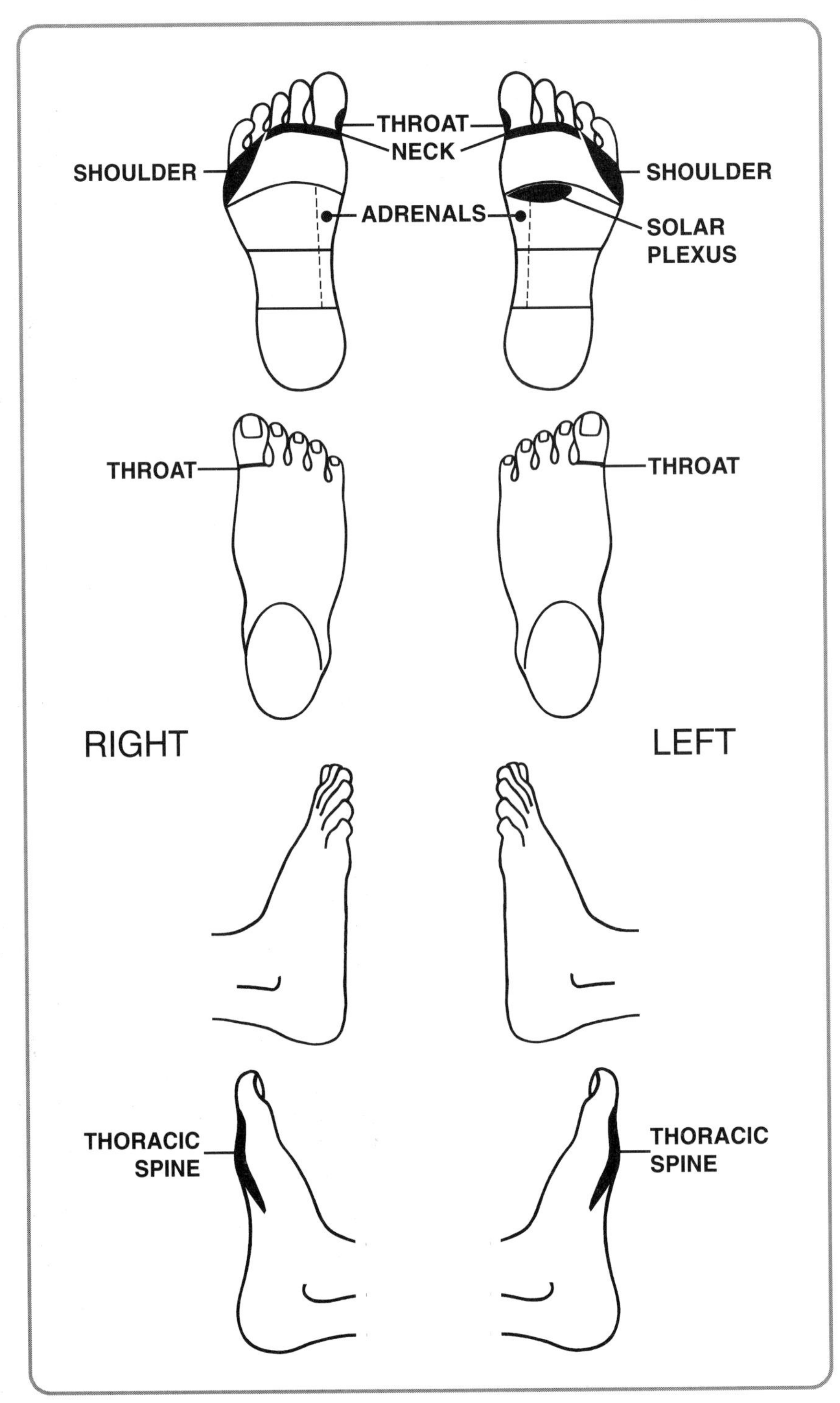

Beneficial herbs, vitamins and dietary advice

LARYNGITIS

As a good immune boost, echinacea, 100–200 mg daily for a 2–3 week period.

Balm of Gilead natural throat pastilles will help ease the huskiness.

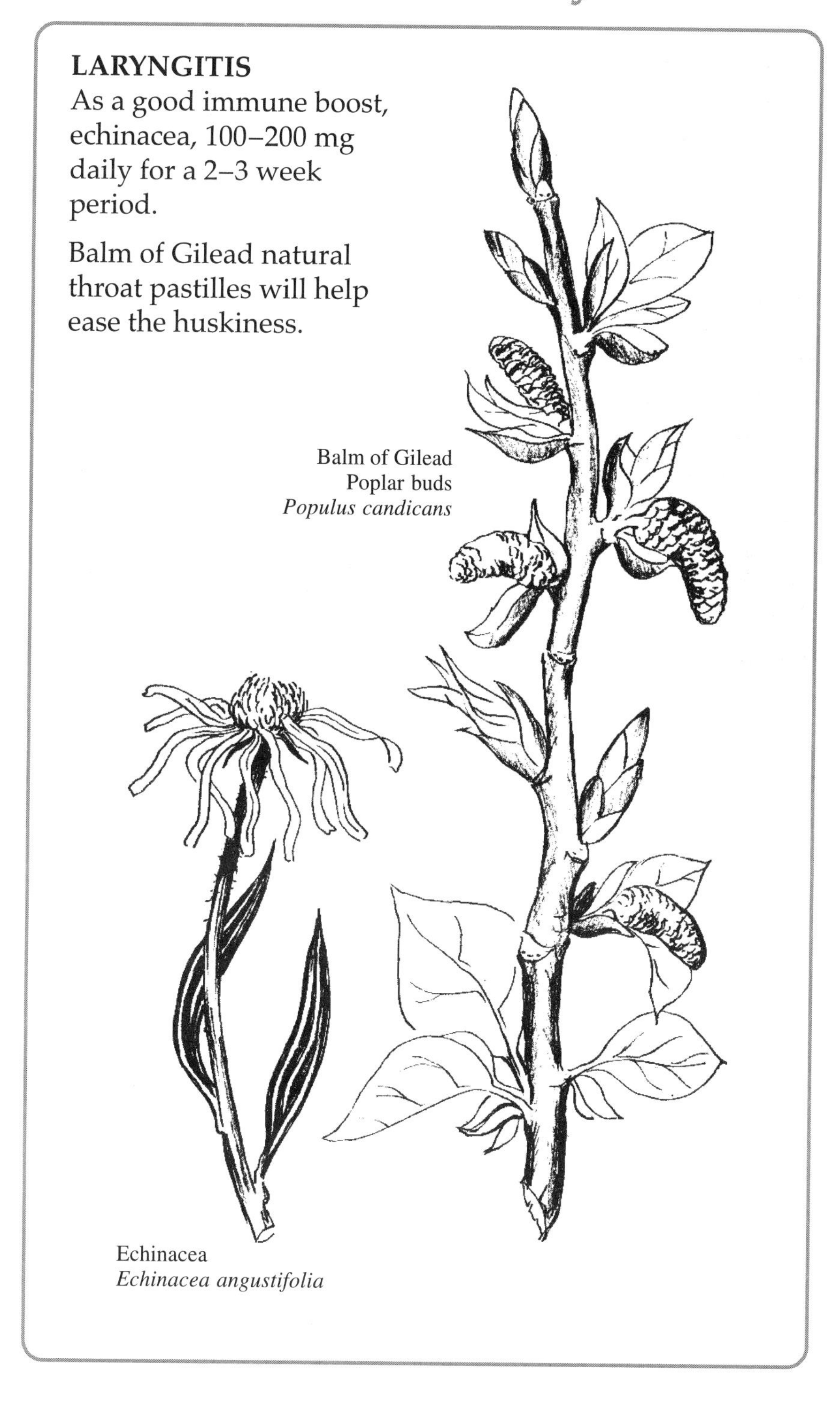

Balm of Gilead
Poplar buds
Populus candicans

Echinacea
Echinacea angustifolia

Martina – Leukaemia

LEUKAEMIA Can you mend a broken heart with Reflexology? I wish you could. Sometimes we can reduce some of the pain – unfortunately, often not enough.

When you are really beautiful, 26, have a fine supportive family, a loving husband, a nice home and everything to live for one would think that life was still worth living, whatever tragedy prevailed, but not so in the case of Martina.

Martina had met her husband whilst on holiday in England. Swiss by birth she chose to leave her native country and settle in England. They had been married just three years when their first planned pregnancy was confirmed, much to the delight of them both. Emma was born, a duplicate of her mother, a child who had an almost ethereal look, with her enormous blue eyes, long blond curly hair and a very heart-warming smile. When she was just four she suddenly became very ill, lost a lot of weight, suffered from constant infections and was totally lacking in energy. A blood test revealed all. Little Emma had leukaemia and despite all the conventional treatments she died just six months later.

Martina contacted me shortly after Emma's death. I think she felt that Reflexology could somehow help heal her mind and reduce some of the agonizing emotional pain that she was suffering. Try as she did Martina could not accept the loss of her little angel and spent every day sitting on the graveside talking to her child. She sat there whatever the weather, in pouring rain or extreme heat; she seemed to have lost all sense of feeling and sensation. Her husband rang me to say how desperate he was to do anything to help his wife to find some reason to continue living. He had tried everything and so had the doctors.

Martina's feet revealed no sensitivity; they were insensitive and non-reactive, which really expressed how she was. I continued with the weekly treatments. Her husband always brought her to me and collected her an hour later, but unfortunately no improvement in her mental state occurred.

She was still coming to me for treatment five months later. Maybe the one-to-one communication helped; the physical contact may have been of benefit too, I don't know. Just one year after the death of Emma, Martina started showing symptoms of illness, a drastic loss of weight, exhaustion and raised glands around her neck, armpits and groin. Her feet, which previously had shown no reaction whatsoever, showed extreme sensitivity in these main lymphatic areas. Blood tests revealed that she too had leukaemia and six months later she died, which was exactly what she wanted. Life without her little girl was not worth living. Her mental state had created the disease and her wish had been granted: she joined her daughter.

A tragic story and one I shall never forget, but a very powerful lesson in just how the mind can control the body. I am sure that if we concentrated our thoughts for long enough we could die of a septic finger!

Reflexes in the feet that revealed sensitivity

LEUKAEMIA
There was no reaction at all in Martina's feet until a year after commencing treatment.

There was then extreme sensitivity in all the main areas relating to the lymphatic system.

Sensitivity was in the neck, armpits and groin.

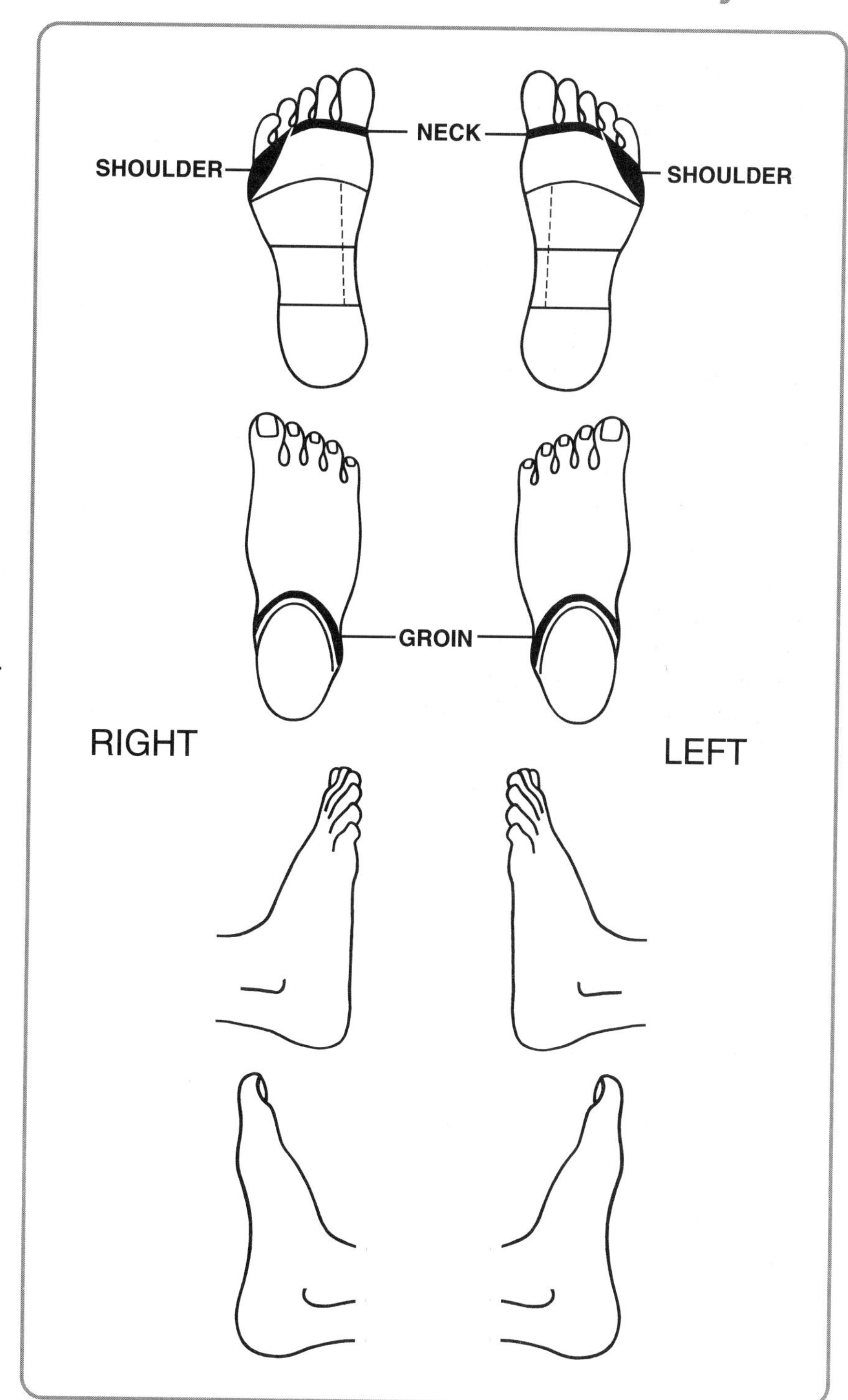

Beneficial herbs, vitamins and dietary advice

LEUKAEMIA
Where there is a deficiency in the immune system echinacea is recommended as a particularly useful herb to take.

Echinacea
Echinacea angustifolia

Jean – ME, Myalgic encephalomyelitis

ME, MYALGIC ENCEPHALOMYELITIS or CHRONIC FATIGUE SYNDROME, is a condition which can be associated with a lengthy list of symptoms, the most common of which are fatigue, muscle pain, depression, headaches and mental confusion.

A milder form of this condition is called post-viral fatigue syndrome, this usually subsides within a year. ME, however, seems to have no definite end, only periods of remission. The exact cause of the collection of symptoms associated with this condition is not yet fully understood although it seems likely that viral infections or stress precipitate the illness. On the emotional level, sufferers have often been found to have experienced a distressing situation in their lives which resulted in very 'angry' feelings being buried deeply into their subconscious.

Jean contacted me with a typical history of ME. The onset of the illness occurred after a severe bout of 'flu' and she had been suffering with recurring symptoms for a period of two years.

Her doctor was at a loss to offer any further help and so Jean decided to seek some solution to her illness by using an alternative route and she chose Reflexology.

She was 30 years old, married with one son and had, prior to the onset of the illness, held down a full-time job with an insurance company which she disliked intensely, but it was essential that she worked.

After three months off work with ME she had been forced to take on a part-time, less demanding office job and even this was becoming a great strain.

Apart from a sensitivity in the area of the spleen, which, as we know, is a great powerhouse which fights infection, there was very little else that proved sensitive in her feet. I gave Jean a good general treatment which she found very pleasant and totally relaxing. In fact, she went to sleep during the treatment.

There was very little change in her debilitating symptoms until the fourth treatment, when she said that she suddenly felt an upsurge in energy and was able to cope with her job and the household chores without collapsing into a heap at about 3.30 p.m.

Jean continued regular treatments for another two months and the improvement was maintained. She followed the dietary advice that I suggested and took the vitamin and mineral supplements, which I am sure contributed to the excellent end result. Jean continued to have one treatment every six weeks for a further six months and maintained her renewed health.

Reflexes in the feet that revealed sensitivity

ME
There was very little sensitivity in the feet apart from a reaction in the spleen, which is the main organ of immunity.

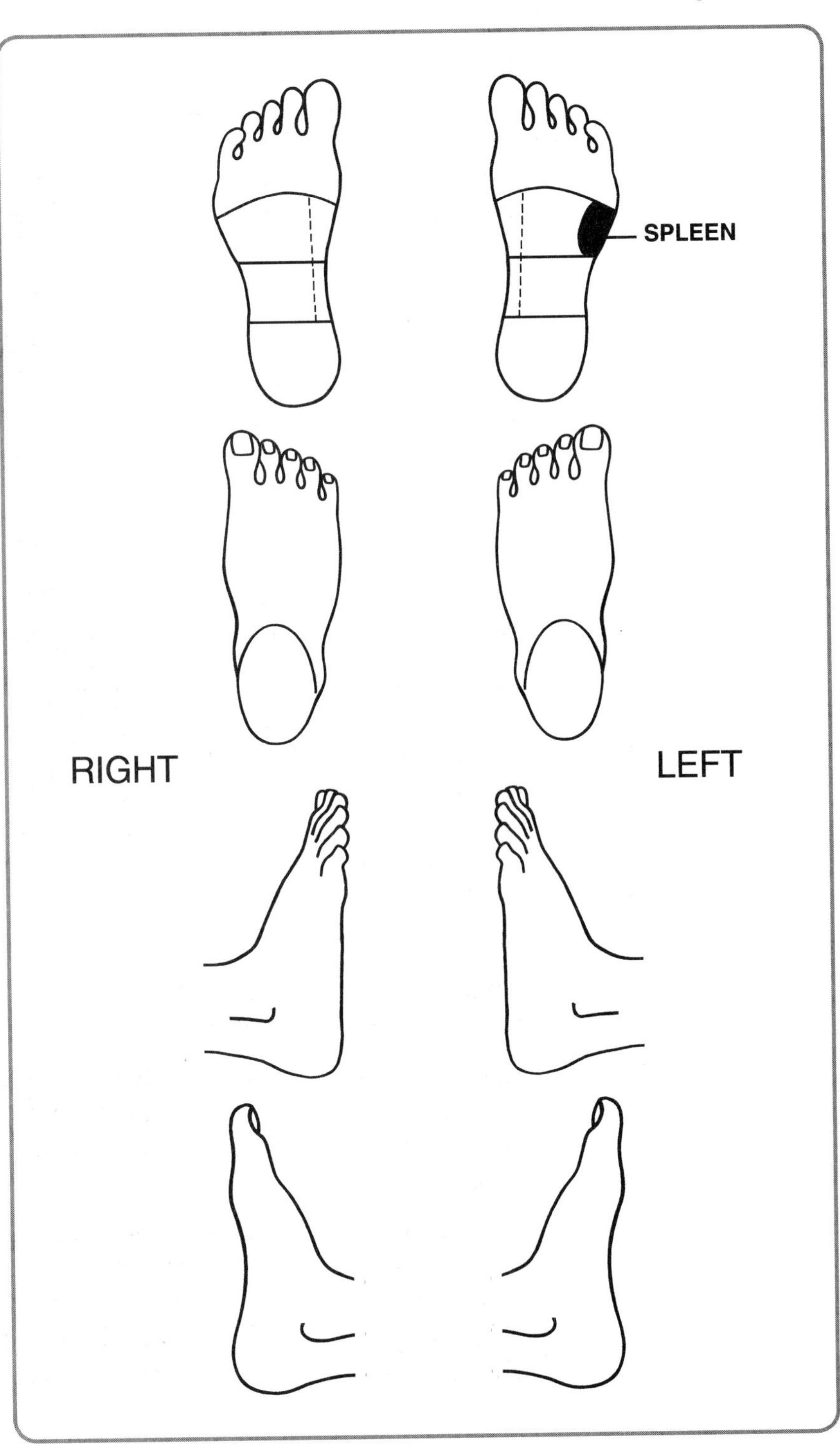

Beneficial herbs, vitamins and dietary advice

ME

Rest is essential. A common mistake is to feel better and then to relapse when normal activity is resumed. A healthy diet high in vitamins and minerals is recommended. As allergies, candida (yeast overgrowth) and hypoglycaemia (blood sugar swings) can feature strongly in this condition it is important to avoid yeasty foods, sugar, artificial additives or chemicals as well as tea, coffee and alcohol.

As there are so many different symptoms and therefore requirements for this condition, the following supplements are recommended for the immune system.

Echinacea *Echinacea angustifolia*

Evening primrose *Oenothera biennis*

Co. Enzyme Q: 10–30 mg daily. This is the biochemical spark involved in energy release.

Echinacea: 1000–2000 mg daily for two–three week periods. This helps to support the immune system which is severely depleted in ME sufferers, leaving them vulnerable to infections.

Magnesium: 150–450 mg for fatigue. Vitamin A: 2664 iu.
Vitamin E: 100 iu. Selenium: 200 ug, and zinc: 15 mg or a good multi-vitamin and multi-mineral supplement daily.
B 50 complex: daily. Vitamin C: 1 g daily.
Evening primrose oil: 500–1000 mg daily.

Janet – Menopausal problems

MENOPAUSAL PROBLEMS Janet telephoned me regarding the unpleasant symptoms she was suffering due to the menopause and asked whether Reflexology could be of benefit.

As I had treated several similar cases before, I was able to encourage her to give Reflexology a try and see if she could avoid going on hormonal treatments which she was very much against.

Janet was a young-looking 50-year-old who seemed to have enjoyed life to the full, had raised three children who had all now left home and gone their own ways and was just ready to enjoy the easier part of her married life and start getting out and about with her husband.

However, her menopausal hot flushes, lack of energy and complete lack of interest in life generally made any attempt to become more actively involved in activities impossible. Her sleep pattern was greatly disturbed; at least three to four times a night she would get up, suffering from hot sweats and take another half an hour or so to get over it and settle herself down.

I always advise people who go to a Reflexologist for the menopause to seek also the help of a registered herbal practitioner, as there is a very good hormonal preparation that helps the imbalance of the hormone function during menopause which, combined with the Reflexology, gives amazing results.

I feel that Reflexology could be efficient in treating the case on its own merits, but because the average person could not possibly have a daily treatment, then the herbal preparation supports the imbalance of oestrogen which gives rise to the symptoms being experienced. There are rarely any major areas of sensitivity in the feet unless the patient suffers from a lot of other health problems, and in Janet's case this was so.

There were slight sensitivities in the ovary and in the pituitary area in the brain and a little sensitivity in the thyroid, but other than that her general health seemed, as she had confirmed, to be good.

After the first treatment Janet telephoned the following day to say that she had had the best night's sleep for months and in fact was only disturbed twice by hot flushes and had therefore felt much more energized the following day. We continued with the treatments over a three-month period together with the herbal preparation which she got from a herbal practitioner, and at the end of the period of time she reported freedom from hot flushes altogether, an increase in energy, and, as she described it, was back to her normal self.

Reflexes in the feet that revealed sensitivity

MENOPAUSAL PROBLEMS

There were slight sensitivities in the pituitary, thyroid and ovaries.

Other than that, the feet revealed very little sensitivity.

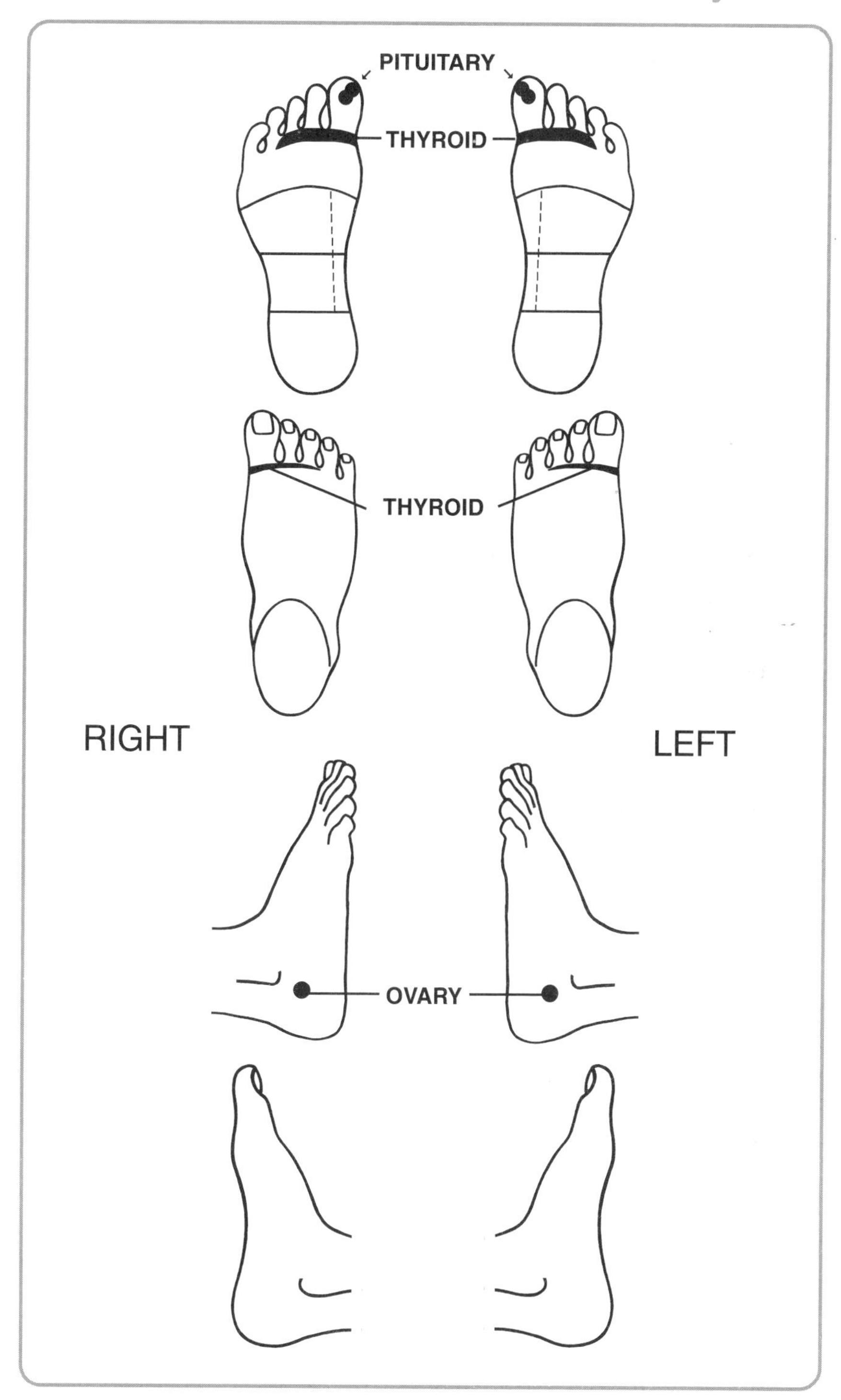

Beneficial herbs, vitamins and dietary advice

MENOPAUSAL PROBLEMS

It is essential to avoid all stimulating food and drink such as caffeine, alcohol, highly coloured and spiced foods and curries.

Sage is a very beneficial herb and can be taken in tablet form or as a herbal tincture. This effectively relieves the flushing.

A good mineral supplement will also be of benefit. This should include zinc, potassium and magnesium.

Avoid highly salted foods as these tend to encourage the body tissues to retain fluids and increase the bloated feeling that some women experience.

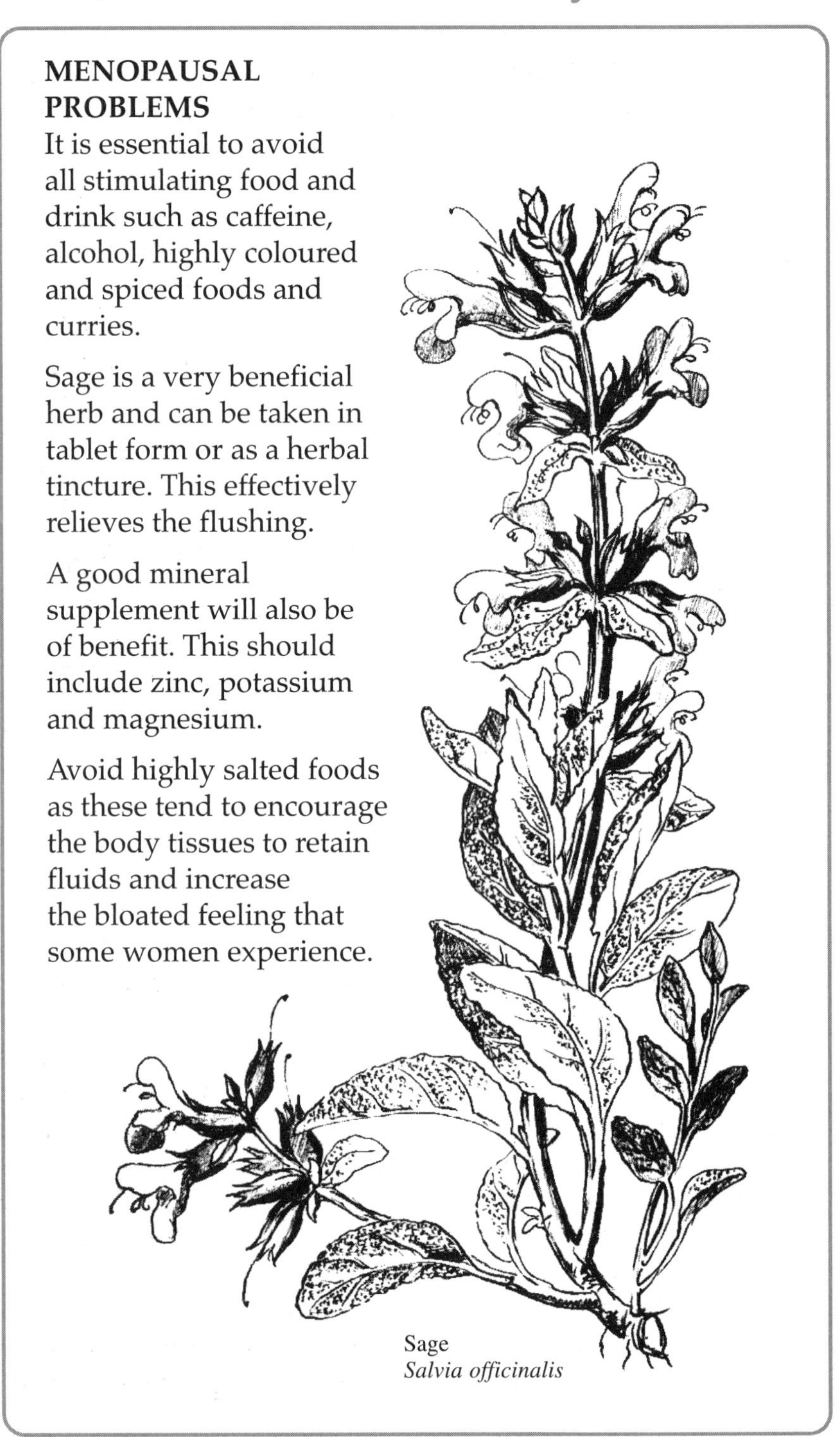

Sage
Salvia officinalis

Cynthia – Menstrual conditions

MENSTRUAL CONDITIONS Penny contacted me regarding her young daughter, Cynthia, who was only 15 but had suffered such disabling menstrual pain both the week prior to and during the week of her period that she was constantly away from school and unable to follow any of her sports and activities.

She was a very pale, rather thin-looking girl who was embarrassed about her state and worried about missing so much schooling. On working through her feet the main area of sensitivity was in the liver, which obviously is a very vascular organ, receives a major part of the blood supply through it, and there was congestion in the uterus and the pelvic area. There was also excessive sensitivity on the left foot in the area of the large intestine and sigmoid colon. I felt that her condition was probably being exacerbated by constipation, poor diet and lack of exercise, which unfortunately made these problems become worse.

I suggested to her mother that she would probably need to bring her daughter for treatment for at least 10 to 12 sessions in order to get permanent improvement and that some attention to her diet would need to be followed in order to maximize the benefits of Reflexology.

I find increasingly that in menstrual pain, particularly in teenagers who tend to eat a lot of fast foods like beefburgers, chips and so on, pains are worsened. Following a low fat diet will give a dramatic improvement to the situation – Reflexology will do the rest.

Cynthia was a very cooperative patient and was keen to help herself, so we were on the right track. After the first appointment she reported that her tendency to constipation had been greatly improved. In fact, following the treatment she had had several bowel actions the following day, which was most unusual. The lack of congestion would have a significant effect on her next period, I was sure.

The following week her period arrived and the first day was as usual painful and disabling, which kept Cynthia away from school. She came to me for her third appointment the following day and reported that she was able to return to school with very little discomfort.

She was keeping to the low fat diet and was, because she was suffering less pain, starting to get some regular exercise, brisk walking with her dog in the evening and swimming too.

We kept on with the Reflexology sessions and attention to dietary support. Cynthia lost the grey pallor which she came with, looked much brighter and fitter, and within the first two months of a weekly treatment session we decided

Cynthia – Menstrual conditions

to lengthen the gap between treatments and just wait and see what happened.

Cynthia attended for treatments over a three-month period of weekly sessions and her menstrual pain had diminished considerably after the first month. She reported improvement in her bowel action. Her frequent constipation had been a problem for many years and I rather feel that the congestion in the pelvic area increased the discomfort she was experiencing.

She followed a low fat diet, improved her pattern of eating to a healthier one and decreased the amount of chocolate which she consumed.

The general result therefore after the three months of treatment was extremely favourable. She was able to follow her education without the usual week away from school and enjoy a much better quality of life accordingly. The treatment was of immense support during the stressful time of taking her 'O' levels, which incidentally she did very well in.

She is now married with a family of her own and recently brought her husband to me. He was suffering from sciatica. He too is a great believer in Reflexology.

Reflexes in the feet that revealed sensitivity

MENSTRUAL CONDITIONS
There was considerable sensitivity in the liver which is a vascular organ and any imbalance here can affect menstruation.

In Chinese medicine they talk about a sluggish liver function for all conditions concerned with blood flow. I find that the same findings link up with Reflexology.

Sensitivity in the uterus, ovaries and fallopian tubes was to be expected. The congestion in her descending colon and sigmoid area in the left foot was apparent.

This confirmed the history of constipation which was causing pain and discomfort.

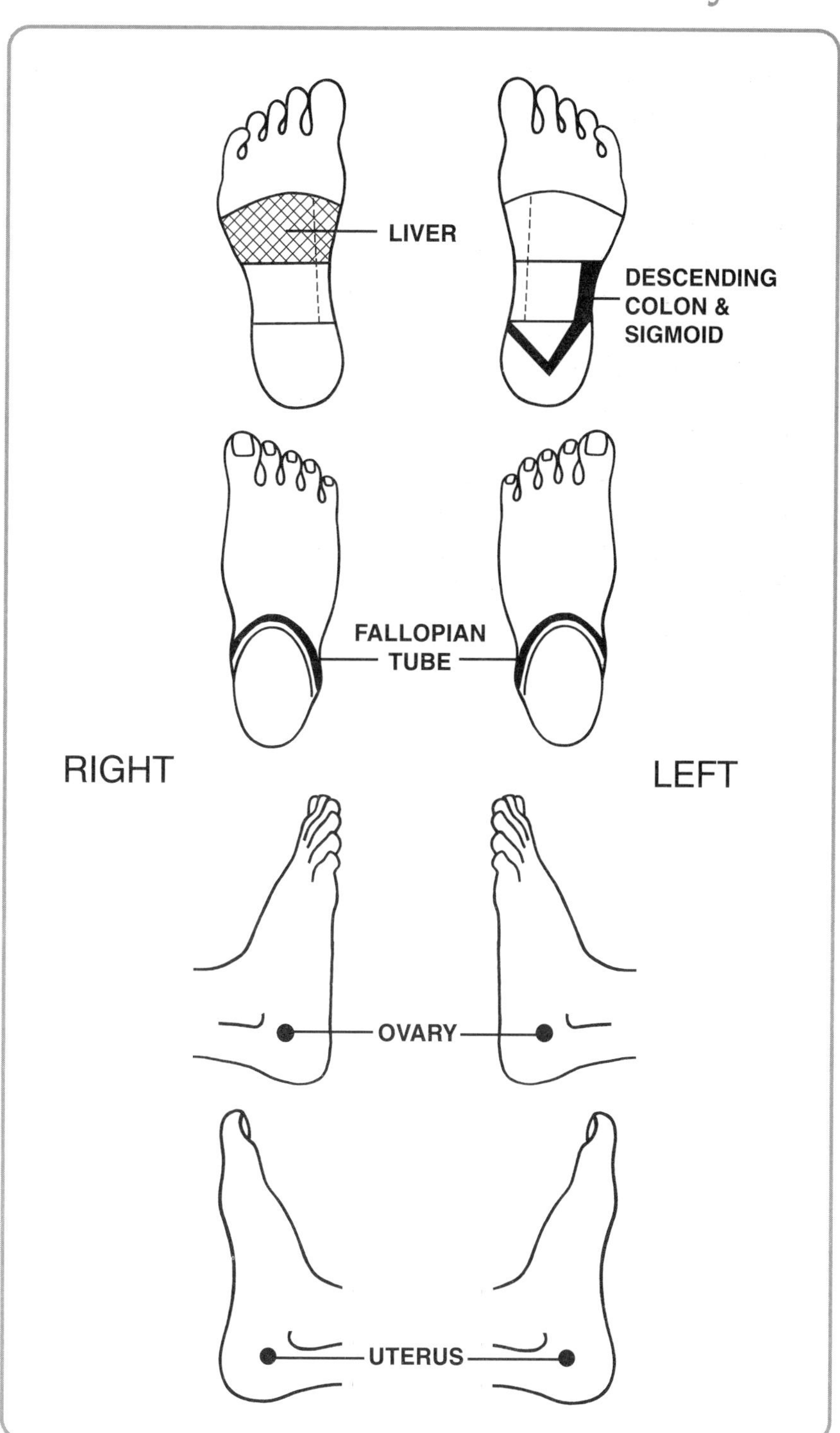

Beneficial herbs, vitamins and dietary advice

MENSTRUAL CONDITIONS

Heavy or painful periods can be eased by black haw, motherwort and raspberry leaves. These have a tonic and relaxing effect on the muscle of the uterus.

A diet rich in the minerals potassium, zinc and selenium is helpful. Potassium often helps to relieve muscular spasm.

A low fat diet helps considerably in relieving the pain of menstruation. Stick rigidly to a low fat diet for a three-month period and just see the difference.

Once some relief has been achieved exercise is essential to stimulate circulation and tone up the muscles of the intestinal area and pelvis.

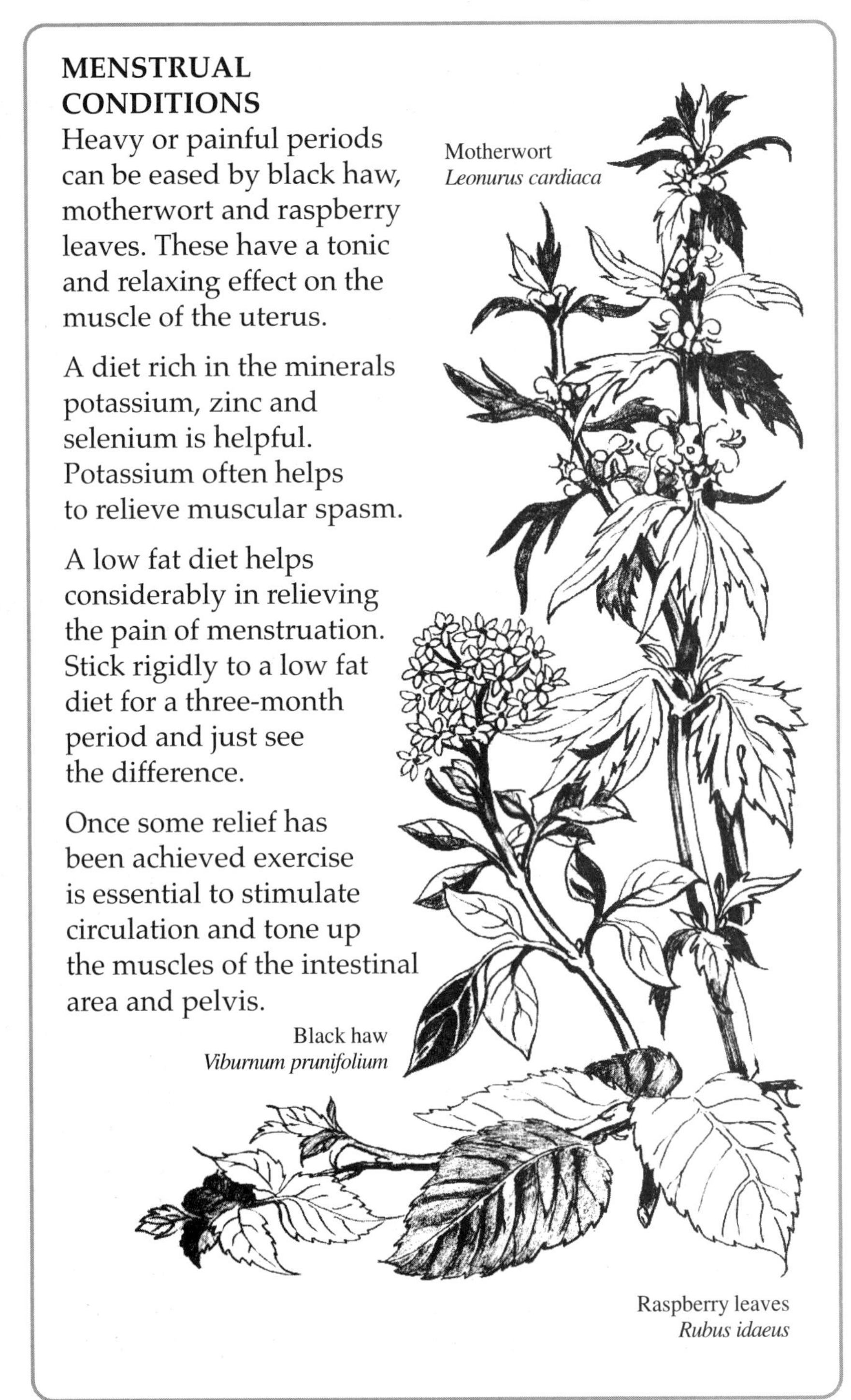

Motherwort
Leonurus cardiaca

Black haw
Viburnum prunifolium

Raspberry leaves
Rubus idaeus

Jill – Migraine

MIGRAINE is a recurring headache, commencing with constriction of blood vessels of the brain followed by expansion which allows the engorgement of vessels. It may be single- or double-sided, with nausea, vomiting, speech difficulties, visual disturbances, emotional stress and tension.

Half of all migraine patients suffer from anxiety, and one in five experiences depression. Causes are many and varied: alcoholic, coffee and caffeine stimulants; gluten food allergies; dairy products; chocolate; citrus fruits. Sometimes it is related to carbohydrate metabolism. It may be associated with emotional disturbance, nervous or physical fatigue, liver, stomach or kidney disturbance or the pill.

Symptoms may include temporary blindness or sight may be only half the visual field. There may be flashing lights, throbbing headaches, reaction to loud noises, which worsen it, nausea, vomiting and depression. The condition can sometimes be linked to the menstrual cycle.

Jill was 42 when she came to me with extreme problems of migraine which had been a part of her life for seven years. The attacks had become so serious that her job in the BBC, which was demanding, stressful and involved very long hours, was about to come to an end as she had had several warnings about her absenteeism, which was getting worse. She did in fact spend at least seven days in bed every month with such bad migraine that she was unable to sit up without vomiting. She frequently lost the vision in one of her eyes, and had tingling and numb sensations in both her arms. The usual doctor's medicines which had been prescribed had very little result. The treatments given to her gave such serious side effects that they were almost as bad as the condition from which she was suffering.

The quality of her life, she said, was such that she often wondered whether it was worth going on, and the pain was so extreme that she had on occasions considered taking an overdose in order, she said, to end it all.

Reflexology had been recommended to her by a work colleague who had sought out a Reflexology practitioner for a similar condition, with great results. As is usual in the treatment of migraine, the target and most sensitive areas that present themselves in the feet are the liver and stomach, and I always feel that it is a toxic liver that causes the frequent eruptions of toxins into the bloodstream which start the whole procedure going. Therefore, the approach to treatment from Reflexology would be to improve the liver function – namely, to help detoxify and also strengthen the functioning of the stomach.

Jill – Migraine

The sensitivity in her liver reflex was such as I have never before experienced. Even the slightest feather-like contact brought tears to her eyes, which told me that her liver was in an extremely delicate state, a lot to do with the condition but more to do with the vast volumes of drugs she had consumed over the past seven years.

Apart from her stressful job, which she enjoyed, her lifestyle seemed quite pleasant. She was married with a couple of teenage children who didn't seem to cause much stress, and all in all I would say that were it not for her migraine she would have had quite a pleasant lifestyle.

The reflex areas in her cervical spine, the top of the brain too, told a lot of stories, as did the neck area. We often hold a lot of stress and tension in our shoulders and neck. I'm sure you have all heard it said: 'It's a real pain in the neck.' I gave her a very light, general treatment, but was not able to work out the liver area as efficiently as needed due to the extreme sensitivity she was experiencing.

The following morning her husband telephoned me to say that his wife had had such a severe reaction to the treatment that she was back in bed, vomiting with not such severe head pains but had been up all night with excessive bowel actions and vomiting attacks. I explained to him that although this was distressing, I was sure that we were on the right tracks and that if she could just tolerate this situation and return for some more treatment we would then be able to improve her migraine greatly. I advised the patient to drink a lot of pure lemon juice to flush the liver out and keep off all solid food for a couple of days. Jill did exactly as she was told, as she was so anxious to find a solution to this condition which was ruining her life.

She returned to me four days later and said that she felt rather weak and wobbly but that the migraine attacks or reaction to treatment, or whatever it was, had subsided and she did actually feel a little bit clearer in her head. The second treatment produced a similar reaction to the first, only much less severe and the third treatment brought about a rash which covered her whole body, which I am sure was another way of nature eliminating waste. On the fifth appointment she said that for the day following that treatment she passed a lot of very dark-coloured urine, which again, I am sure, was the kidney eliminating a lot of waste material.

The usual pattern of a week of migraine per month did not continue, as during the next month the migraine did start but lasted only one day and she was able to return to work. She did not have the vomiting or the nauseous

Jill – Migraine

feeling and the head pain was very minimal. 'I really can't believe it,' she said. 'This is an absolute miracle. I've tried so many other treatments but to no avail.' And Jill did return to me for a further nine weeks on a regular basis and eventually we got the migraine attack down to just a very muzzy feeling in her head, and for the first time in seven years she was able to manage three months at work.

Thereafter she came to me once a month for one session of treatment, which seemed to keep the condition at bay. This is highly recommended, particularly in the treatment of chronic illness, as it stops the toxic state occurring or building up in the body as it had done before.

In my opinion, migraine is all to do with digestion, poor elimination and stress.

The sensitivities which were revealed in this patient's feet were very interesting and initially caused some confusion.

There was extreme sensitivity in the heart, the brain and the kidney areas, which certainly did not seem to have any explanation in the case of a migraine sufferer as the patient was only 42 years of age and had no history of high blood pressure or heart disease, was a non-smoker and drinker with no family history of coronary disease. This was worrying.

However, she was being treated by a new drug for migraine, and upon investigating the side effects of this new medication it did mention that the drug caused a contraction of the arteries in an attempt to restrict blood flow to the brain.

What I was picking up in this case was the arterial constriction.

As soon as Jill experienced such an improvement in the frequency and severity of her migraine she stopped the medication, and within a week the previous sensitivities in her heart, brain and kidney area disappeared.

The more I work with Reflexology the more amazed I am at how accurately the feet detect what is going on in the body.

A sensitive reflex has a story to tell.

Reflexes in the feet that revealed sensitivity

MIGRAINE
There was extreme sensitivity in the reflexes in the neck, head and very top of the brain. This indicated tension in these areas. The liver sensitivity was such that even the lightest pressure was hardly bearable. This sensitivity was due to the large quantities of drugs that she had taken over a long period of time and the poor eliminating ability of the liver which was the cause of her problem. The main causes of migraine are: dietary, poor elimination and stress. Sensitivity which appeared in the heart and kidney reflexes did not have any connection to her physical condition. I am sure that these were caused by a new migraine drug which Jill was trying that did have an effect on the vascular system.

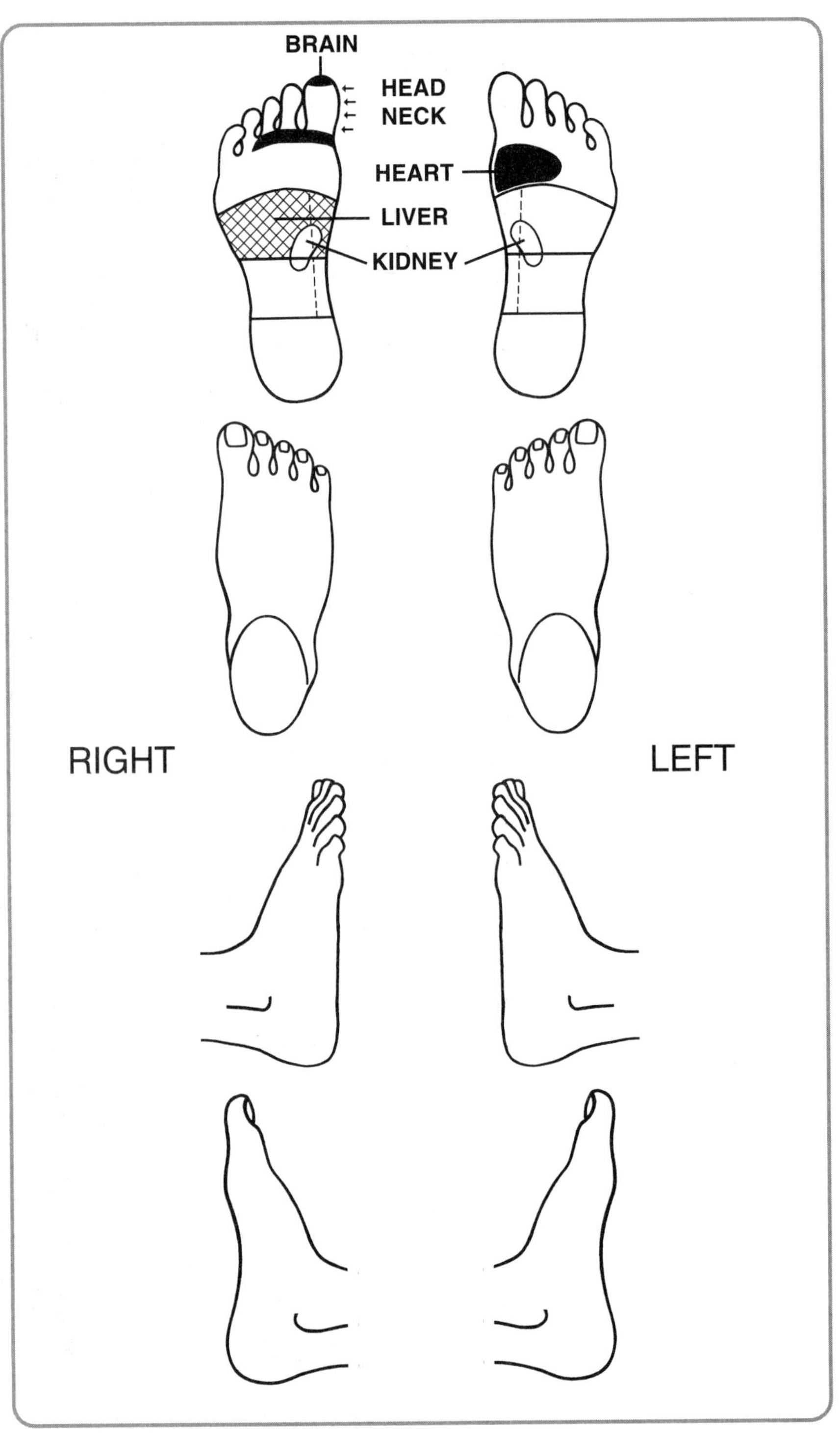

Beneficial herbs, vitamins and dietary advice

MIGRAINE

A low fat diet is to be recommended for migraine sufferers. Fats in the diet put a stress on the liver, and as this is the target area for the condition it would be as well to try this regime for several months. Cheese, chocolate, alcohol, tea and coffee are to be avoided.

Herbal preparations to improve the function of the digestive system would be recommended. Feverfew has relieved many chronic migraine sufferers. There are records of its use for headaches since medieval times. Meadowsweet and dandelion root, plus a bitter tonic such as hops are useful herbs for this condition. Chamomile tea is a soothing beverage with anti-inflammatory benefits.

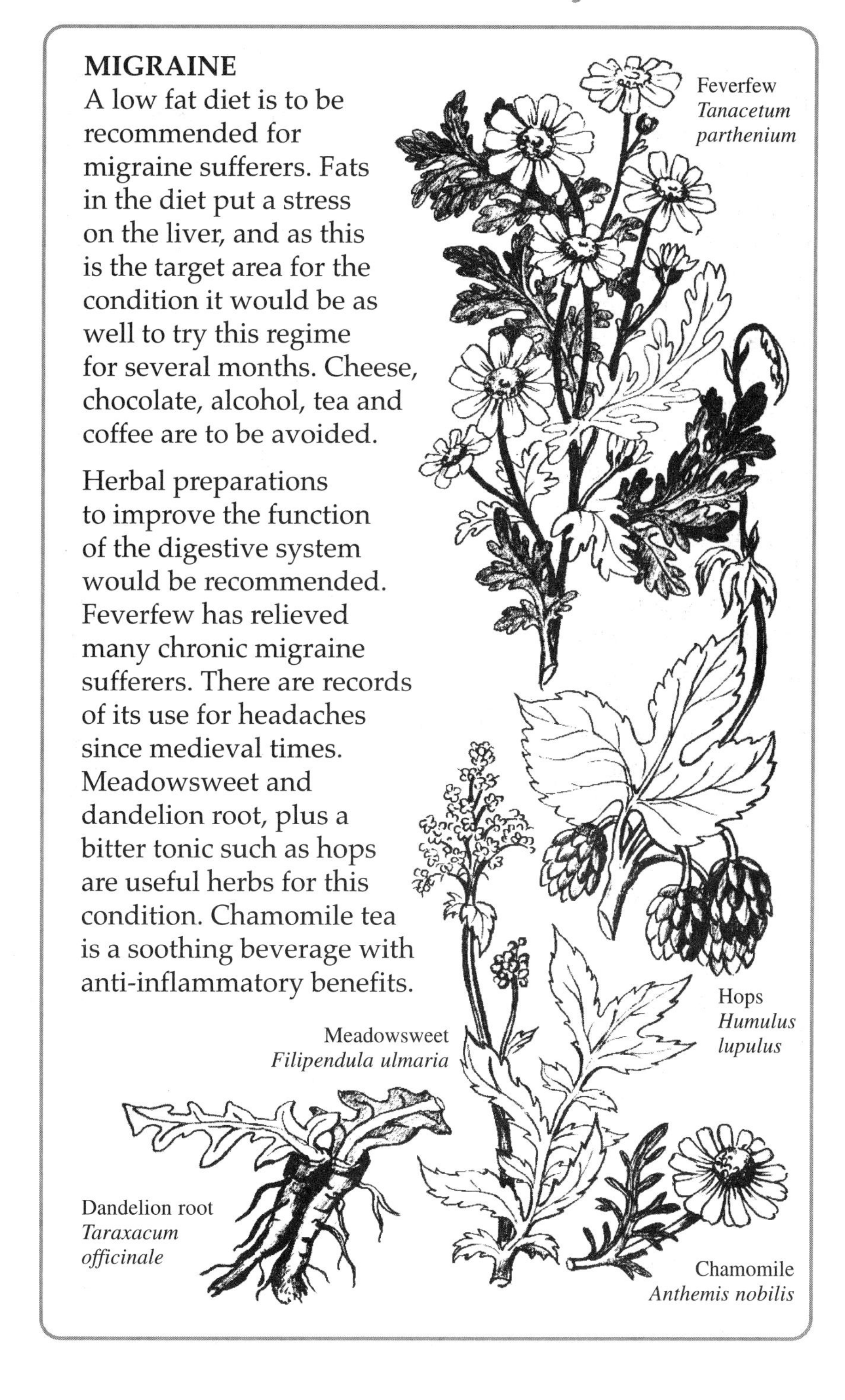

Mary – MS, Multiple sclerosis

MS or MULTIPLE SCLEROSIS The nerve fibres of the brain and spinal cord are enclosed within a white sheath made of a fatty substance called myelin, and without the presence of this they are unable to conduct impulses. Multiple sclerosis is a disease characterized by demyelination of the nerves so that its symptoms are correspondingly variable and diagnosis is made difficult. The disease progresses in episodes followed by partial recovery but is usually progressive. Young or middle-aged adults are the usual victims. Tingling and numbness in an area of the body, weakness of the hand and foot, blurred vision and slurred speech are the usual symptoms.

Mary came to me with a long-term history of multiple sclerosis; in fact, the early symptoms began when she was only 17. As I got to know Mary on a more personal level during the long periods of time she attended for treatment with me, I got the impression that her relationship with her mother was a rather difficult one and she did seem very fixed in a lot of her ideas.

Her relationships with men proved very unstable and brought forth much suffering. One of her husbands was an alcoholic and she was badly treated during this marriage. Another relationship ended in the death of her husband after a long, debilitating illness whereby she had to give him as much physical and emotional support as she possibly could, which became very difficult with her increasing disability.

I did not meet Mary until she was in her late thirties, at which time her disability had progressed to the state where she was using elbow crutches to get around but was still able to drive her hand-controlled car.

The main problem which caused her the most distress and disability were the muscular spasms that occurred in her low spine and legs, which became so severe on occasions that she was unable to move at all and would then have to be taken into hospital where she would lie flat for 10 to 12 days, being treated with muscle-relaxant drugs and basic physiotherapy. Eventually the situation would improve and enable her to go home, though in a very weakened condition, suffering from the side effects of the large doses of anti-inflammatory, pain-killing and muscle-relaxant drugs which she had been on.

I must confess that when I met her I was very unsure of whether I would be able to offer any help, mainly because of the long span of 20 years which had intervened between the commencement of her illness and the present.

However, she appeared to be quite confident inasmuch as if there was a possibility of relieving her episodes of muscle spasm and keeping her out of hospital that would be a near miracle as far as she was concerned.

Mary – MS, Multiple sclerosis

Once I commenced treating her feet I found the main sensitive areas, as always, on the spine and brain. The whole of the area was extremely sensitive to any form of touch. The urinary system also appeared to be very sensitive, and Mary did confess to me that she occasionally had bouts of incontinence, which were occurring more frequently than she liked.

Despite her disability Mary led quite a full life, involving herself in as many social and charity events as was possible, and she seemed to have good relationships with her sisters and their young families.

I started treating Mary weekly, and within a very short period of time she revealed how much freer her body felt. Her comments were, 'I really can't explain how I feel but I just know that something happens when I have this treatment which makes me feel better altogether.' Treatments continued on a weekly basis until we reached the six-month period and Mary realized that for the first six months in the past ten years she had not been to hospital. She was overjoyed at this benefit.

We then reduced the treatments to fortnightly sessions and she continued, and still does, to have her fortnightly treatments, and during the last three years she has never had a return to hospital as an in-patient for this distressing condition.

She also is delighted with the fact that she has not had progression of the illness. In fact, her bladder weakness has returned to normal, incontinence is a thing of the past and she is still mobile, walking with her elbow crutches and driving her car.

Although this is not a case in which there have been any outstanding results, it is 20 years since the onset of the illness and, as very little can be done to help these multiple sclerosis sufferers on the medical side, there is very little to lose in trying something on the complementary approach.

I wish the results had been more outstanding, but as the patient is overjoyed at her improved health and freedom from painful episodes in hospital, I feel that we have made some good strides in at least managing a very difficult situation.

Reflexes in the feet that revealed sensitivity

MULTIPLE SCLEROSIS

A little sensitivity showed in the urinary system. This represented the weakness and episodes of incontinence that Mary had experienced from time to time.

The whole area of the spine and brain were acutely reactive. This indicated the deterioration of the spinal nerves.

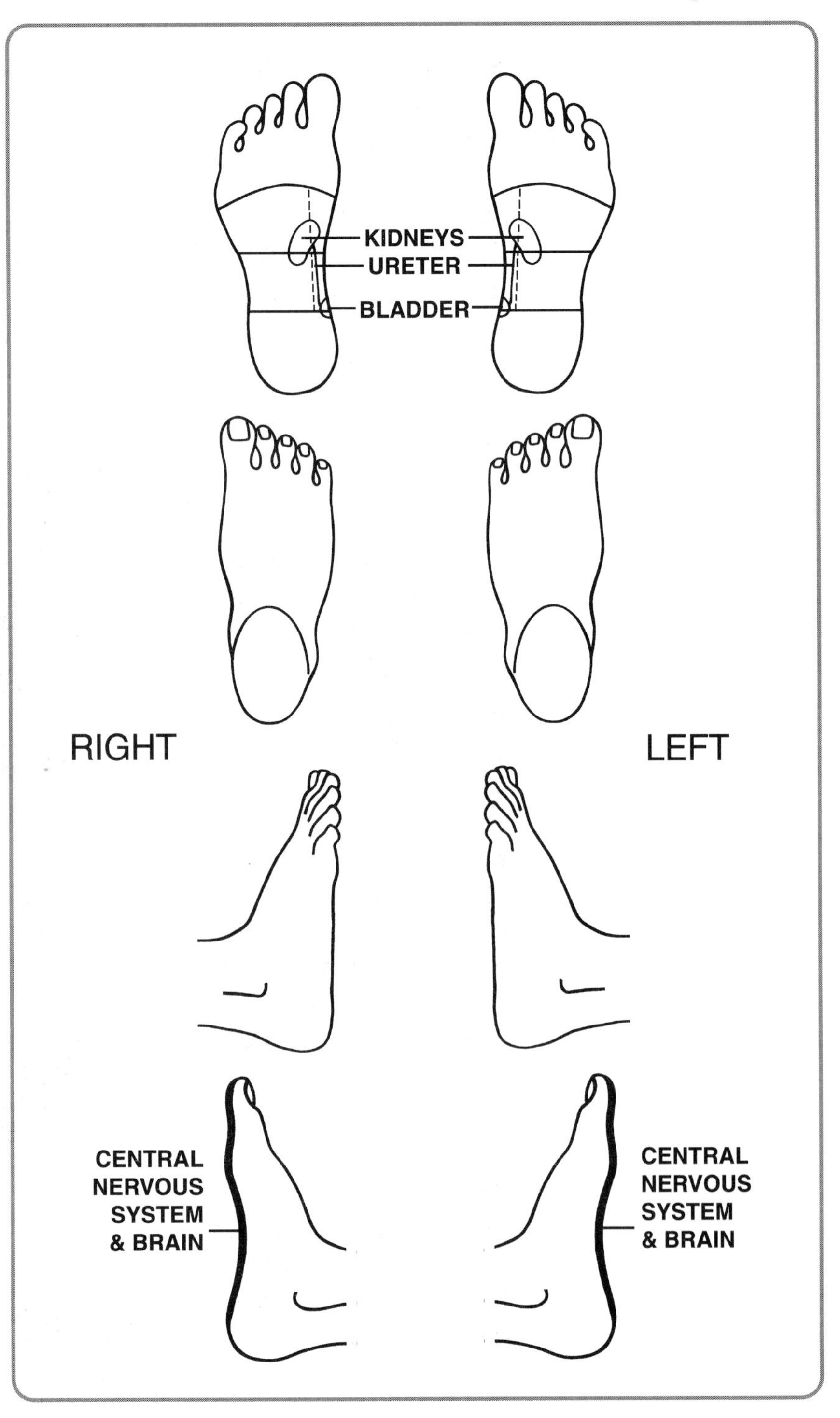

Beneficial herbs, vitamins and dietary advice

MULTIPLE SCLEROSIS
Many experts now believe that diet and lifestyle changes may have a significant impact on the progression of the illness.

A reduction in saturated fat intake and the use of essential fatty acids found in evening primrose oil and fish oils may be of help. Meat intake should be reduced.

A natural approach to treating this disease will cause no harm and may be of benefit.

Anti-oxidant nutrients, vitamin E and selenium are sometimes recommended. High potency fish oil: 1–3 g daily. High potency GLA: 1–3 g daily. Vitamin B complex formula. B vitamins are paramount in nerve health, especially B12. A high-potency, broad spectrum multi-vitamin and mineral complex formula.

Avoidance of all white refined products, white flour and white sugar. Follow a diet low in dairy products.

Evening primrose
Oenothera biennis

John – Spinal condition

Unlike the limbs, the spine is not a lever. This may appear to be stating the obvious, but many of the problems which the back incurs arise from using it as if it were. Nature designed the spine for both support and flexibility, and did so by wedging it in the pelvis at the sacroiliac joints and then guying it with muscles. It is when these muscles are not properly used and become slack that the intervertebral joints and discs develop displacements which may lead to pressure on the nerve roots as they emerge from the spine.

John was a middle-aged man who, for 18 months, had been unable to put his heels to the ground because of extreme pain. He had been to a chiropodist and an orthopaedic surgeon, who could find nothing wrong with his feet but prescribed insoles which gave him a little more support, but he still had very painful heels.

He had heard about Reflexology from a colleague and as a last resort thought he would give it a try. Having the utmost confidence in the principle that where a sore spot occurs in the feet, at the corresponding part of the body is the root cause, I proceeded with the treatment.

John's major sensitivity was in his lumbar spine and sciatic nerve in particular, the right side. He said that his right heel was far more sensitive than the left so I knew that we were on the right track. He had suffered back trouble on and off for years.

'As far as I am concerned, John, there is nothing wrong with your feet.' He looked amazed. 'There must be. I can't stand on my heels.' 'Nerves arising out of the lumbar spine control the functioning of your legs and I feel that there is compression in that part of your spine. My treatment sessions will be focused on a lot of work on the spine and let's see what happens.' I gave John a good treatment, working extensively on the whole of the spinal area.

The next morning I had a telephone call from a very satisfied patient. 'It's amazing, I can stand on my heels,' he said. 'They are still painful, but such an improvement.'

We carried on with a further six sessions. Each week the sensitivity in John's feet became less and less and in the sixth week he was elated at being able to walk properly for the first time in 18 months. 'Why did the doctor not find the cause?' he asked. 'Doctors unfortunately often look no further than the painful part and if no structural problem is found, become mystified and did as they recommended to you, prescribed pain killers and insoles, neither of which could ever cure the cause.'

Reflexes in the feet that revealed sensitivity

SPINAL CONDITION
When John came to me there was evidence of acute sensitivity on the bases of both heels, which radiated up the back of the legs.

The origin of John's problem came from the lumbar spine.

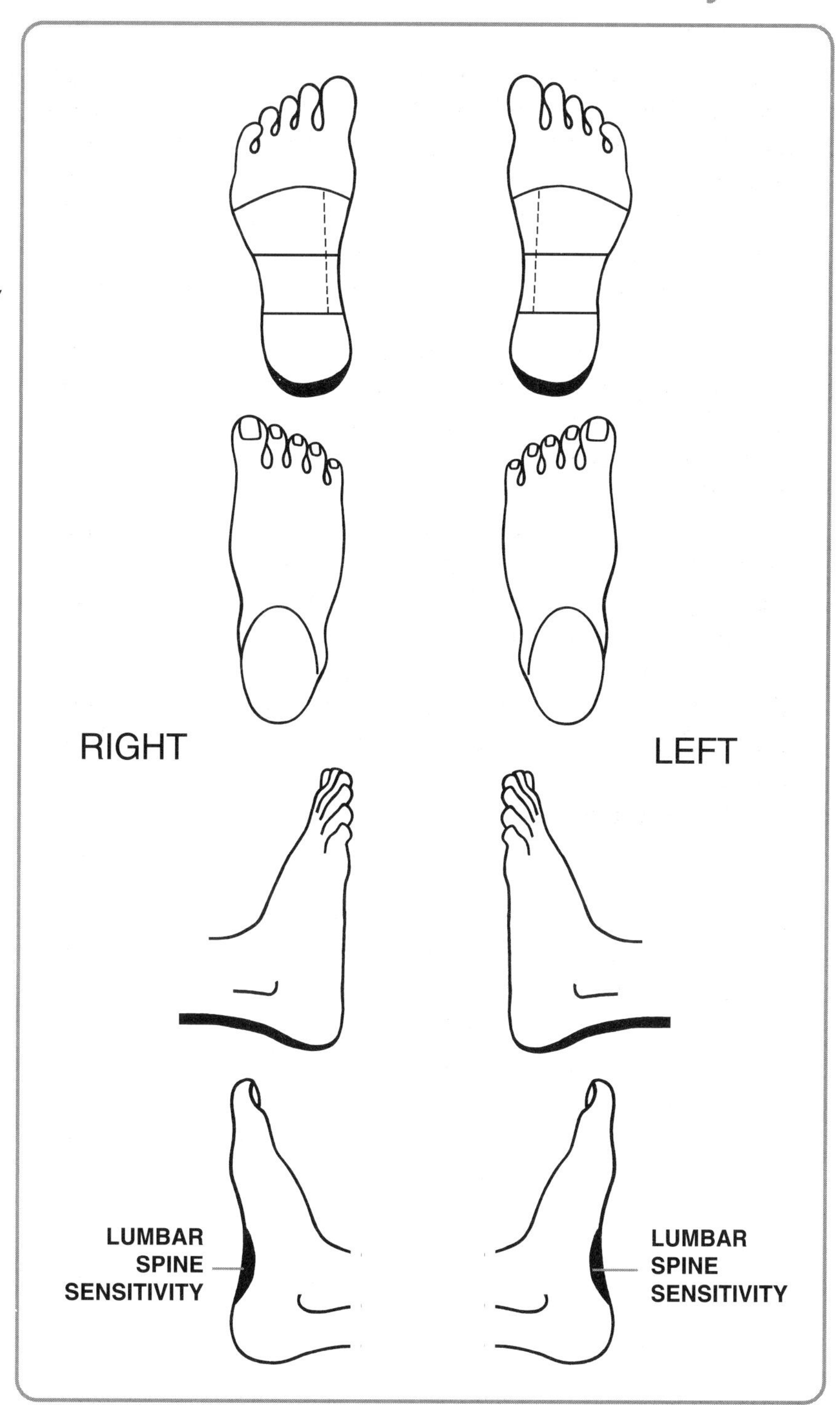

Beneficial herbs, vitamins and dietary advice

SPINAL CONDITION

Poultices are very effective in treating arthritic joints, inflammations, tension in muscles and bruising.

Poultices are made by adding hot water to a herb to make a paste.

Two herbs to use would be slippery elm or linseed meal obtained from the herb flax. When the right consistency is reached spread the paste on a piece of flannel, apply to the skin and cover to maintain the heat. The benefits of a poultice are twofold: the heat helps to relax local muscles easing tension and pain, and the warmth and moisture help to soften the area, allowing the therapeutic constituents of the plant to be absorbed more easily.

Any inflammatory condition of a tendon or joint will be eased by taking vitamin C: 1–2 g daily for its role in collagen formation. Vitamin E: 200 iu and beta carotene: 15 mg daily for their anti-oxidant activity.

Flax
Linum usitatissimum

Slippery elm
Ulmus fulva

Philippa – Tinnitus

TINNITUS and deafness may go hand in hand, tinnitus being the reaction of the organ of corti in the cochlea to some kind of stimulus such as inflammation or pressure, while perceptive deafness is the failure to react to that stimulus. Tinnitus is a very common and often distressing disorder experienced as a continual noise in the head and ranging from a high-pitched whistle to a deep, booming vibration. As such it is masked by external noise which pushes it into the background and this is sometimes used as a form of treatment. The greater majority of cases, of which there are about 100,000 in the UK, arise for no obvious reason.

Philippa was only 13 when her parents brought her to me for treatment. She suffered frequent bouts of 'ringing in the ears'. 'More often than not it is a buzzing sensation,' she said. An ENT surgeon had found nothing abnormal in her ear function and was at a loss to know what to suggest next.

Philippa was a tense, very pleasant, sensitive girl, but I was more worried about her rather over-protective parents, particularly her very dominant father, who seemed more concerned about the effect this problem would have on her education than the misery it was causing her in her everyday life.

As I started treatment I was utterly mystified, as no sensitivities appeared in her ear reflexes at all. Wondering if there could be a displacement in the vertebrae in her neck (sometimes this can cause such noises) I worked extensively in this area; again no sensitivity occurred.

Her diaphragm area and that solar plexus was again telling me stories; her adrenal glands were acutely sensitive. This picture in her feet represented to me a young girl in a very stressful state. The diaphragm often becomes sensitive in those who are anxious, as a rapid heart beat and over-breathing are common. I also took into account that Philippa was probably rather nervous at this, her first treatment with a Reflexologist.

Was the anxiety causing ringing in the ears or did the ear condition cause the anxiety?

It was difficult to get any response as mother and father answered all the questions, and try as she might, Philippa could not get a word in edgeways. Mother and father talked over each other, one constantly correcting the other on the facts of the case, and so on.

Philippa was a child of much older parents. Her brother was in fact 12 years her senior.

I had one desire and that was that her mother and father leave the room

Philippa – Tinnitus

while she had her treatment, but I knew that this was going to be a problem.

Every point in the foot had to be explained to them and if it was sensitive, then why was it?

The whole situation was quite hopeless. The second and third sessions were much the same as the first, and at one point Mum and Dad became quite heated in a discussion about their daughter.

Deciding that we were not going to get anywhere with these stressful treatment sessions, and because Philippa had shown no signs of any improvement, I asked the parents if they could leave their daughter with me on her own and go off somewhere together for an hour, as I found their constant, rather excitable discussion off-putting to me as well as to their daughter.

So often the cause of the illness is the person sitting next to the patient! And it was so in this case.

On the fourth treatment I had Philippa to myself and put just a little pressure on her to talk about herself.

'How do you get on with your parents?' I asked. Immediately her expression changed to one of pain. 'Not bad', she said, 'but they are always picking at each other over anything and everything. It goes on week in, week out. They are both OK on their own but when we are all together life is difficult.'

'I don't think there is anything physically wrong with your ears at all, in fact I am 100 percent sure of that. What is wrong is the stresses that you are living under. Your parents need the treatment, not you.'

There was such relief on that girl's face. 'I think you are creating this noise to shut out what is going on around you. The stress of your parents.'

I summoned up some courage when her parents returned: asked Philippa to go out and sit in the car, and had a chat with them.

'I can't help your daughter at all, but feel sure you could do so much for her if you could calm down the bickering which she says is constant.'

I waited for the onslaught, which did not come. They both became so sheepish. Big, bold Dad looked like a little boy and Mum had tears in her eyes. The outcome was remarkable. Mum and Dad both came to me for treatment. Mum came for her migraine headaches (stress again), and Dad suffered from high blood pressure (more stress).

They were both relieved of these conditions; in fact Mum only experienced very rare attacks of mild migraine. Dad's blood pressure dropped to within normal limits; and what about Philippa? Her ringing in the ears completely disappeared within the next few months.

Reflexes in the feet that revealed sensitivity

TINNITUS
An acute sensitivity in the adrenal glands indicated stress.

The solar plexus area was sensitive also, an indication of a very anxious young girl.

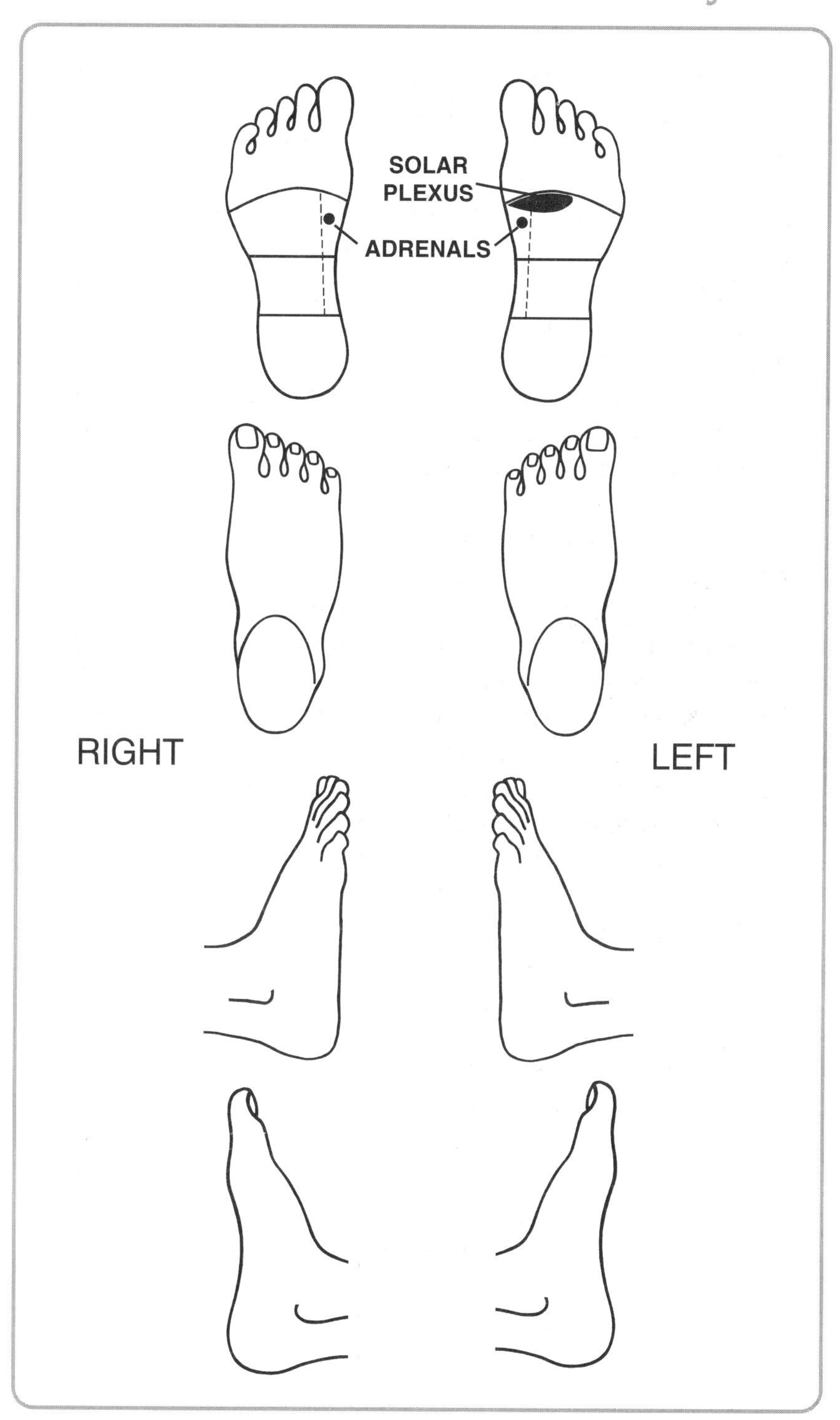

Beneficial herbs, vitamins and dietary advice

TINNITUS

I recommended that Philippa's parents take the herb valerian, which is recommended in cases of high blood pressure and insomnia and for general stress relief.

There is also detailed information on high blood pressure in Case history 12.

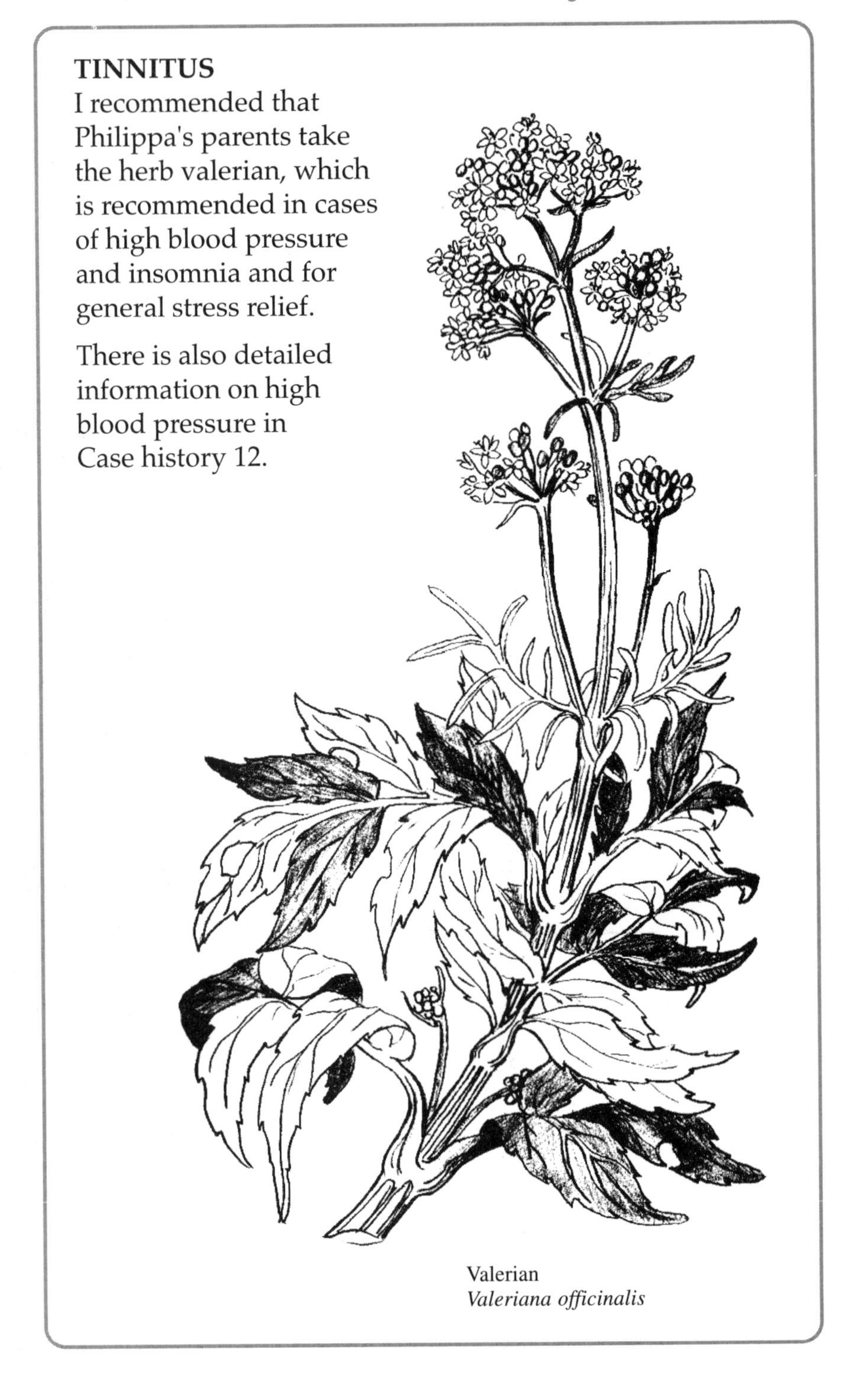

Valerian
Valeriana officinalis

'Yesterday was the past.
Tomorrow is the future.
Today is a gift
and we call it the present.'

Conclusion

Conclusion

'It does not take a sledge hammer to crack a nut.' How often do we find in life that there is often a very simple solution to a health or emotional problem that we had overlooked in our rush to find some other, often quite aggressive way to sort out a problem.

Reflexology is a gentle treatment, a holistic approach to helping the body to heal itself, which it was built to do. This treatment puts the body into the right gear to balance the functions, reduce mental and physical stresses, and the results are good ones.

We are dying today from diseases of the fork. What we put into our mouths is the fuel upon which the body can work. Chips, beer and cola are destructive fuels. Fresh vegetables, fruits, cereals and grains are the tools we need to give the body a chance to repair, rebuild and renew. Never before have we had so much terminal illness, coronary heart disease, cancer, AIDS, diseases of the nervous system.

If drugs could give us good health then we should all be fighting fit, as never before have we had so many. The future for all who choose to follow that path will be not only drugs to control disease but further drugs which we will be encouraged to take to prevent illness.

Complementary medicines, or as I prefer to call them 'medicines of the soul', are growing, and growing very fast. They have, after all, been around for a long, long time – acupuncture, 5,000 years, Reflexology, 2,500, and herbalism is the oldest recorded form of healing.

I have witnessed near miracles in my life with simple treatments, attention to diet, lifestyle and a look at what is going on in your minds. Healing is so simple: it takes a lot of hard, destructive work to make yourself ill and some very simple common-sense measures to build back your health and strength.

Your body is your responsibility, yours totally. It does not belong to the doctor or the hospital and it is up to you to decide what to do with it. What about trying? It's all about personal effort and *loving yourself!*

Index

Bold type indicates an entry in Case histories
An entry in italics indicates an illustration

Index

Bold type indicates an entry in Case histories
An entry in italics indicates an illustration

Index

Bold type indicates an entry in Case histories
An entry in italics indicates an illustration

Index

Bold type indicates an entry in Case histories
An entry in italics indicates an illustration